THE GosPOOL

of BANK POOL

according to

"The Beard"

Hallelujah!

The knowledge and reminiscences of an Old–Time pool hustler and true apostle of the game.

Freddy "the Beard" Bentivegna

TABLE OF CONTENTS

Foreword:

These are my observations of players encountered during my career. My apologies to the old-timers whom I didn't see play and had to leave out. The opinions come from what I've actually seen and experienced.

I hope no one will be offended by what I say. It's all in fun and the truth is I deeply love the game and all of the pool players, regardless of lifestyle or character. The sinners and the rogues I love best of all. I have the greatest respect for pool ability, knowing the great commitment it takes to play high-speed pool.
Freddy "the Beard" Bentivegna
Chicago, IL
March 30, 2006

THE POOL PLAYING SIGNIFYING MONKEY

Anonymous

Deep in the jungle, way back in the sticks, The animals had a poolroom and a champion Baboon that called hisself "Slick."

He took on all comers that came into town and broke every sumbitch that laid his money down.

But then one day, up from Coconut Grove, came a cool, pool playing Monkey, you could tell by the cut of his clothes.

He had a long black coat, black slacks and pigeon–toed shoes. A blood red hat and a two–piece cue that he was gonna use.

The Baboon was the furst one he see when he walked thru the door, cause the Monkey tripped over his pallet that was laying there on the floor.

"I just got in from Skunk Holler. Does any a you muthafuckers . wanna play one for a dollar ?"

The Baboon told the Monkey, "Boy, get you a cue, I'll play you some pool you little muthafuckah, you!"

The houseman said, "It's the Baboon's break." But the Monkey said, "There'll be no cheating, and there'll be no mistake. An unfair advantage, you're not gonna take."

So the Monkey flipped "tail" and the Baboon "head." It was the Baboon's break just like the houseman said.

The Baboon broke, and he ran to the eight. But it bubbled in the corner for a fatal mistake.

So the Monkey got down like a hunter on a gun. When he rose back up, he had a smooth sixty-one.

The Baboon jumped up and down and cried, "That aint right! Muthafuckah, before you leave there's gonna be a hellova fight !"

The Monkey told the houseman, "You better call this man's wife. I done took his money and I'm about to take his life."

Then the Baboon said, "No, I aint thru. I'll play you one more, you slick-ass muthafuckah, you."

This time the Monkey broke and he ran the one, two and three, Looked up at the houseman and said, "I gotta go pee."

Then he pissed out the window and he shit on the floor, Got back down and made a cool combination on the five and the four.

He made the six, seven, eight and also the nine, in different pockets and at the same time.

The eleven was in front, he couldn't see the ten. So he played a two cushion kick and he knocked 'em both in.

He played the twelve in the corner and the thirteen in the side, with a lot of high-top english, he gave the fourteen a ride.

Then he reached in his pocket and pulled out some Gin, took a long drink and knocked the fifteen on in.

He raised up from the table,
put his foot on the stool.
He said, "I may be a signifying Monkey,
but I can play me some pool!"

A grammar school poem from the 1920s or '30s.

COMING UP IN CHICAGO — BENSINGER'S FOREVER!

An interview with Freddy "The Beard" Bentivegna by Steve Booth of Onepocket.org

Steve Booth: Freddy, where did you come up playing pool?

Freddy The Beard: I came up in Chicago, in a bowling alley that also had five pool tables. Bowling was big then, so you had to sign up and wait for lanes. I was about 14, and I'm on the waiting list. One of our guys says, "Listen, there's a poolroom next door. Why don't we shoot pool while we're waiting for our lanes? " So we went next door to play pool. We never returned to the bowling side. That's true. They called our name, but we never went back and we never bowled again.

SB: So it was a neighborhood place?

FTB: Yeah, and the equipment was hideous. There were no pockets on some of the tables; there was just a hole.

SB: The ball dropped right to the floor?

FTB: They had those high ashtrays, and they'd put them under the pocket and the ball would go plunk and roll around in there. The cloth was taped up with two–inch wide electrical tape. They were pretty tough to play on. That's where I beat my first guy from **Bensinger's.**

I used to have to sneak in there (**Bensinger's**) because I was underage. They had this real high counter by the door. So I used to duck by the old guy who was about a hundred years old who worked the counter, and sneak off into the back. When I was in the back, about fifty feet away, I'd say, "Turn the lights on!" The guy didn't know who the hell it was, and the balls were already there. He'd turn the light on and I got into action.

When I first started going up there, I never won. I'd just try to last. I would try a new guy each time and each guy would beat me. I kept thinking, "Man, they've got to run out of guys who can beat me pretty soon," but they never did.

Finally I got a couple of them to take a ride out to my joint, **Nap's** poolroom on 26th street in Chicago. I said, "I'll play you guys over there." I had such an advantage it was ridiculous. The first guy I played was **"Mexican Johnny" Vasquez**. I beat him and he quit. There were tracks for the banks; you just shot the ball into that track and it would go right down the tape into the pocket. So Johnny quit. We were only playing for, who knows, three or four dollars a game.

Then I played another hustler, "**Gus the Greek**," and I broke him. He stayed for the whole show. He had taken the bus down and wanted me to give him a quarter to take the bus back to **Bensinger's**, but I said no and let him walk — the son-of-a-bitch – that's what they did to me. I'd have to walk from downtown because I didn't have sense enough to ask for bus fare. I was too proud. They'd break me and I'd lose every quarter. I'd make sure I had nothing when I left.

SB: So you started at Nap's, but then you'd foray up to Bensinger's where the competition was brutal.

FTB: Bensinger's at that time had some really good players. There was **Isadore "Pony" Rosen**. Pony was a top player. Everybody that came through town had to go through Pony. He'd only bet five or ten a game, mind you — he couldn't play for more than that, but there'd be two or three hundred bet on the outside.

SB: I've heard of him, so he was a One-Pocket player, too?

FTB: Yeah, and he played all games well, but there were a jillion tough players up there. **Joe Sebastian** from New York hung there, and he could run a million balls. I didn't really hang out there until after I got out of the army. I was twenty years old when I got out of the service; I did three years.

I started hanging out up there because there wasn't anything as exciting as playing at **Bensinger's**. It was something. I mean, I used to tremble when I got up there. I didn't care about winning, I just wanted to last as long as I could around those guys.

SB: That was one of the great poolrooms, along with Ames in NY.

FTB: Well, **Bensinger's** on Randolph Street was the original poolroom modeled in the book, **The Hustler**. Then they moved to the North Side. They actually considered shooting the movie **The Hustler** there. But the ceilings were too low at the new **Bensinger's** on Clark and Diversey. That's why they decided to go to New York and shoot it at **Ames**. **Bensinger's** was first considered because the name of the place in the book was **Benningtons**, but he was writing about **Bensinger's**.

SB: You mean the place Tevis described in the book, was Bensinger's?

FTB: Yeah. It was a famous place at the time.

SB: So you're talking about the original location.

FTB: Yeah, the original room on Randolph Street. A lot of people don't realize that pool was so big in Chicago that at one time the Bensinger family used to have nine poolrooms in the Loop. They had nine places, but there were fifty rooms in the Loop with thirty or more tables!

SB: That was in the '20s and '30s?

FTB: Yeah. That's how big pool was then. Then they just all started fading away.

SB: So they all started out as high-class rooms, but by the time you came in they were getting kind of worn and Bensinger's became the action room.

FTB: Yeah, but it was still a gentlemen's room. A lot of business guys would come in there and play billiards in a suit and tie. It was a no-nonsense place. Matter of fact, I would really love to create another room just like that, with that club atmosphere.

They moved to the North Side and they started to lose that image. Then it got even worse. Bensinger died and **Artie Bodendorfer** bought it. When Artie ran the place, it was a good action room. Later **Bob Siegel** bought it from Artie and he ran it right into the toilet. He let people come in and take over— gang guys, druggies, pimps— a hideous crew.

There were big rats that took over the joint at night. After one o'clock the rats owned the room and you couldn't go into certain areas.

SB: I remember reading somewhere, maybe Winning One-Pocket, about a rat dropping off a pipe or something.

FTB: That was my story! A rat slipped off the pipe onto the table and knocked the balls around and snookered me! It was brutal. Somehow **Bensinger's** got a bad reputation; guys would say, "Don't go there because you can't get out with the money."

A lot of tough guys did hang out there; the **O'Sheas** (the fighting brothers) hung out there. But "not getting out with the money" had nothing to do with getting stuck up or being bullied. It had to do with nobody could win! We broke everybody who came through the door. That was the real reason they couldn't "get out with the money." They couldn't get past me or Artie; I'll tell you that!

SB: I didn't realize that Artie actually owned the room for a while.

FTB: Oh yeah, and he put on the greatest show ever seen. When he ran the counter (he worked about twelve hours a day behind the counter), he played the whole time. He'd play pool, run back and hand out the balls, go back and shoot, ring up a sale, go back and shoot, answer the phone, go back and shoot, and when the joint closed he'd play after hours!

Of course, he was a kid then. Plus he'd never wash; his T-shirt used to get brown. He was always in action; he didn't have time to do anything. I don't know if he ever slept more than two or three hours a night. Yet he never lost. How about that: brand new room; hustled all day, played every game except Snooker; played 3 Cushion, One-Pocket, 8-Ball; running back and forth to the counter.

Artie played every son-of-a-bitch who came in there. After one o'clock he'd close the door and play guys like **Cardone** [**Billy Incardona**] and **Bugs** [**Rucker**] and whoever else and beat every living human. For a guy who played tough action, Bodendorfer had the greatest batting average in the history of pool; that's all I can tell you.

Bill Incardona

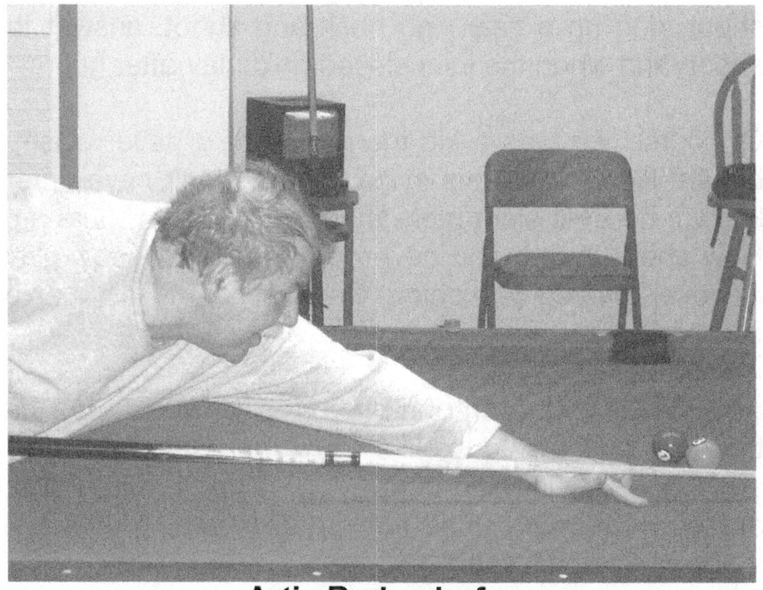

Artie Bodendorfer

John "Cannonball Lefty" Chapman
Photo courtesy Illinois Billiard Club

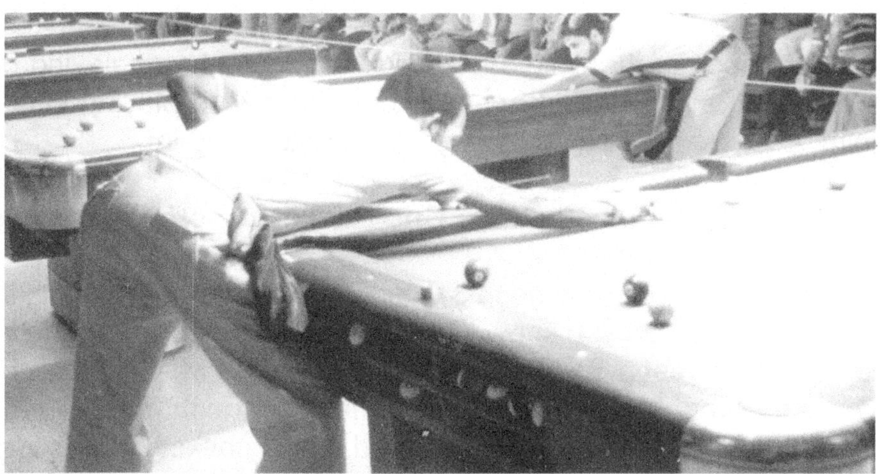

Cannonball Lefty
Photo courtesy Illinois Billiard Club

Jersey Red
photo courtesy Bill Porter and Mike Haines

SB: Whoever came in? It didn't matter who came in?

FTB: We're talking about guys like **Steve Cook**, **Jersey Red**, **Sonny Springer** — a million guys would come in — "**Cannonball Lefty**," **Bugs**, **Marvin Henderson**. **Joe Procita** was there. **Boston Shorty** hung out there for a long time. Shorty and Artie played a five day match. They had to play so many hours a day, and Artie ended up beating Shorty. This was when Shorty was Shorty, if you know what I mean.

SB: That would have been in the late 60's or 70's?

FTB: Yeah. Shorty hung out there for a long time. He played a lot of Three–Cushion there.

SB: He was a real good billiards player.

FTB: Nobody in the United States could beat Shorty playing billiards. His oil was just too stifling. And nobody could beat Artie playing One-Pocket in that joint. After a while you couldn't get people to come in!

SB: So 3 Cushion helped the One-Pocket of both those guys?

FTB: Artie played pretty good 3 Cushion. He never lost playing that either. If he played, he'd win, if you know what I mean. If somebody spotted him, he'd beat 'em. **Dallas West** used to come around once in a while, and his batting average with Artie was .000. He never won. Playing straight pool, Artie would put him on a 5' x 10' with flat Snooker rails and 4 inch pockets; it was impossible to run twenty balls on that table! Artie made sure he took care of himself. He never gave a guy an even-enough shake where the guy could unleash his arsenal.

SB: So he'd pick the table depending on the player.

FTB: Well, he'd make sure that things didn't go too much your way, so you were always uncomfortable. If you wanted to bet twenty, you had to bet forty or fifty. If you wanted to bet fifty, you had to bet two hundred. If you wanted to play three out of five, you had to play six out of eleven. Whatever it was you wanted, Artie wanted something different. Artie and **Ronnie Allen** were the greatest managers in the world.

The Beard, Marshall "Squirrel" Carpenter & Truman

Myself & Truman Hogue

Truman -- A real Banking Devil

They call setting a game up to your advantage "managing." Usually the game is over before it even starts.

SB: So he had to feel like he had some kind of little edge in the match–up or he wouldn't play.

FTB: The two of them [Artie & Ronnie Allen] were going to play up in Wisconsin and they spent two hours in negotiations. They debated and negotiated over what table, how much to bet, the rules, they finally got stymied on what cue ball to use.

Now Artie's with a friend of mine, **Race Track Phil**, a raving lunatic who had just won about fifty thousand at the track. Phil loved Artie and he wanted to see the game. He's the kind of guy that will blow ten thousand just to *see* a game. Phil didn't care who won, okay?

Now he wants Artie to play Ronnie; he wants to see that game. I mean, what a game, Ronnie and Artie, playing even! But Artie wouldn't play; he wouldn't concede the things that Ronnie wanted. My friend is threatening Artie; he put the gun on Artie and said, "I don't care if ya lose, but if ya don't play I'm going to kill ya." But Artie said "No! No! No!"

Phil was like a wild man; he was screaming and cursing, "Just play, I don't care about the money." And he didn't care about the money! He just wanted to sweat the game. But on the threat of death, Artie would not make a game that he didn't like.

It came down to not letting Ronnie put his own cue ball in. And Ronnie, by the same token, wouldn't play without his own cue ball! Everybody wanted to see the game; I was there and I was dying to see the game.

SB: But it didn't happen because neither one of them could get one tiny little edge in the making the game.

FTB: That's right. It was an irresistible force meeting an immovable object.

SB: That's pretty funny; so those two never played?

FTB: No, they never did play.

"Race Track Phil" Guagliardo & Me

Sonny Springer & Minnesota Fats
photo courtesy OnePocket.Org

SB: It sounds like Artie was a real strong One-Pocket player early on.

FTB: Yeah, he learned the game right away. He used to play with **Pony** every day, and finally Pony had no chance with him. The only guy that beat him pretty good was **Nick Varner**. Nick beat him fifteen games of One-Pocket for fifty a game when Nick first got to town.

But I know how Nick plays and I knew Nick couldn't beat Artie playing One-Pocket, so I was dying to get Artie to play him some more. I had played with Nick; I knew he couldn't beat Artie!

But what Artie did instead, was bet on Nick; he took a piece of Nick's action and he steered him into playing guys around Chicago. He got a ball from Bugs, and stuff like that, and Nick won a lot of money and Artie had about 30% of the action.

Then Nick went to NY with his father to play in that year's World's Straight Pool championship, and Nick won it. He was playing so good he won the championship. So now Nick comes back to Chicago because there was so much action here and I guess he's figuring Artie will steer him around some more, but Nick's burned out.

Artie knows Nick isn't going to get any more good games; he just won the World's championship. Plus he already beat everybody his last trip up here; he's not such a hot commodity anymore.

So there's only one thing left; the only value Nick's got left is his own bankroll and for Artie to play him himself. Nick thought Artie didn't want to play, because he had beat Artie so bad and had never asked to play again. He didn't realize that Artie was such a pragmatic kind of guy. He didn't want to play him anymore because he figured he could do better taking a piece of him. But once all that wore off he challenged him.

Naturally Nick had to play; he really couldn't believe that Artie wanted to play him. It might have even hurt his feelings a little bit, but they played anyway and Artie killed Nick. All along I'd been hounding Artie to play him; I told him I'd stake him to play. I had bad luck because I wasn't there when they started playing. I was out chasing some young broad. Artie was beating Nick so bad that Nick's father tried to get him to quit. "This is no good," he says, "You can't beat the guy." But Nick came with a fabulous line: "I can't quit; I'm learning too much!"

SB: That's pretty funny.

FTB: So I missed out on that score because Artie would give you a piece, or he'd let you stake him. He loved to get staked. He had his own money, but he liked getting staked and he played real good getting staked. But if Artie bet his own money it was worse. He's one of the few guys that played real good getting staked — and liked to get staked — but if he played for his own money he was fifteen or twenty percent better.

SB: Really.

FTB: There was really no defense against his game; Artie was an animal. And the crazy thing was he didn't really like pool. Maybe that's the reason he played so good.

He really didn't like pool. That's probably why he quit and went to Las Vegas. He just quit playing pool; it was just too much pressure on him. Pool was just a means to an income, or he was just too scared of getting beat — I don't know what it was — some kind of psychological trauma involved.

I talked to **Wimpy** about that. I said, "Listen, **Wimpy** [**Luther Lassiter**], there's a kid in Chicago that never loses." I told him about Artie and Wimpy says, "Boy, I sure feel sorry for that kid." I said, "What do you mean, you feel sorry for him? You feel sorry for a guy that never loses?" Lassiter says, "Yeah, do you realize the pressure that guy must be under?"

And then I thought about it for a while. And maybe Wimpy was right, because Artie eventually had to get psychiatric counseling. It ain't normal to never get beat. I knew them all; some of the best guys ever. "Cardone" had a great winning record for a while, but his average with Artie was very low; maybe one time out of ten, he'd come out ahead.

SB: You're saying Artie was to One-Pocket what Lassiter was to 9–Ball? I guess Lassiter went through that with 9-Ball.

FTB: Yeah, nobody could beat him either. Of course, Lassiter ducked **Harold Worst**. Maybe because he was the reigning world champion and he figured what the hell, why would I want to risk my crown? Worst wanted to play him too. As a matter of fact, Worst invited anybody in the world that wanted to play.

Wienie Beanie tried to get Wimpy to play Worst, saying, "This guy wants to play 9-Ball for five and ten thousand dollars; let's go." But Wimpy said "No, I got these exhibitions. I have the exhibitions and the posters and the world championship..." He didn't want to risk it. Plus, he already knew that Worst had beat his guy, **Don Willis** (Willis beat Mosconi a couple of times). Willis was Wimpy's road partner, so Wimpy knew that Worst had executed one of the all-time 9-Ball monsters. Don Willis had a batting average at 9–Ball about the same as Artie's at One-Pocket. It wasn't so much that Wimpy was afraid of Worst; he's just thinking, "Why the hell should I? I could win a few thousand but if he beats me, I lose all this notoriety and all these exhibitions."

SB: Could you tell us a little more about Harold Worst?

FTB: Worst was from Grand Rapids, Michigan. To me, he was the most phenomenal human playing pool that ever breathed. Forget about anybody else. I mean, I played with Mosconi, he ran 160 and out on me. I watched him never miss. Mosconi had more talent than anybody, but Worst was the most frightening pool player. Everybody who played Worst trembled. When they played Harold Worst, if you looked at their right hand, their hand was shaking like they had palsy. The guy was so intimidating...... if he had lived a couple more years... But I guess he wound up beating everybody anyway, doing everything.

SB: He did — including 3 Cushion, too.

FTB: He was the world's 3 cushion champion! He won the world championship down in Argentina. I heard he had to sneak out of the country after he beat **Navarro** and won the title. They were so hotheaded they were talking about killing him. He was only 21 years old when he won.

Worst had some billiard training by no less than Willie Hoppe.

SB: Did he pick up One-Pocket at Johnston City?

FTB: Yeah. But his first appearance in a pool tournament was in Tampa, FL. He walked into the tournament room, nobody knew who he was, and he says, "I'm the world's greatest 9-Ball player, and I want to play anybody who rolls 9-Balls."

photos courtesy Bill Hermicudas

Harold Worst

Eddie "The Knoxville Bear" Taylor

Luther "Wimpy" Lassiter

"Who is this guy?" they asked themselves. **Squirrel** is there. **Eddie Taylor**, **Danny Jones**, **Fats**, etc. are there. Worst didn't even know the rules they were playing by! He was used to playing *shoot-to-hit-it**. And they were playing *push-out.**

SB: That was like in '62 or something?

FTB: No, it was past that. I forget when that was. **Portland Don Watson** was there; I think he won it.

SB: Oh yeah, it was an all-around [1964].

FTB: Yeah. Anyway, they said, "We'll get somebody to play," and they didn't get any *short-stops** either, even though they didn't know who he was. They said, "Who is this bum?" Somebody said, "Some billiard player from Michigan."

So who do you think they opened up with? Eddie Taylor! The only thing that bothered Worst in pool was that he'd get snookered and wouldn't have any shot, because he knew he could make anything he could see. That was the only thing that scared him. But now they are playing push–out.

Worst asks, "You mean to tell me, if I get snookered I can push out and have another chance to make the ball? " And they're saying, "Yeah, yeah."

These are the top push-out guys in the country! So he'd push out for something ridiculous and they'd say, "Go ahead and shoot" and they'd laugh and he'd whiz it in the pocket. Worst thought they were idiots. "You mean you're going to let me shoot this? "

So Worst barbecued Taylor. Then they brought in **Jimmy Moore**— there was no stalling with these guys! And he beat Jimmy Moore. Then they brought in Danny Jones, and next they brought in Squirrel. Then they finally started to do their work on him. Now these are the smartest hustlers in the world and this guy Worst ain't got a clue about hustling, so they set to work on him. I think he gave Danny Jones two games on the wire going to 11. Then he gave Squirrel the break or two out of three breaks or something.

**shoot to hit it*: Today's Nine Ball rules. You must make an attempt to hit the object ball every shot. Failure to hit the object ball gives opponent ball in hand.

**push-out*: The old rules for Nine Ball, whereby, when you were snookered on the next ball, you could push the cue ball out for a shot. Your opponent could then elect to let you shoot, or shoot the shot himself.

**short-stop*: A lifetime pool player whose ability is just under the top players.

Now they started to pound him. They outmaneuvered him. He was getting steered around like a stepchild. I hate to snitch on him, but **Wienie Beanie** was his advisor — Wienie Beanie! So you take it from there what kind of advice Beanie was giving him. Beanie's first allegiance was to the hustlers.

So they did get to Worst, as far as winning the money, but nobody could stand up to him in a square shake. Another thing about Worst was that he would bet all you wanted to bet. He was like **Jew Paul [Paul Bruslov**] in Detroit. The line was open. Worst would bet until you were done betting. So whatever game he made, you could break him with that game, because he bet all you wanted to bet.

In Johnston City he would play anybody, any game, except banks. All the other games he played, 8-Ball, 9-Ball, One–Pocket, straight pool, or snooker. He beat **Sammy Blumenthal** playing snooker! (That happened in Johnston City, not in Jacksonville, where Sammy was unbeatable.) Worst was just a freak.

SB: Didn't he die at like 41 or something like that?

FTB: I don't think he got to 40. The most phenomenal guy I ever saw play pool, and I've seen some good players. This guy would rocket the game ball in. He would make the game ball look like a ham sandwich and he would hit it at 600 m.p.h. right down the middle of the pocket.

Worst was ferocious. Even the top guys ducked him. Taylor ducked him and Wimpy ducked him. That's the true story. I hate to snitch on those guys, but they ducked him. Not that they couldn't beat him for sure, because anybody could win once you're in that level...

Worst was very abusive. He was obnoxious and very contemptuous of everybody. He'd say, "Doesn't anybody want to play anything? Do any of you guys have the nerve to play anything? "

Worst wasn't well liked. I remember **Cornbread Red** went up to Eddie Taylor and said, "Bear, when are we going to take off this Dutchman and make him shut his mouth? " And the Bear said, "I'm going to get to him, Red, I'm going to get to him." But he never did.

Then Wimpy and Worst played 9-Ball in a tournament match and Wimpy beat Worst. Wimpy had got a lot of lucky rolls and Worst was steaming. So after the match was over Worst says, "I'll see you in the back room, Mr. Lassiter, for $200 a game, 9-Ball. Everybody flocked to the back room because they wanted to see that game — Worst against Wimpy — $200 9-Ball — but neither guy showed up.

SB: I didn't realize that Harold got into action quite that much.

FTB: He bet all you wanted to bet. And just about every time he was in a game, he was in a trap. These were sharp hustlers. They were monsters he was dealing with — road guys like Beanie and Taylor and their advisors.

Every game he made he had the worst of it, every single match. He was playing **Babyface [Alton Whitlow]** 130 to 100 at straight pool. That was the game.

Babyface says, "This is the greatest match I ever had in my life and I can't win a game." Who could give Babyface 130 to 100? But Worst would do it. He just shoved his way through the mess; he didn't know there was such a thing as a bad game. I think he was playing **Sonny Springer** and he's giving Sonny 8 to 6. I'm not sure if it was 8 to 6 and the break or just 8 to 6, but they were playing One-Pocket and they were playing for $200 a game and Worst was eight games loser or something like that— getting robbed. He knows he can't win now.

Wienie Beanie had told him "Go ahead and play, Harold, it's a good game. Go ahead and give him 8 to 6." Giving Sonny Springer, one of the great undercover One-Pocket players, two balls, put Worst in a trap. Understandably, Sonny was pounding him.

Worst eventually realizes he's in a trap; that they had bagged him up. So what did he do? I don't remember the math but he raised the bet. Instead of quitting, he doubled up or tripled up and ran eight–and–out four games in a row and got even and he quit.

My memory is a little weak here, Worst might have made it $400 a game, which is a lot of money, we're talking 1965 or 1966. He raised it to $400 or $600 a game and he ran eight and out four games in a row on a guy who had the mortal *nuts** and then he quit because he knew the game was no good.

**nuts:* To have a tremendous advantage over your opponent in the game or session you are playing.

Billy "Cornbread Red" Burge
photo courtesy Bill Porter and Mike Haines

Alton "Babyface" Whitlow
photo courtesy Conrad Burkman

Squirrel & Cornbread
photo courtesy Bill Porter and Mike Haines

Ed Kelly, Eddie Robin, Myself & Artie Bodendorfer

SB: I've been impressed as I've done these interviews; it's quite a combination of skills that you guys have. It's not just the pool playing; there's a whole lot of other stuff going on that is impressive. One thing I've noticed is that you guys all have quite the memory for different players and different situations; you know where you played a guy, when, what the game was, how they played and what the money was. Then there's the whole *lemon business and the psychology of drawing a guy into a game that is very interesting. I want to talk about that some more. I appreciate your time today, Fred.**

FTB: Remind me to tell you the story about when I was just a kid, with my first wife — but I don't think we were married then — she was just my girlfriend. I had been off cheating with some other girl who had given me a big hickey on my neck. Now what do you do in that spot? How do you beat that situation? This is with a girl who was very suspicious and used to inspect my clothes. So I had to come up with a super-move. Only a pool hustler could escape that kind of trap.

SB: I want to hear it.

FTB: You know **Doc Richie Herbert**?

SB: The guy that owns Chris' Billiards in Chicago now?

FTB: Yeah, Doc reminded me of that story because he had a part in it. It's a real good story and only a certified pool scuff would qualify for an escape. You have to be a guy that had went out on the road. So how do you get out of that spot?

She's on the way to meet me in the next ten minutes and I have a hickey the size of an apple on my neck. **END PART I**

**lemon, to lemon someone*: The practice of conning a weaker player into believing that you are even weaker than they are. A pool con job.

START PART II

SB: Where we left off, your girlfriend is on the way and you've got a hickey the size of an apple.

FTB: Right, and she was very suspicious; she used to smell my body and sniff my clothes, not very trusting. So Doc and I are in front of **Bensinger's** poolroom, where I'm supposed to meet her. We came up with a scheme. Doc drove his car over to the front of the poolroom and we lifted the hood. Then Doc starts the motor and says, "Get underneath the car like you're fixing it. When we spot her coming, I'll give you a kick when she's right here." As soon as she's in range, he nudged me underneath the car and I let out a scream and I come out cursing, covered with grease and oil and I yell at Doc, "You dumb son-of-a-bitch, you leaked the goddamn hot oil all over me!" And of course my neck is all red. She looked at it, all sympathetic, "Honey, we better get you home right now and I'll put some salve on that for you."

SB: So you turned it to your advantage.

FTB: It's an example of thinking on your feet at the last second.

SB: So you had your own room in Chicago for a while?

FTB: Yeah, North Shore Billiards. It was the second greatest action spot in that era, next to Detroit. Nothing was like Detroit because those guys bet $15,000 or $20,000. But we were like $3,000 a game, $5,000 a game, $5,000 or $10,000 sessions on a regular basis. Everybody was hanging around there — every player. **Buddy Hall, Louis Roberts, Larry Hubbart, Allen Hopkins, Nick Varner, Jack Cooney**.

I mean, everybody, even **Earl Strickland**. Ask Earl. Earl slept on the floor. We let him sleep upstairs underneath the tables. Earl, he didn't have a buck then, and he's big enough to talk about it now. He's not ashamed, that's just what he went through when he first came up here, before he started beating everybody. He got his start at North Shore, my joint.

SB: He was a teenager then?

FTB: Yeah, just a kid.

SB: But he got real strong, real early didn't he?

FTB: Right then, right from my room; he launched from there and it was 100 m.p.h. When he was with us he played okay. But all of a sudden, boom, he's a monster and he started winning tournaments. **Keith McCready** played there. Everybody was there and they were playing all over the joint, not just on one table.

SB: But Earl is one guy even though he hung out in your room, he never really picked up One-Pocket, did he?

FTB: No, he liked to play 9-Ball; that was it. He played a little banks on the South Side but he's not a banker either. He was there to play Nine Ball. Now Nine Ball really wasn't that big in my room. It was mostly One-Pocket or banks, but tremendous action, 24 hours a day.

SB: Why do you think Chicago had such a strong One-Pocket tradition?

FTB: Well, we had some great players, we learned from Pony. Pony was our guy and Artie had his own style and **Bugs** [Leonard Rucker] had his own style. I had my own style, kind of a mixture between Artie and Bugs.

SB: Because you're a real good banker too, of course.

FTB: Right. Artie wasn't, Artie couldn't bank a lick. I used to play him eight to six. He couldn't even play Nine Ball. He couldn't beat anybody playing Nine Ball. He played a little straight pool; actually he played pretty good straight pool. It's hard to believe that he had that kind of speed at One-Pocket without that bank power. His moves and percentages were just so good.

SB: He controlled the cue ball real well then?

FTB: Basically it's percentages. The shots that he took were sound. After a while he would break a guy down. The guy just kept looking at Artie doing the right thing; never making a mistake, never doing the wrong thing, hour after hour, day after day. And he could play for days without any drugs.

SB: So it was his cue ball control and the fact that he just always picked the right shot?

FTB: That's right. His percentages were just unbelievable. He knew exactly what to do.

SB: And that's something that he didn't just learn; he also must have invented some of that himself.

FTB: Yeah, nobody plays like he did. At first he used to play Pony, just to learn, then he told me Pony couldn't teach him anything anymore. Then he started robbing Pony playing even. Finally, Pony dropped dead playing him! As a matter of fact, Artie's probably got the record, two guys dropped dead playing him . That's the kind of pressure he puts people under. He's had two people drop dead at the table. Artie had Pony like seven to nothing and Pony fought back and tied it up. He needed one ball. He was shooting at the game ball and it was just too much and he gave out and dropped dead in front of Artie. And another guy, not a famous player, Ray Falchero, did the same thing.

SB: That's brutal! So he's probably one of the smartest One-Pocket players you ever ran into?

FTB: Not probably. Artie was the smartest. There's nobody smarter than he is. Like I told you, he was no great shooter. He couldn't beat anybody playing Nine Ball, couldn't beat anybody playing banks. He was a nice straight pool player, but he couldn't beat any of the New York guys. So how did he beat you? Good question.

SB: How about the black players, like Kenny Romberg?

FTB: Remus was his name.

SB: That was his nickname?

FTB: No, his name was Remus, his nickname was **Romberg**.

SB: Oh, I got that backwards! It seems like they had parallel One-Pocket pool in Chicago, you had the white rooms and the white players and then you had the black rooms and the black players.

FTB: There was always action in the black rooms. It used to be a guy could have fun if he wanted to play One-Pocket around Chicago. One-Pocket or banks. There were plenty of bankers and plenty of One-Pocket players.

SB: And that's part of the reason why Chicago had such good One-Pocket players and they had all those good bank players too?

FTB: Well, it's a certain style. We call it the Chicago style of One-Pocket; it's a little "squeezy." California's got a different style, because Ronnie (Allen) was the main player out there. Ronnie was the power guy, with power shots and scrambling balls, but here in Chicago we just kept putting you behind balls and frozen to the rail.

SB: Was Clem from around Chicago?

FTB: Clem (**Eugene Metz**) was from Cincinnati. Clem was maybe the safest player ever. I would have liked to have seen him and Artie play; the game may never have ended!

SB: That's what I hear about Clem.

FTB: He's another guy that didn't like pool. I'll tell you how tough Clem was: he beat **Eddie Taylor** and **Johnny Vives** playing One-Pocket. The bad thing was, as good as he played ... if you beat him he was liable to stick you up! He was hardcore. Tough as it was to beat the guy, if somebody did luck out, they were liable to get stuck up. He might put the gun on you, that's how rough things were then.

SB: I believe he did spend some time in jail.

FTB: He led a motley kind of a life, but I liked him.

SB: Well, there is a little of that around pool.

FTB: But he didn't like pool! He'd rather do anything else.

SB: I never understood that, being that talented but not liking it.

FTB: To him it was just a way of making money. The same thing with Artie, I guess. They got away from it as soon as they could.

Cliff Joyner & Jack Cooney
photo courtesy Conrad Burkman

John "Rags" Fitzpatrick
photo courtesy Bill Bell

John "Rags" Fitzpatrick
photo courtesy Bill Bell

SB: I would think in order to get that good, especially at One-Pocket, you would have to like it to some degree. Tell us about your upcoming book, *Banking with the Beard*.

FTB: About 90% of the secrets that I know are in there. I'm giving them up because my son is not really into pool; I was going to just leave it for him. But he's not interested enough in pool. So my ego finally got the best of me. I wanted some recognition. Everywhere I look, I see people getting recognition and half of them can't even play!

SB: Well, there are a lot of players that can do things, but they can't explain what they are doing and if they try, they explain it wrong anyway!

FTB: Exactly

SB: But you are very good at explaining things and I'm sure that comes through in the book. I notice that in the front of your book you credit Gene Skinner.

FTB: Gene was a great player in the '30s and '40s. Then he went to work at the race track and kind of got away from pool. But in his career he played everybody. He's one of the few people to play Mosconi One-Pocket and beat him.

SB: Oh, really? How did he lure Mosconi into One-Pocket?

FTB: You're asking me to remember something he told me 20 years ago. He beat **Jimmy Moore** playing One-Pocket too. He was a great all-around player; he played in those 3 Cushion Billiard Tournaments too.

SB: 3 Cushion billiards?

FTB: Yes, there were ten guys that always finished one through ten at those tournaments, but he was just under those guys at the next level. He used to keep Fats broke too; they used to play all the time. He played **Marcel Camp** a lot too. Gene was a great player and he bet his own money.

Gene Skinner

photos courtesy Macguy

SB: Was he out of Chicago?

FTB: No, he was from Fullerton, California, but when the race track —Arlington Park— was open, he'd be here. That's how I met him. He took me under his wing and showed me how to play One-Pocket. In one week I learned so much from him that when I went down to Johnston City a week later and played in my first tournament ever, I came in fifth! I beat some great players, **Cisero Murphy, St. Louis Blackie, Steve Cook, Wade Crane**, etc. I had Ronnie Allen dead to rights, three games to two and seven to nothing, that was for second place! I went for a bad shot, a three-ball combination. It didn't go and Ronnie got five and ended up winning that game. It was "winner breaks," and he broke real good and got three off the break and out-managed me from there. Ronnie ended up winning the tournament. But with Skinner's stuff, I improved two balls in one week.

SB: That was a little unusual back then to have somebody actually tell you stuff.

FTB: Well, the reason he did was because he had already quit playing pool. He was one of the few guys that would release anything. He kind of liked me and he did it for nothing. If he was still into pool he wouldn't have shown me anything.

Believe me, they just didn't do it. As a matter of fact ,I was just out at Artie's house in Vegas, and he's got a pool table in his garage and he leaked a few secrets to me for the same reason. No way on earth would he ever tell me anything back when we were playing, but we don't compete anymore. So he drizzled off a few things. Listen, I think I'm pretty smart at pool, I'll put my knowledge up against just about any human, especially at banks and at One-Pocket I think I'm pretty smart there too, but Artie is a friggin' genius.

Now I understand it. I finally understand how he was able to beat everybody. He really had a plan. And another thing, I'm going to put this on your web site: Artie issues a challenge, anybody thinks they know more One-Pocket than he does, anybody who thinks they have a better understanding of One-Pocket, that goes for any human, he'll put up thirty thousand. You get a panel of five knowledgeable people to judge and each guy has an hour to display what they know and then the panel will decide who knows more.

SB: Boy, I tell you as a spectator that would be pretty incredible!

FTB: Yeah, a rich One-Pocket freak might put up the money just to learn the stuff.

Wade Crane

Ronnie Allen

photos courtesy Bill Porter and Mike Haines

Cornbread Red

SB: Absolutely. It might be worth thirty thousand.

FTB: I only got few minutes with him and I'm not a humble kind of guy, so for him to humble my knowledge, that was really something. I wouldn't bet against him on that 30-grand proposition. While I was at his house I showed him a few banks too. And once I showed him, he never missed them; every time they came up he made them and the creep never gave me any credit, as if all along he knew how to make that bank.

SB: I find it kind of interesting that he ended up making all that money in Vegas by managing the odds, just like what you are talking about at One-Pocket. He had a good strong knack for recognizing an advantage in percentages.

FTB: Now I'll give up one of my secret road stories. Once upon a time there were these hustlers that put a *spread** down for me to play **Archie Karas**. Have you ever heard of him? Archie the Greek, from Las Vegas. He's the highest rolling man of all time. Have you have heard of **"Nick The Greek" Dandelos**?

SB: Yeah.

FTB: Well, Nick the Greek is a nit next to Archie. Nobody has ever gambled in the history of the world like Archie Karas. Karas won about a $50,000,000 at the **Horseshoe Casino** in Vegas!

Karas first played bar pool with the owner of the **Mirage Casino**, **Bobby Baldwin**, basically on his nerve (He started with very little money) and ended up beating him out of over a million bucks. Then he also beat Bobby playing poker. From there he went on to win about $33,000,000 playing dice at the **Horseshoe Casino**.

At one time Karas had all the $5,000 chips in the joint. They had to print a new chip for him, a $25,000 denomination. Nobody gambled like this guy.

Karas even broke the no-limit poker players. High rollers couldn't keep up with Archie because money apparently held no value to him. It was like he had no use for it. He started out dead broke and got up to $33,000,000.

**spread*: Like a picnic spread. What appears to be nice things all laid out for a sucker to fall for.

"Handsome Danny" Jones
photo courtesy Bill Porter and Mike Haines

Front Row: UJ Puckett, Jim Rempe & Me
Back Row: Jersey Red, Allen Hopkins

But now he's on the way down. He's lost most of the money back shooting craps. He's got a few million left, three, four, or five, that was when these guys trapped him. They told him that there's a billionaire in Pennsylvania, an industrialist that likes to play pool and gambles real high (there is such a guy).

Audie Weiss was the guy's name; a super-rich, gambling degenerate who couldn't play pool at all. Archie had been hearing about this guy for years. These guys told him they could get him a game with Audie — the only kind of guy who would gamble with Archie for his stakes. So they take him to Pennsylvania, to this little town. Planted in that town is me. I'm Audie Weiss, the billionaire.

Archie had heard that Audie Weiss was an eccentric, who didn't dress fancy, didn't wear jewelry and was very common-looking. So I'm passed off as Audie.

Archie and I meet. Formal introductions and so on, then we immediately go to the poolroom. We decided to play 8-Ball. I say, "What do you want to play for, Archie?" We kicked it off at $40,000 a game! Archie has $200,000 in $5,000 and $25,000 chips from the Horseshoe in his pocket. The $25,000 chips were like travelers' checks. You couldn't steal them from him because nobody would cash 'em. Karas had to okay it to cash 'em in, because he was the only guy authorized to have that denomination chip. That's what he carried in his pocket instead of money.

The first game is for $40,000. Archie broke, didn't make anything and I ran out. It was an easy layout. He reaches in his pocket and gives me eight $5,000 chips. I break, don't make anything and leave an easy layout. Karas runs out. I give him back the $40,000. Now I was a little shaky. I could beat him; I was a good pool player, but we're playing for $40,000 a game and I don't have a quarter! None of us had that kind of money. There ain't no paying him off if I lose. We don't have anything to pay him with!

I hung in there and we ended up playing $100,000 a game One-Pocket. But now I'm stalling. I had to try to win and stall too! I didn't dare show my real speed. I ended up beating him out of $100,000 the first night. Karas paid me off with four $25,000 chips.

SB: You must have had a tough balancing act; stalling enough to be credible, but you couldn't afford to lose!

FTB: It was a tough balancing act, but I was a good *lemon* man in those days.

After the match was over, we go up to the counter to pay the time. The time is $21. It's a little bowling alley, a cheap joint. At this point I *short-arm* Karas for the time! I'm $100,000 winner, but I'm an eccentric billionaire. I play the part all the way. So I'm patting my pockets and slow drawing him on the time. I keep patting like I can't find $21. He says, "Don't worry about it, Audie, I've got the time." I had him so totally hooked he paid the time! I said, "Oh, thank you, Archie."

It was one hell of a deal. Now we had to stall off the next match because we wanted to get those chips cashed before we played again, We've got to cash those chips in case he finds out who I am. So we had somebody fly back to Vegas with the chips and Archie had to go along to okay getting them cashed.

In order to let some time elapse, I told Archie that I had to fly to Japan for a big business meeting. That would take me out of the country and give me an excuse to not play for a few days. I wouldn't play more until we got our money.

Well, he gave the okay, we got the chips cashed, played again and he lost another $100,000. But the guys that set the operation up were idiots; they weren't experienced "scufflers," real lemon hustlers. They set it up, but they didn't know how to take it off. Archie paid the first $200,000, but he ended up owing another $800,000, which we never got.

SB: So he owed another $800,000?

FTB: When Karas got back to Vegas, these guys screwed it up. They acted so guilty that it woke Archie up. You see, you gotta act like a legitimate thing occurred. I'm supposed to be Audie Weiss. I won $200,000. Big deal, so what? I've supposedly lost millions.

But the steer guys dogged it real bad when it came to collecting. Archie eventually got suspicious and started asking around about a guy that plays One-Pocket, wears glasses and limps. Pretty soon someone says, "I know that guy; that sounds like ***The Beard*** from Chicago."

So that got us and our scam busted, and we didn't get the rest of the money. But it was one of the great cons. Karas was really hooked. He really fell for it. I laid a great stall down. At one point in the game, they were trying to get him to quit because they didn't want him to owe so much money. Archie said, 'No, no, his leg is gonna give out any minute. " Karas thought my leg was going to cave in on me. My leg was really screwed up and I was in a lot of pain, but so what? I could play for days like that.

SB: So you were a pretty good actor then?

FTB: Yeah. Some good lemon men turned me out. I learned my moves from **Bunny Rogoff**, **Hollywood Jack Nicholson** and some other real good lemon men from Chicago. **Jack Cooney** was another teacher. They were great playing the lemon. I learned from the best.

Like I said before, the guys in the Karas hustle weren't real con men. ***They*** fell for my stall, that's how dumb they were. I'm stalling and they believe that it's the real thing even though I had told them earlier, "Don't you guys fall for my acting; it's only meant for Archie. At some point you're going to think this is real, but it ain't, it's just an act." The original steer guy could barely handle it the first day we played. He kept running in and out of the poolroom, he was too nervous to watch.

It was quite a deception. We couldn't show any money because we had nothing to show! But I had some moves for that, too. What the hell, I'm an eccentric billionaire industrialist.

Archie started wondering about how he was going to get paid, so we flashed him a phony checkbook with Audie Weiss's name on it. *What the hell, I got billions, can't I owe you? You think I have it in my pocket?*

SB: That's a good story, and I know you have more.

FTB: I have ten million more!

"Richie From The Bronx" Ambrose

photos courtesy Bill Porter and Mike Haines

"Frisco Jack" Cooney

A 17 yr old Beard in Ft. Leonard Wood, MO

The 19 yr old Beard in Germany, 1960

My "Daddy Cool" days in Germany

The Beard — Broke And Hungry In Bensingers

The Beard In Action On Table #13 (5' x 10')

More Action On Table 13 (5' x 10')

The Beard's Captain America days in Johnston City IL 1972

My Wife Theresa & I In Front Of The Cue Club In Johnston City

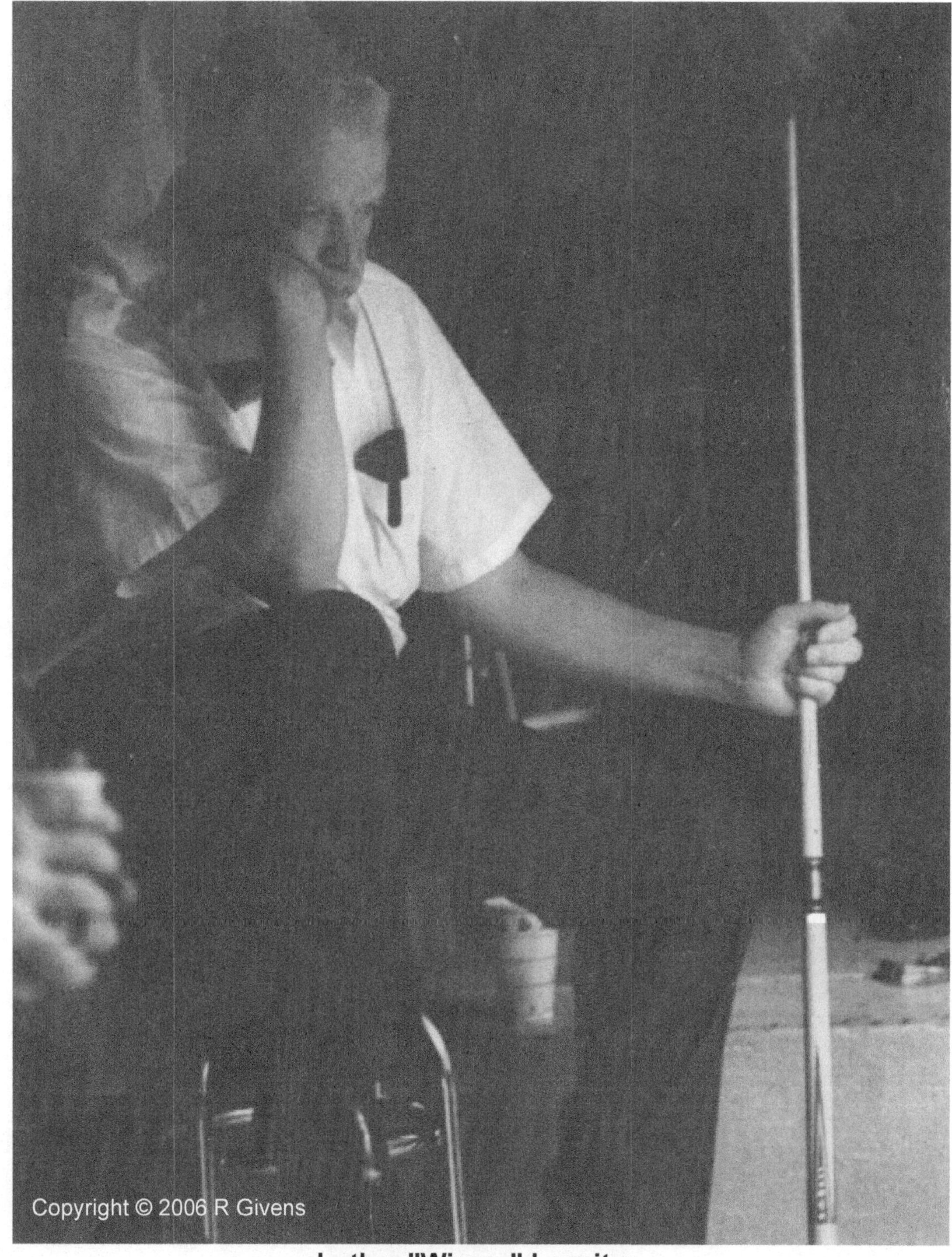

Luther "Wimpy" Lassiter

LASSITER

Luther Lassiter had such a deep dislike for watching an opponent shoot that an unsuspecting observer seeing Lassiter in the chair might have thought Wimpy's best friend or a close relative had just died.

The picture on the left was taken during a straight pool game between Lassiter and Irving Crane. Lassiter had just finished a 92 ball run. Crane replied with 57. While Crane was shooting Lassiter's demeanor was appropriate for a funeral parlor.

Opponent's were well advised to ignore Lassiter's emotional display because Wimpy's dejection only lasted until his next turn at the table and no lead was safe when Lassiter rose from his seat.

If a player made a mistake, Lassiter would return to the table like a hungry lion and run the game out.

Lassiter's depression ceased the instant Crane missed and Wimpy easily ran the 33 he needed to win the game.

Cognoscenti who were supposed to know the truth said that Luther Lassiter was the best shot-maker since Ralph Greenleaf. (Greenleaf was known to shoot combination wing shots on 5' x 10' tables in his trick shot exhibitions.)

AIMS

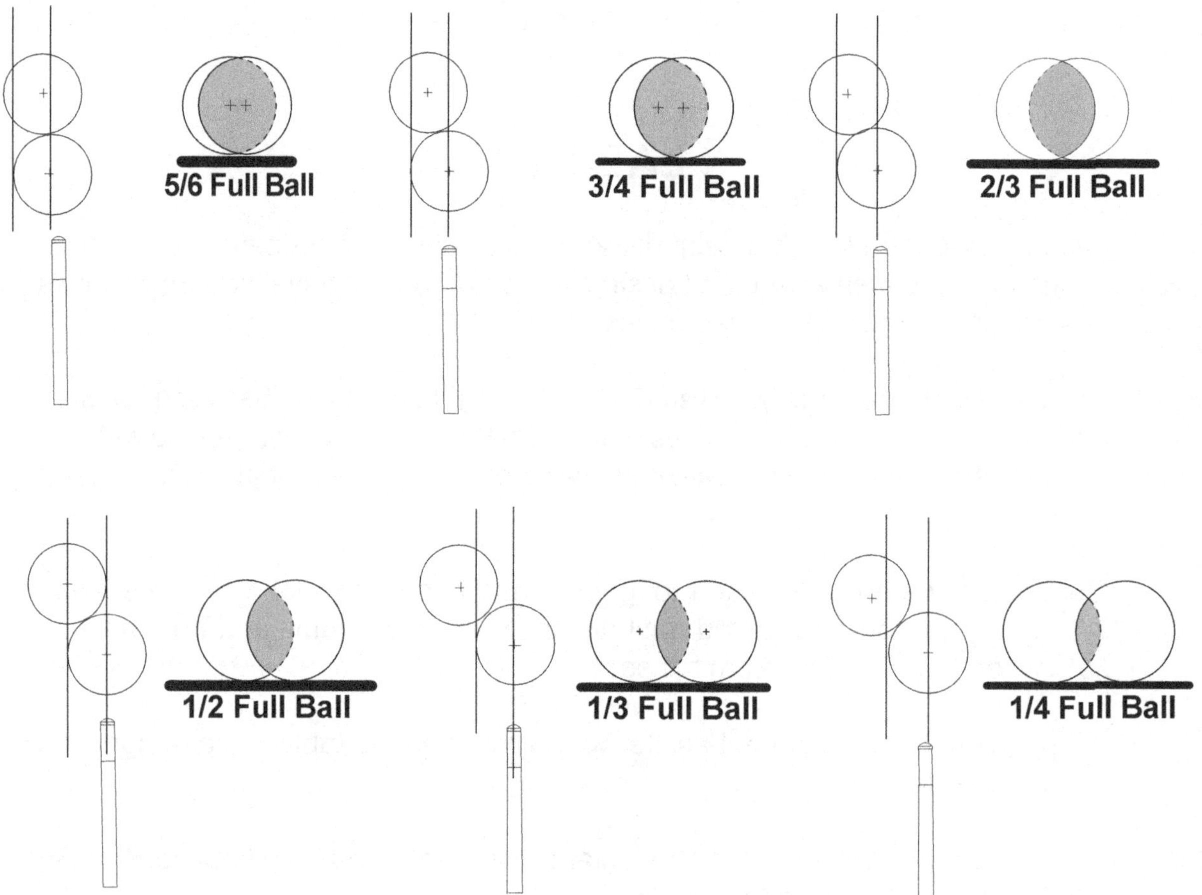

The aims we use in this volume of banking systems provide a rational basis for linking the effects of Acquired English, Cut Angle, Fullness of Hit and Transferred English to accurately control rebound angles. When cutting to the opposite side, you should, of course, reverse the aiming process.

5/6 FULL BALL AIM

Look directly at the Object Ball as though you were lining up a dead straight–in shot. But only cover 5/6 of the Object Ball with the Cue Ball.

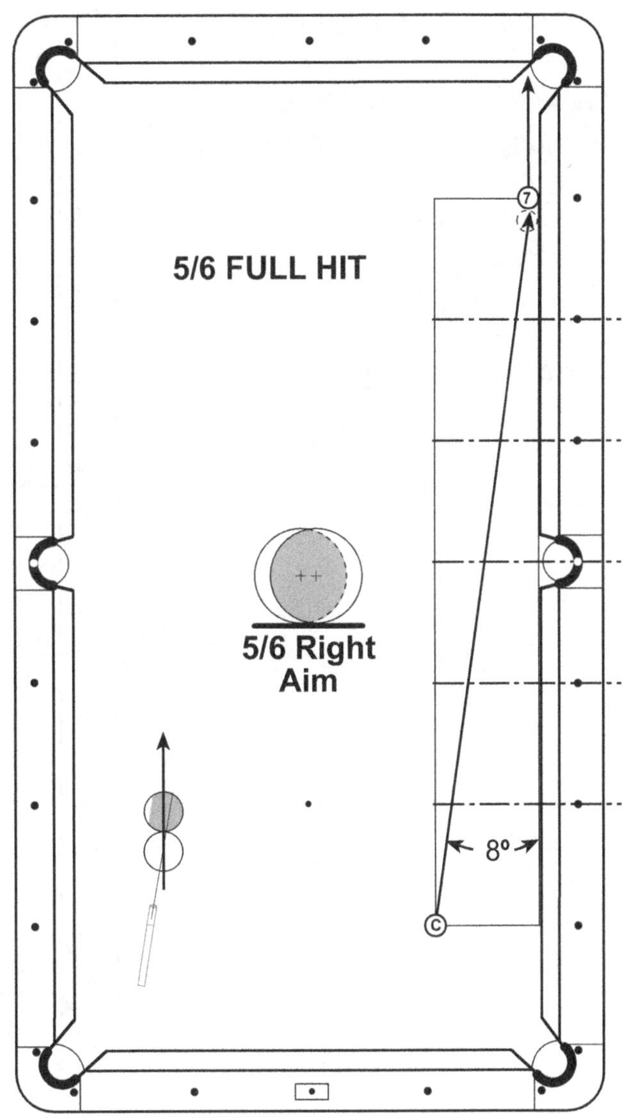

3/4 FULL BALL AIM

Look directly at the Object Ball as though you were lining up a straight-in shot, but only cover 3/4 of the Object Ball with the Cue Ball

This is how a 3/4 Full Ball hit looks in straight-in pool.

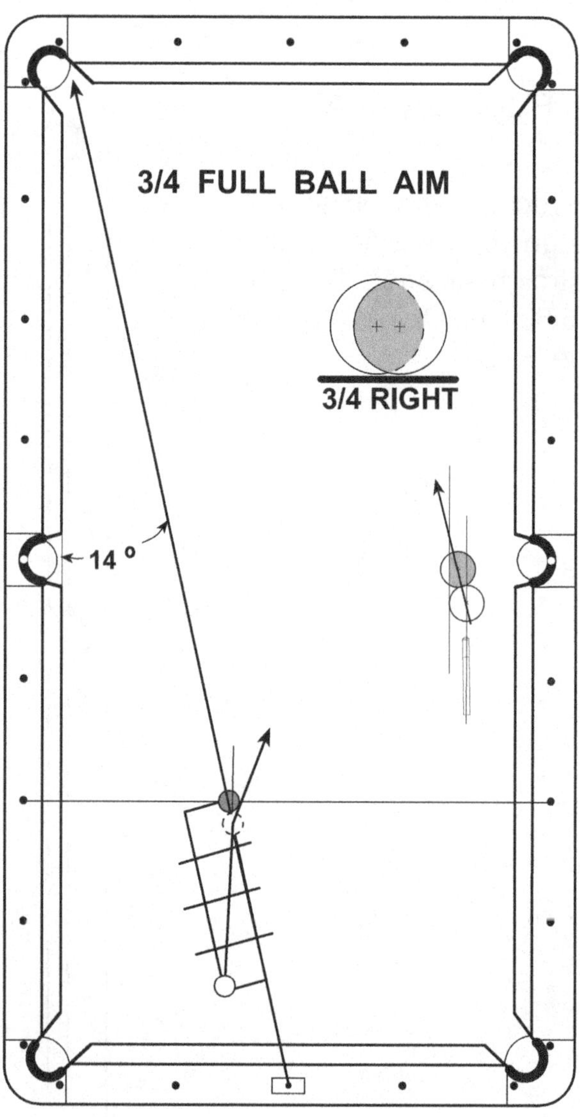

2/3 FULL BALL AIM

Look directly at the Object Ball as though you were lining up a dead straight–in shot.

But only cover 2/3 of the Object Ball with the Cue Ball.

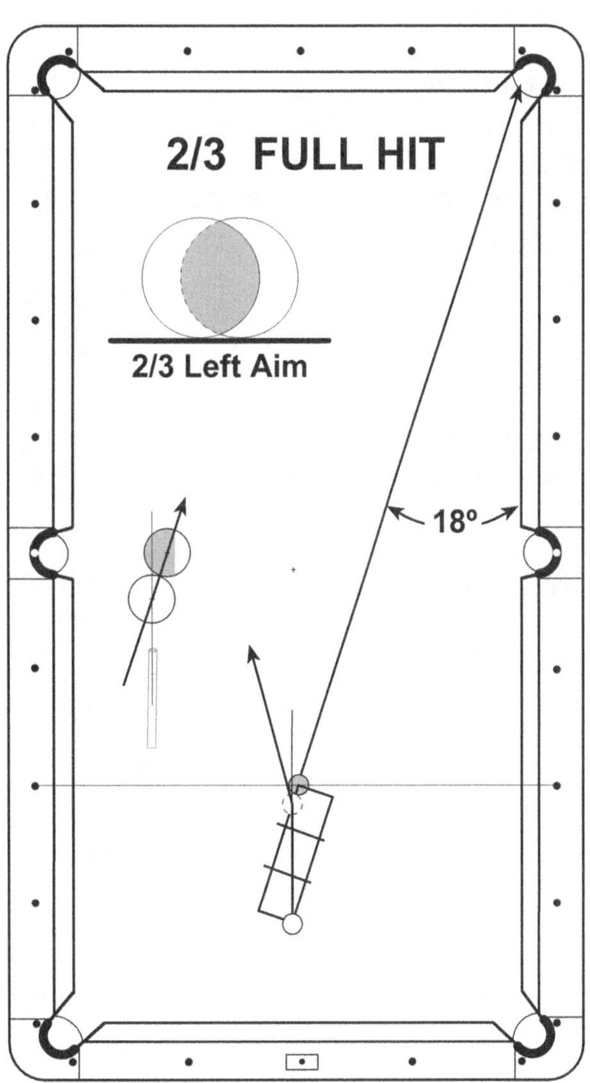

1/2 FULL BALL AIM

Look directly at the Object Ball as though you were lining up a straight-in shot, but only cover 1/2 of the Object Ball with the Cue Ball

Another way of lining up a 1/2 Full hit is to point the tip of the cue through the center of the Cue Ball and aim at the outer edge of the Object Ball.

This is how a 1/2 Full Ball hit looks in straight-in pool.

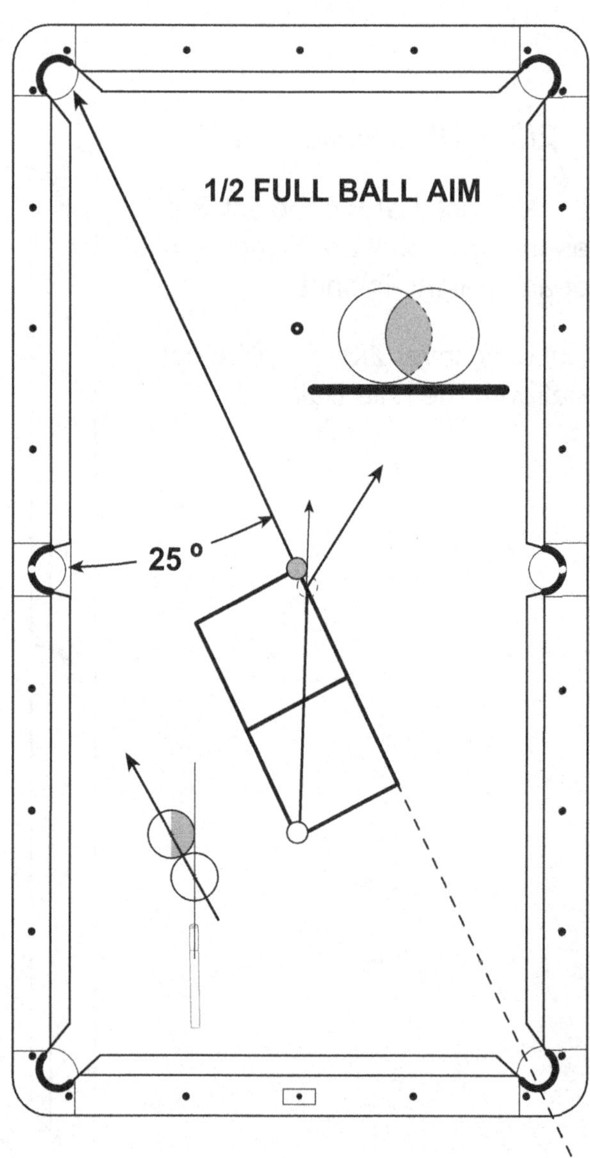

1/3 FULL BALL AIM

Look directly at the Object Ball as though you were lining up a dead straight–in shot.

But only cover 1/3 of the Object Ball with the Cue Ball.

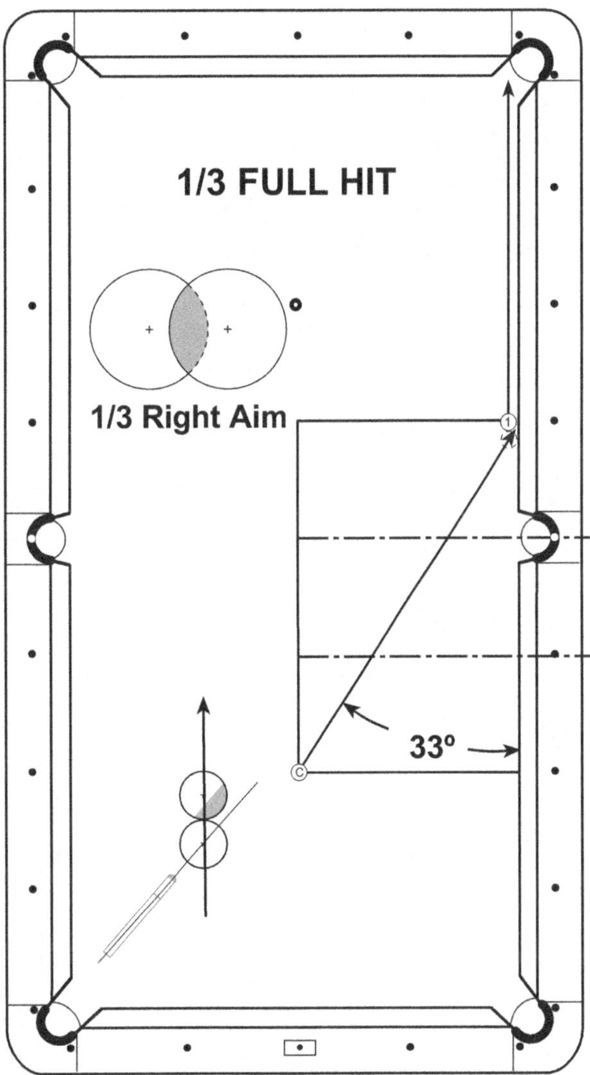

1/4 FULL BALL AIM

Look directly at the Object Ball as though you were lining up a straight-in shot, then cover 1/4 of the Object Ball with the Cue Ball.

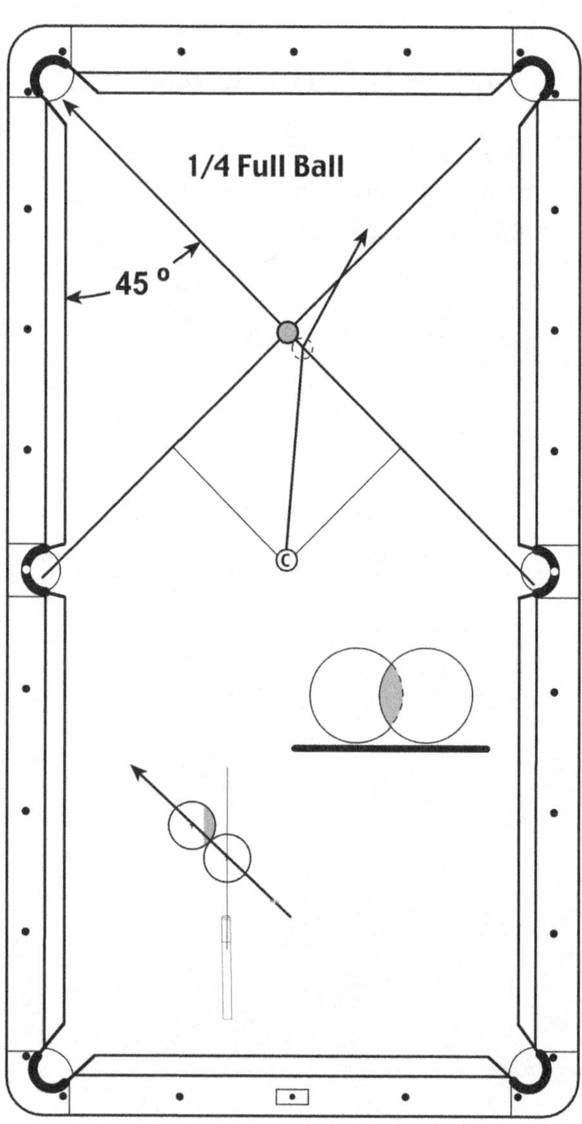

Vernon Elliot, Master Hustler

Young Vernon, A Very Bad Man. Danger! Do Not Play This Man.

DEAD ON BANKS

Do The Math
Diamond 1 ÷ 2 = .5 - .25 = Diamond .25

Subtract .25 Diamond

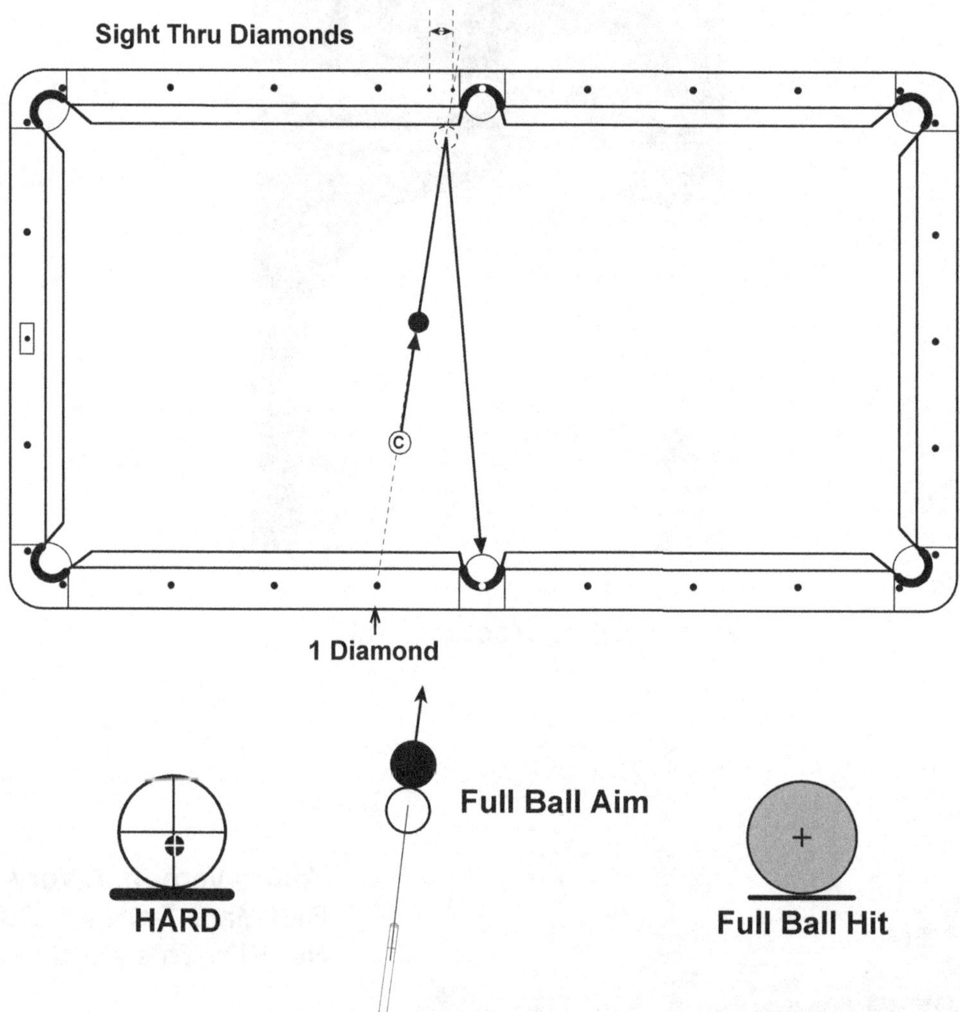

FORMULA FOR DEAD-ON BANKS
Divide the angle — then subtract 1/4 diamond

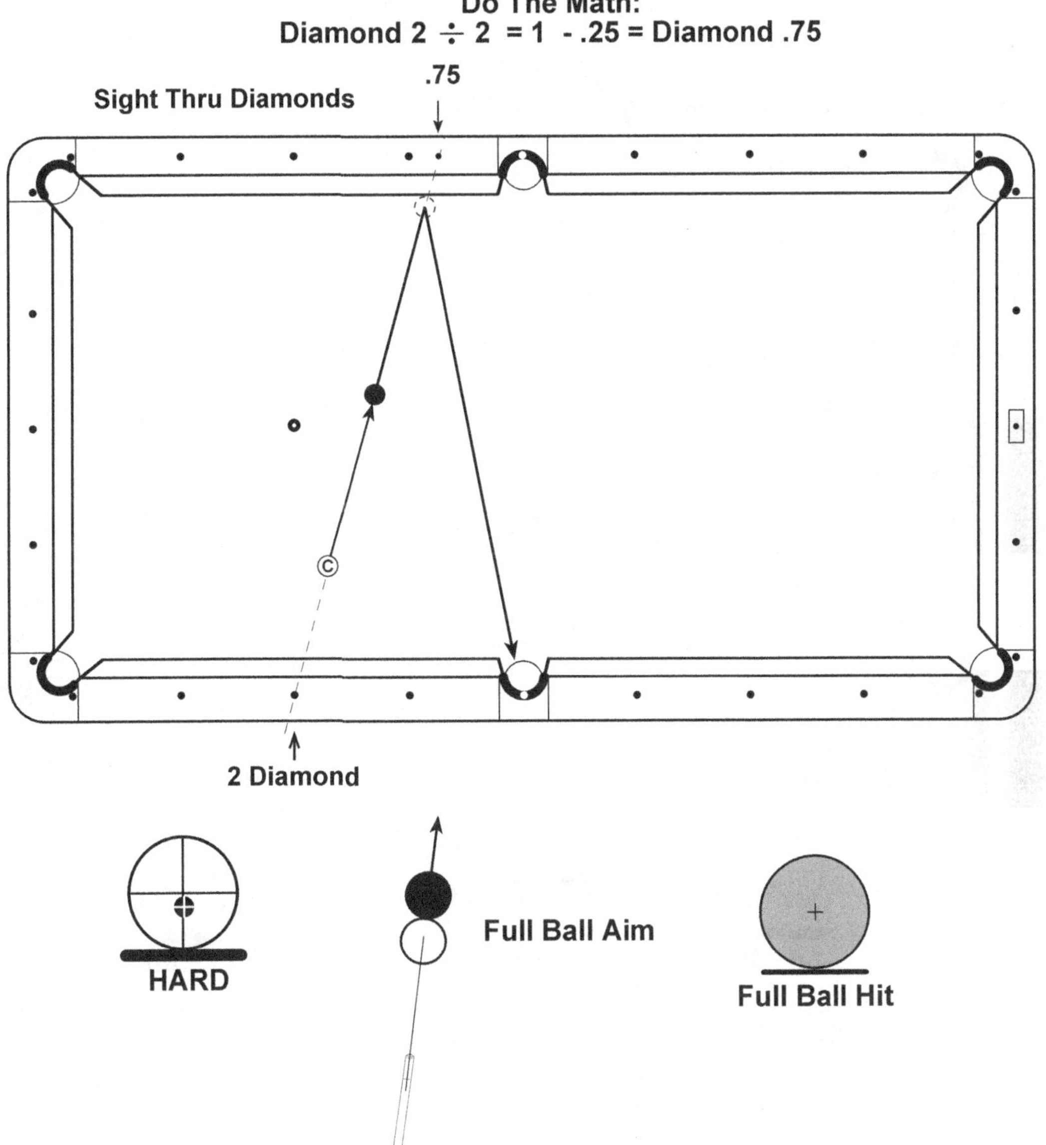
Do The Math:
Diamond 2 ÷ 2 = 1 - .25 = Diamond .75
.75
Sight Thru Diamonds
2 Diamond
HARD
Full Ball Aim
Full Ball Hit

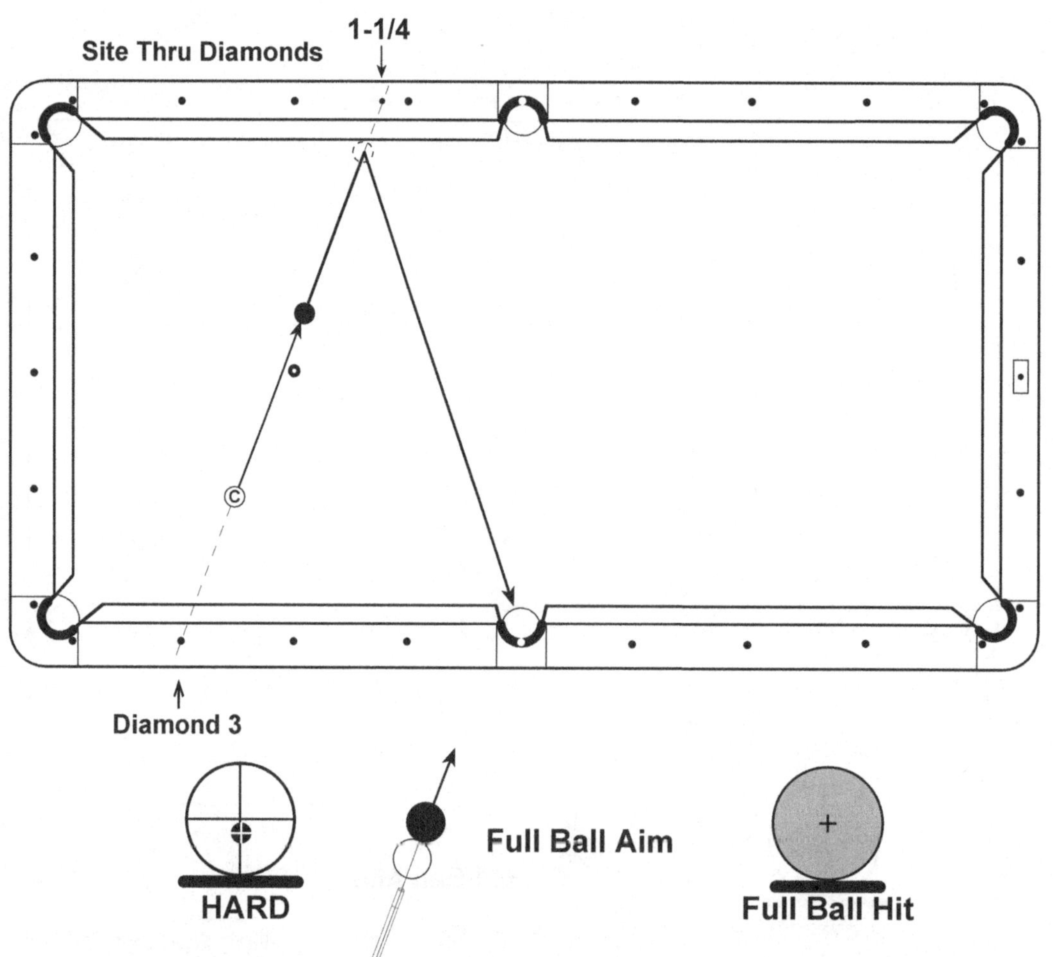
Do The Math:
Diamond 3 ÷ 2 = 1.5 - .25 = Diamond 1.25
1-1/4
Site Thru Diamonds
Diamond 3
HARD
Full Ball Aim
Full Ball Hit

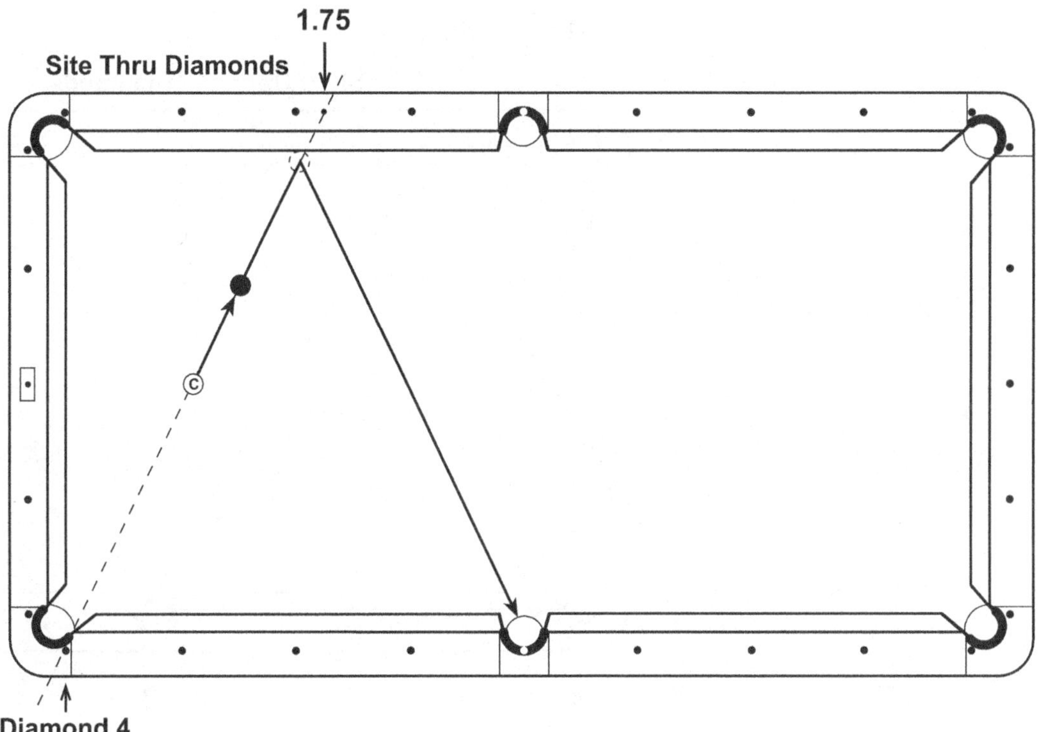
Do The Math:
Diamond 4 ÷ 2 = 2 - .25 = Diamond 1.75
1.75
Site Thru Diamonds
C
Diamond 4

HARD

Full Ball Aim

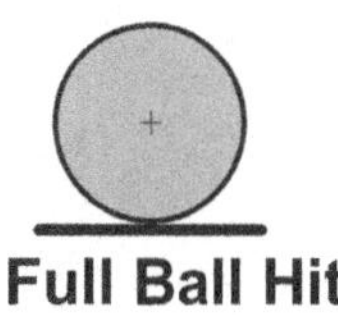
Full Ball Hit

Extended rail, divide the angle system

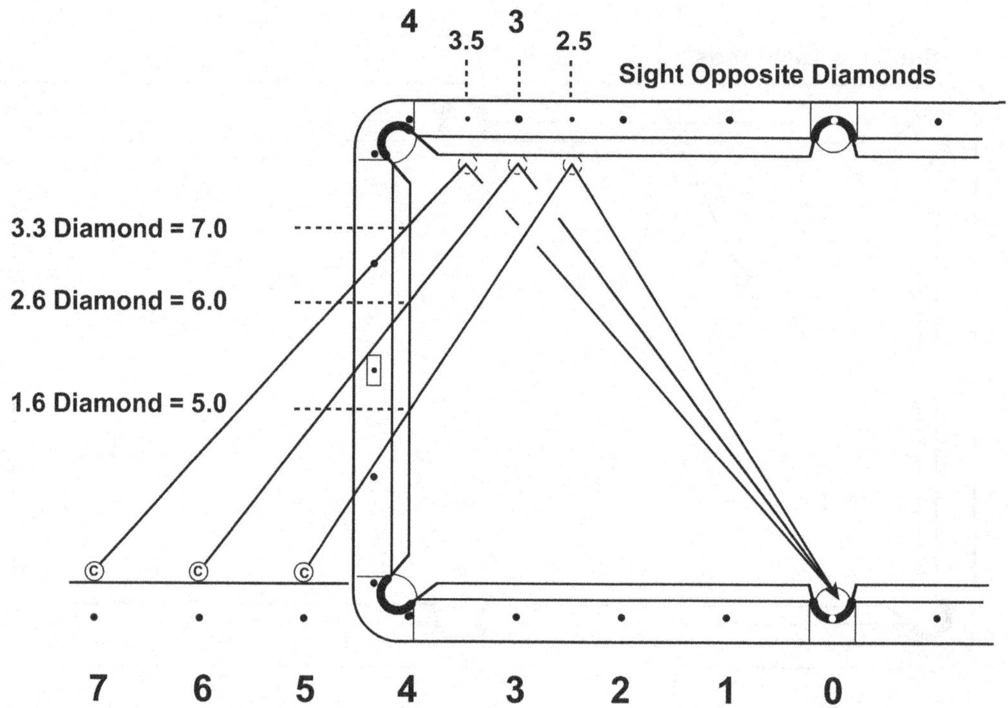

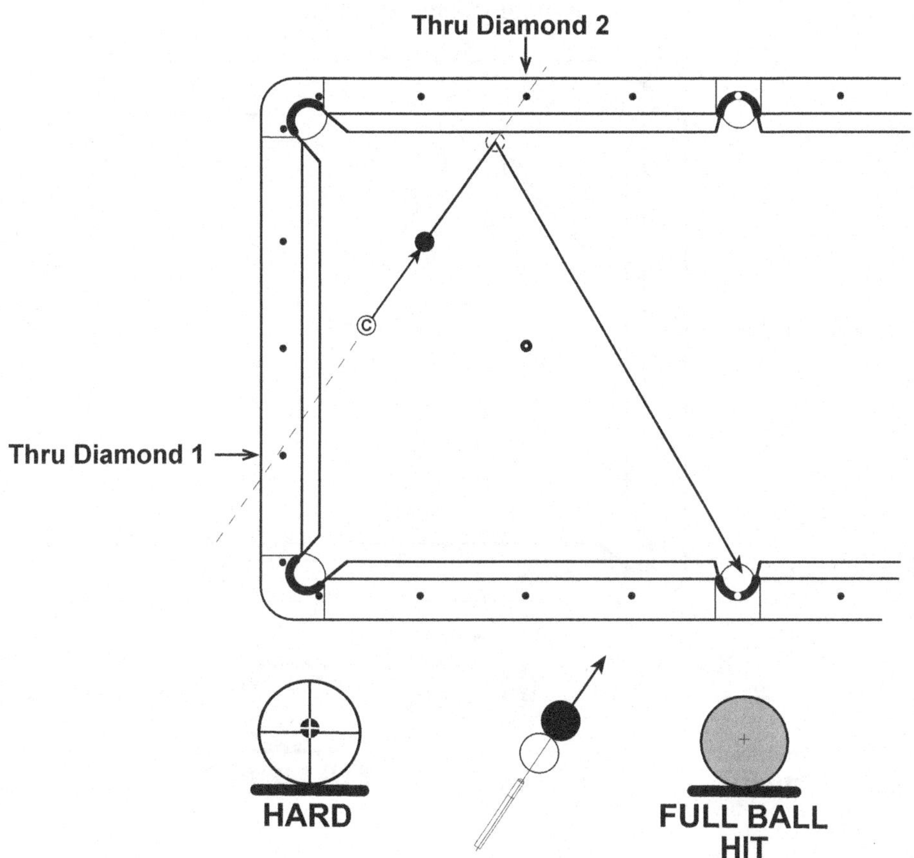
Thru Diamond 2
Thru Diamond 1
HARD
FULL BALL HIT

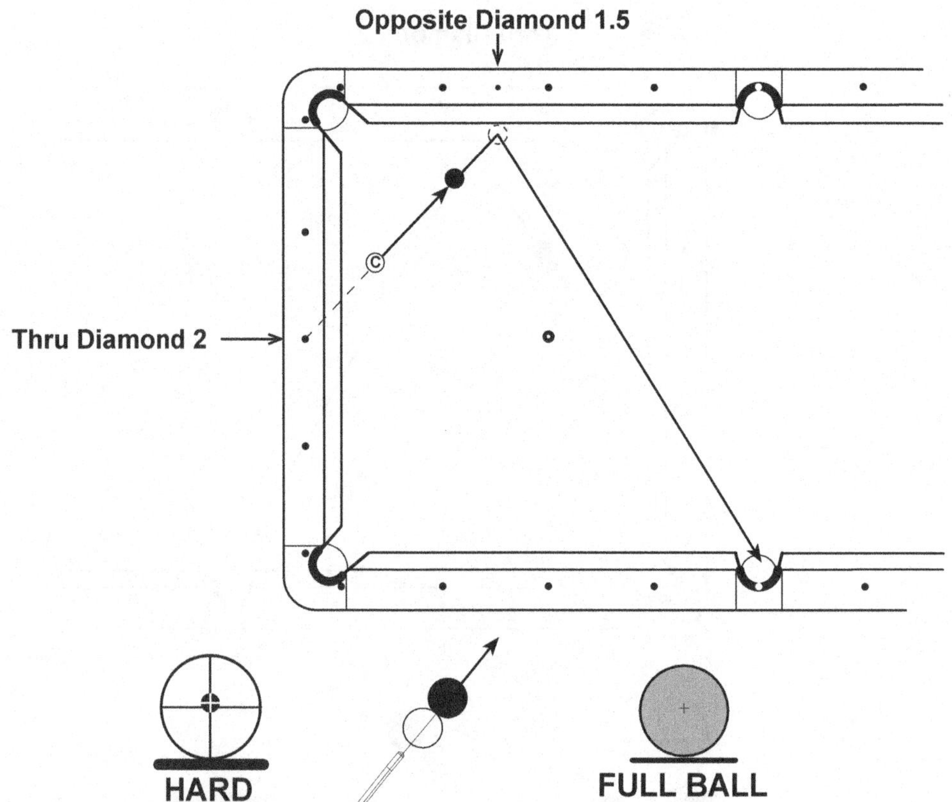

Opposite Diamond 1.5
Thru Diamond 2
HARD
FULL BALL

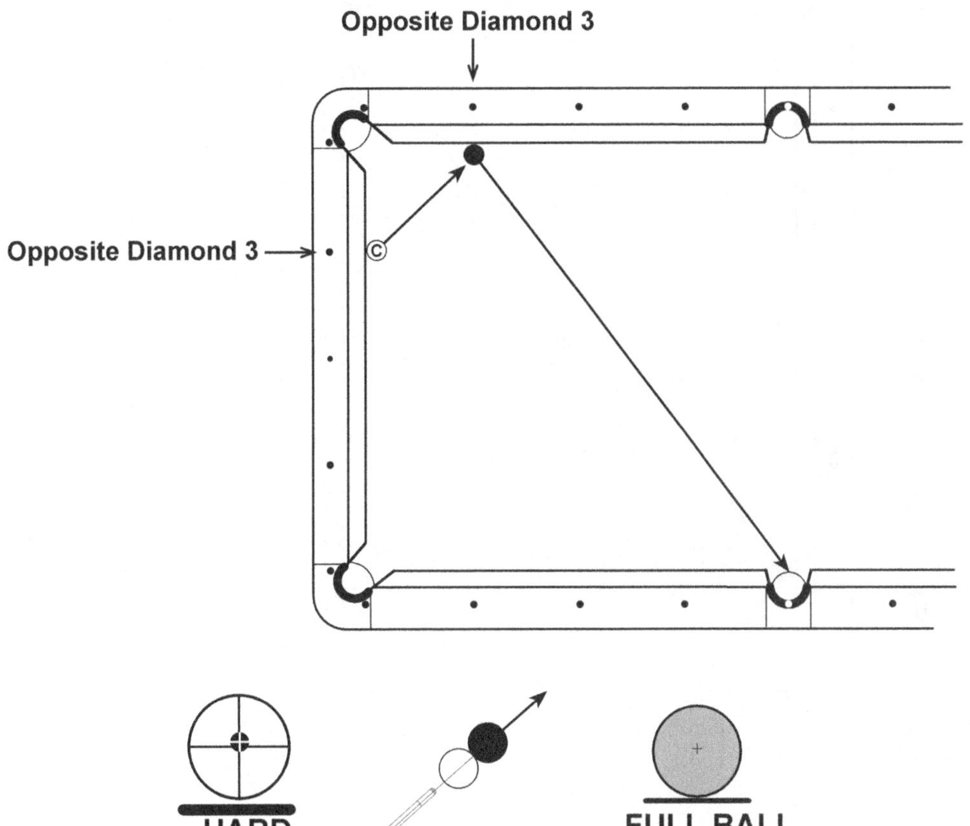
Opposite Diamond 3
Opposite Diamond 3
HARD
FULL BALL

2:1 Tracks For Long Cross–Corners

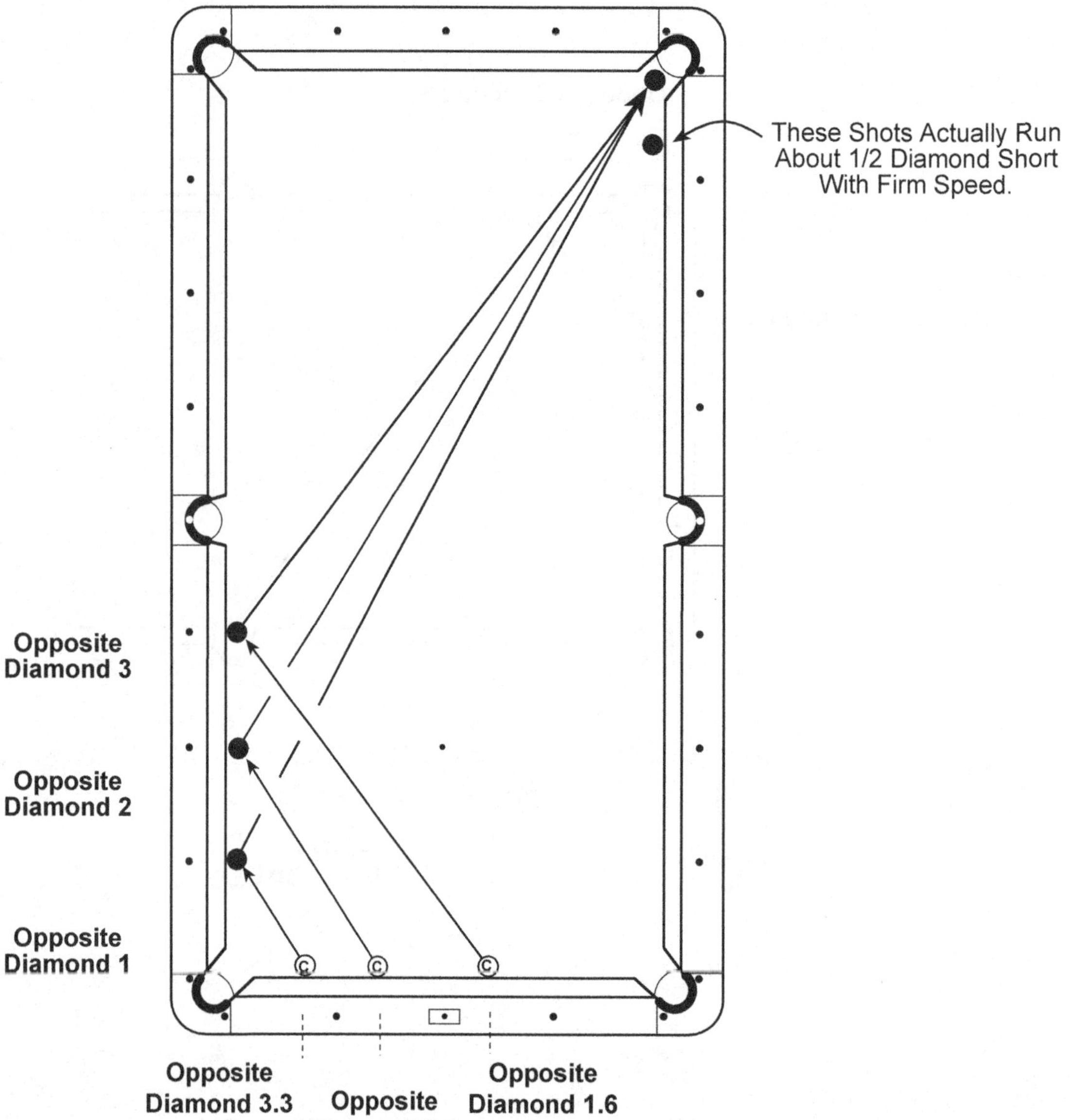

Long Cross-Corner Dead-On Banks

Adjustment for 2:1 Tracks +.25 Diamond

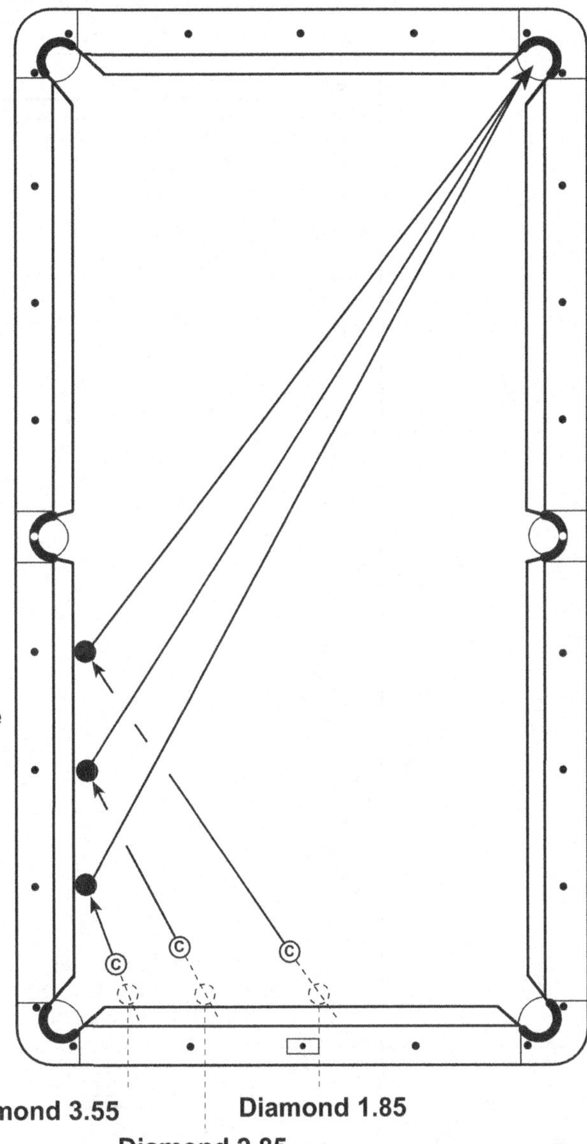

Diamond 3.3 + .25 = Diamond 3.55
Diamond 2.6 + .25 = Diamond 2.85
Diamond 1.6 + .25 = Diamond 1.85

2:1 Track Angles For Straight-Backs

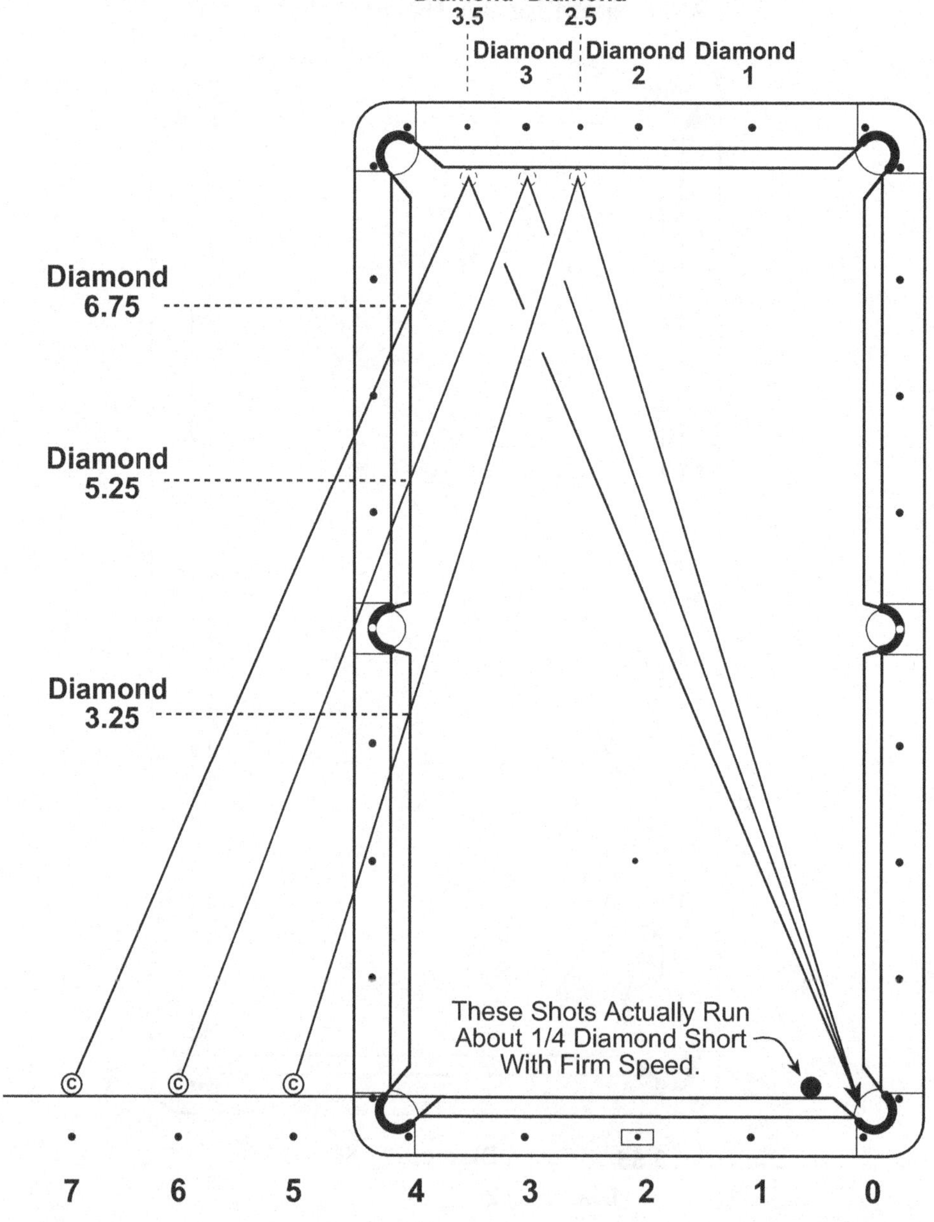

DEAD ON BANKS

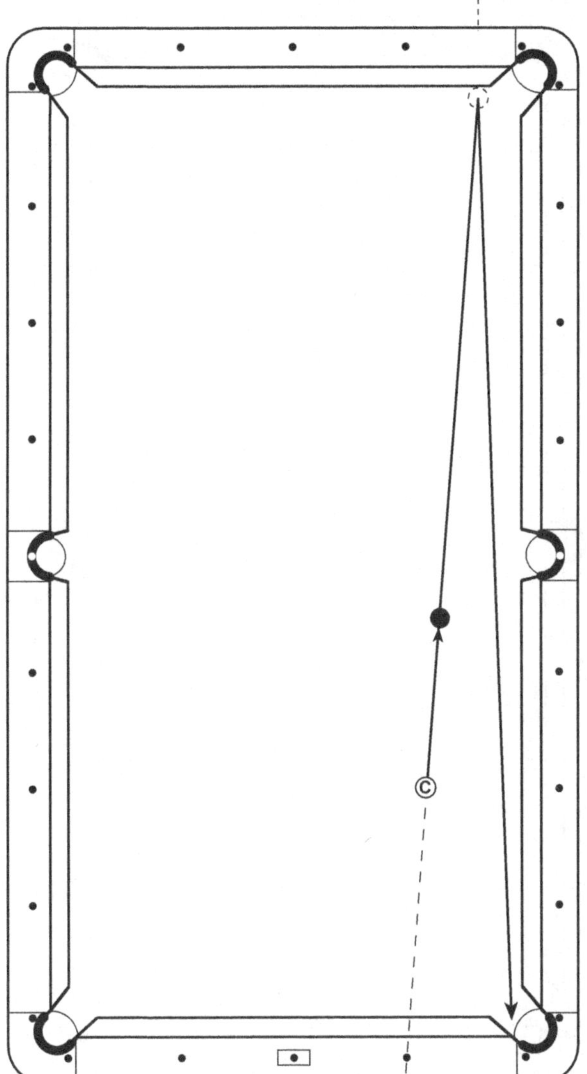

Diamond 1 to Diamond .25

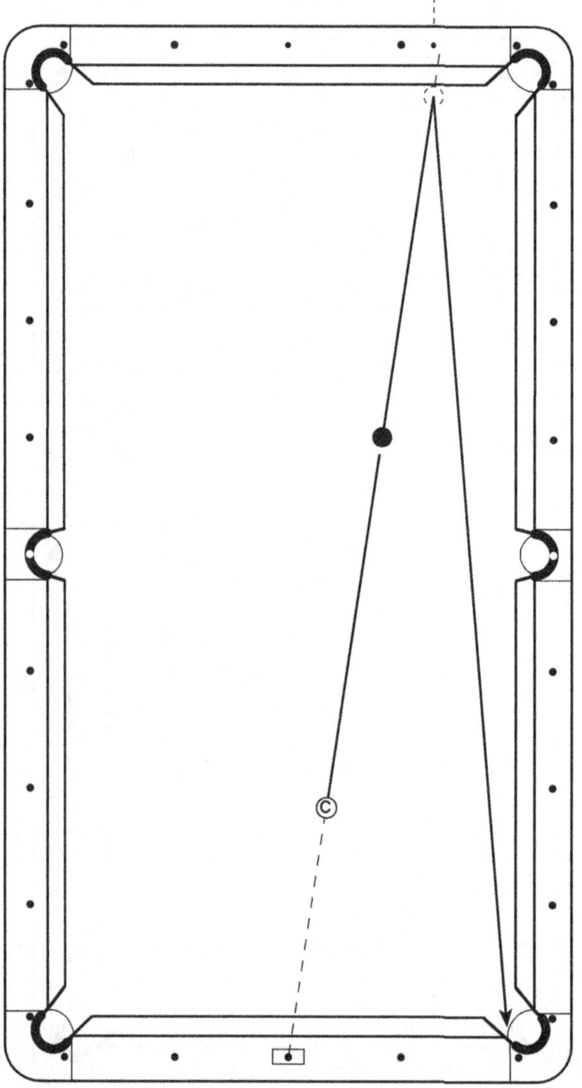

Full Ball Aim

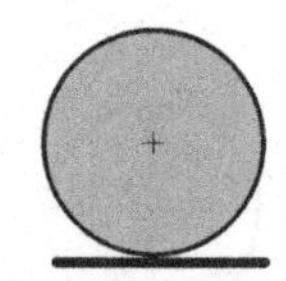

Do The Math:
Diamond 3 ÷ 2 = 1.5 - .25 = Diamond 1.25

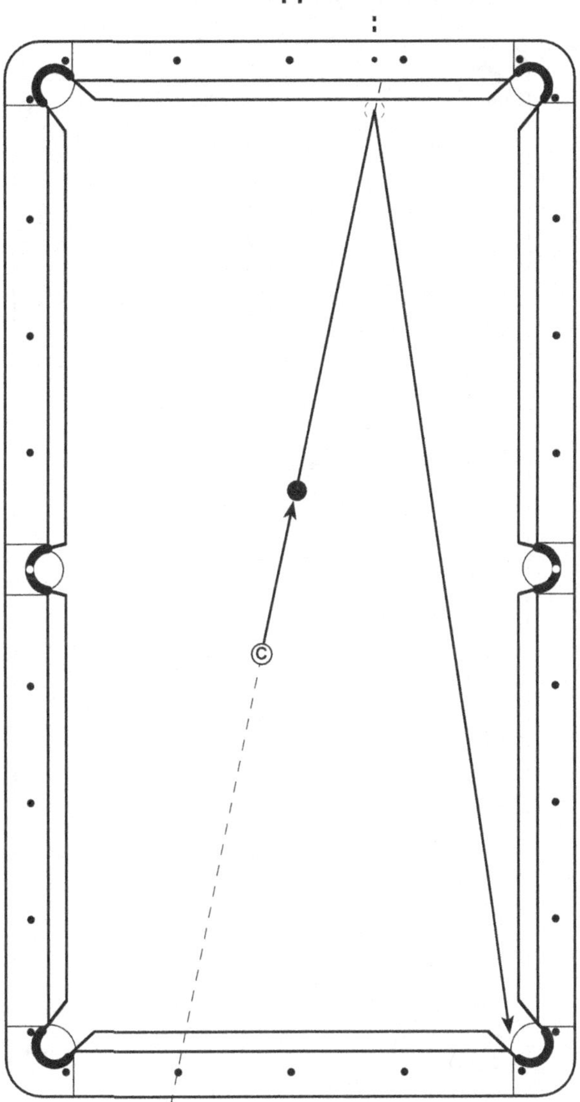

Diamond 3 to Diamond 1.25

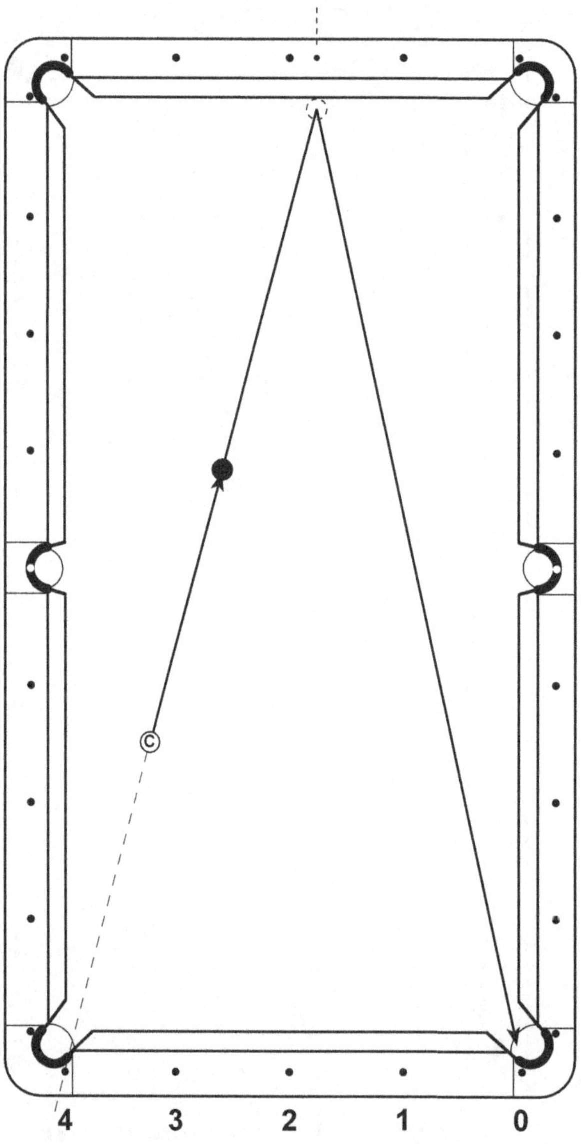
Do The Math:
Diamond 4 ÷ 2 = 2 - .25 = Diamond 1.75
Hit Opposite Diamond 1.75
4
3
2
1
0
Diamond 4 to Diamond 1.75

HARD

Full Ball Aim

FULL BALL
HIT

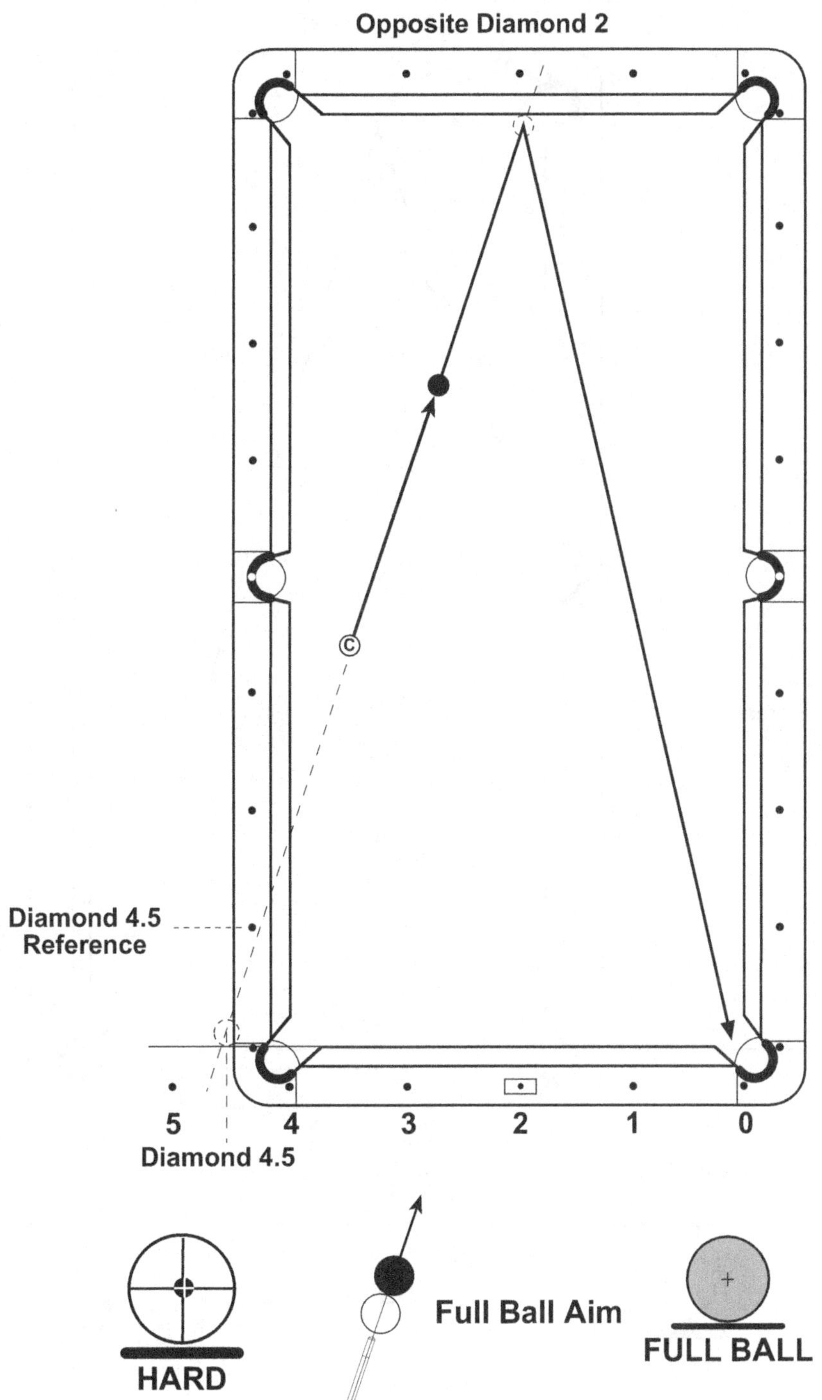
Do The Math:
Diamond 4.5 ÷ 2 = 2.25 - .25 = Diamond 2
Opposite Diamond 2
Diamond 4.5
Reference
5
4
3
2
1
0
Diamond 4.5
HARD
Full Ball Aim
FULL BALL

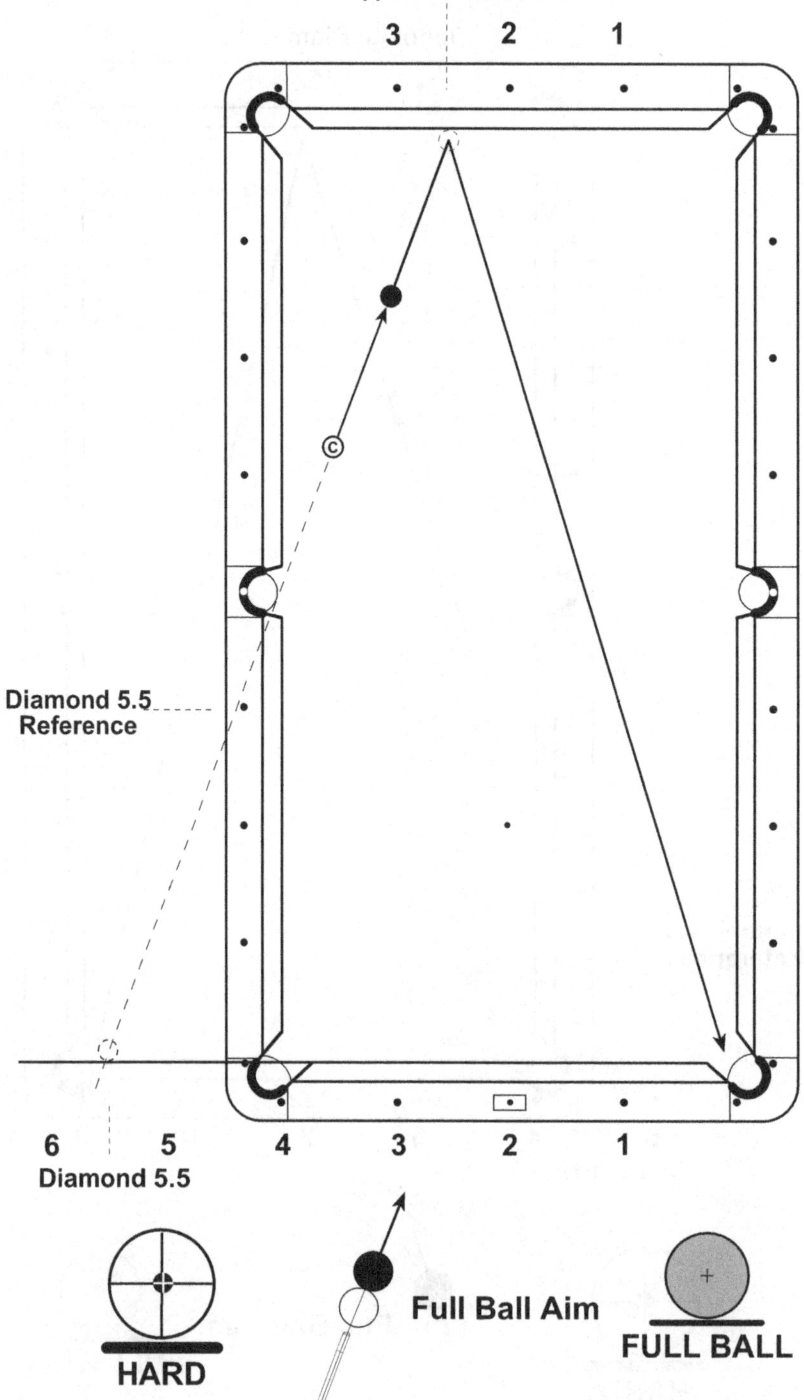

Do The Math:
Diamond 5.5 ÷ 2 = 2.75 - .25 = Diamond 2.50
Opposite Diamond 2.5
3
2
1
Diamond 5.5
Reference
6
5
4
3
2
1
Diamond 5.5
HARD
Full Ball Aim
FULL BALL

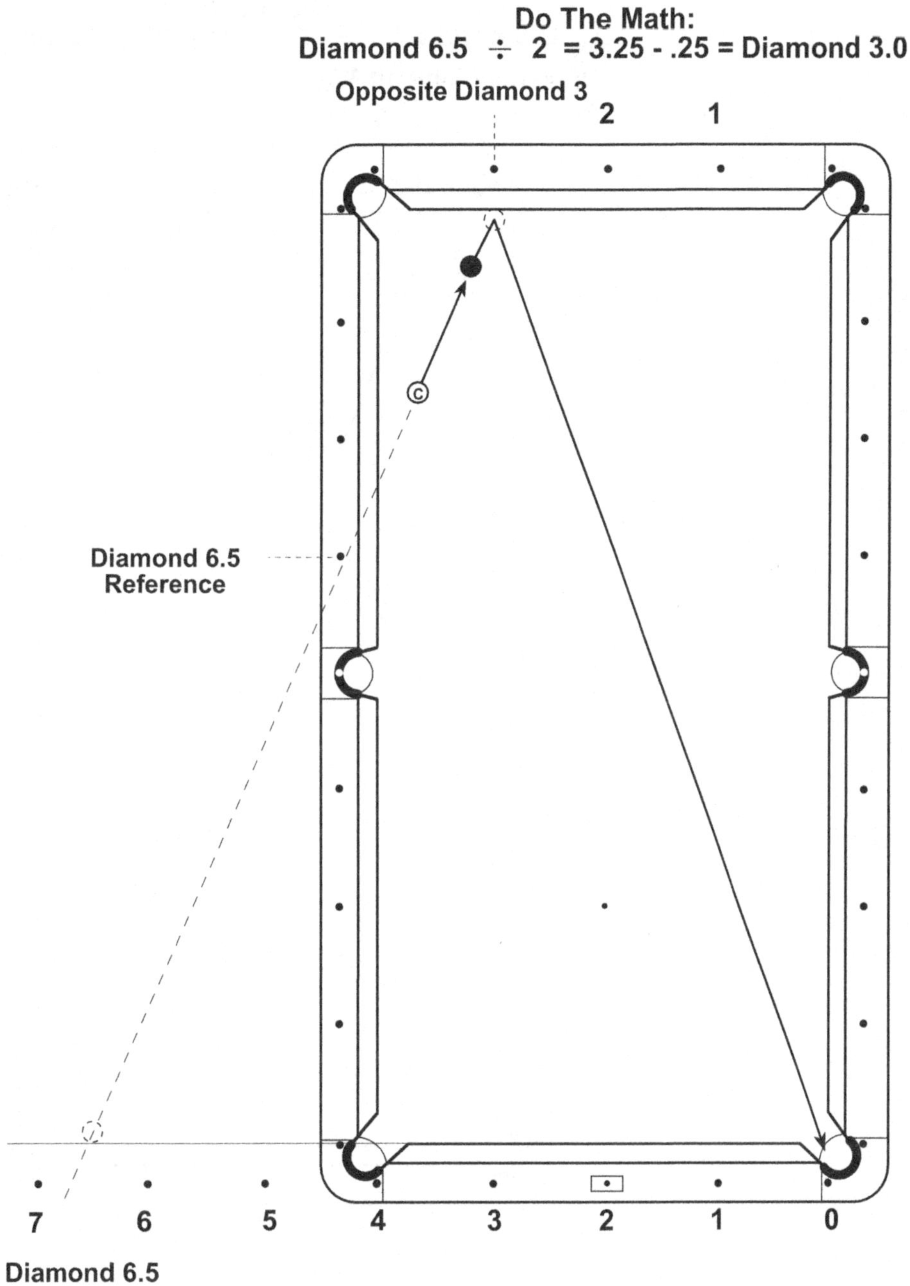

Do The Math:
Diamond 6.5 ÷ 2 = 3.25 - .25 = Diamond 3.0

Opposite Diamond 3

2 1

Diamond 6.5 Reference

7 6 5 4 3 2 1 0

Diamond 6.5

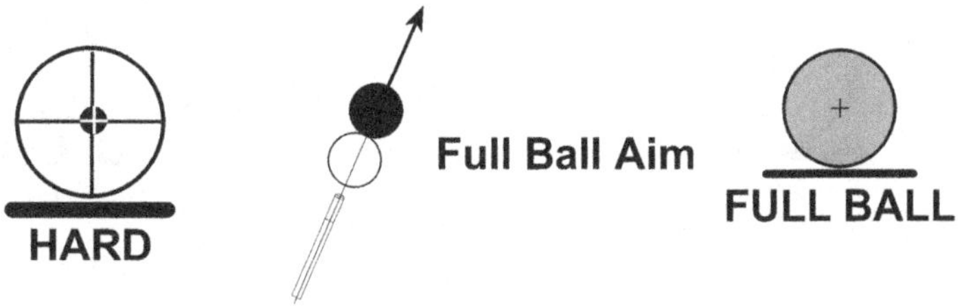

HARD

Full Ball Aim

FULL BALL

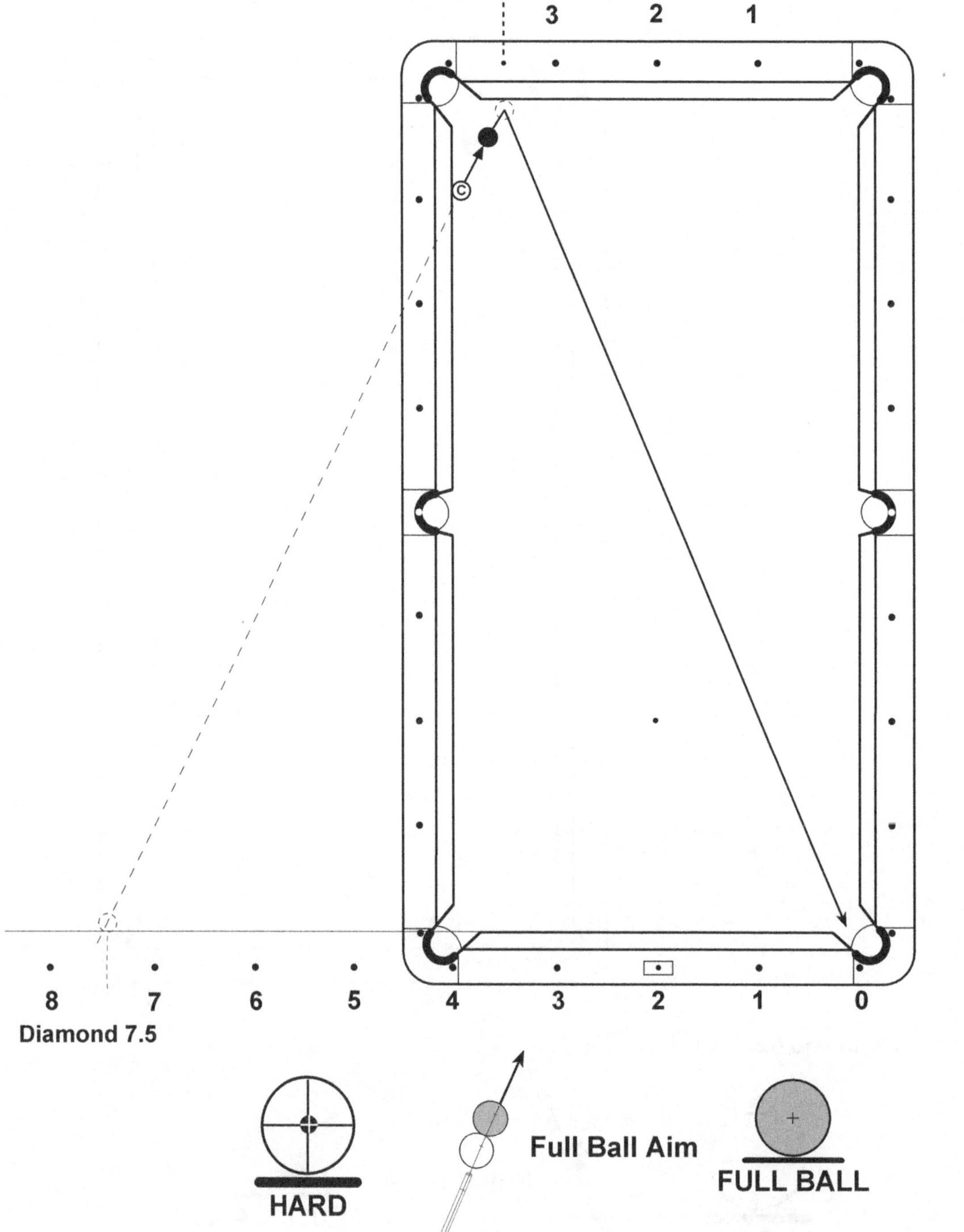
Do The Math:
Diamond 7.5 ÷ 2 = 3.75 - .25 = Diamond 3.50
Opposite Diamond 3.5
3
2
1
8
7
6
5
4
3
2
1
0
Diamond 7.5
HARD
Full Ball Aim
FULL BALL

2006 Hall Of Fame Awards, One-Pocket & Bank Pool Inductees: Bottom, L to R, Steve Cook's Father, Leonard "Bugs" Rucker Top, L to R, Artie Bodendorfer, Cornbread Red's Son-In-Law, Steve Lomako, Marshall "Squirrel" Carpenter, Truman Hogue & Yours Truly

Who Was Better? Then Or Now?

Players of my era would destroy players of today. **Bugs Rucker, Ronnie Allen, Jersey Red, Artie Bodendorfer, Boston Shorty, Eddie Taylor, Cincinnati Clem Metz** etc, were vicious competitors who would *shark**, cheat, psyche and even *tushhog** opponents in order to win.

Now consider this. Players of the '30s and '40s would have probably destroyed the players of my era! **Marcel Camp, Gene Skinner, The Eufala Kid, John "Rags" Fitzpatrick, Johnny "Irish" Lineen, New York Fats, Hubert Cokes, Alton "Baby-Face" Whitlow, Tommy the Greek, James Evans, Isadore "Pony" Rosen** et al, played even harder than the Ronnie Allen-era boys.

The economic conditions of the Great Depression developed players of a determination and ferocity that has not been seen since those rough times. Depression-era players were hungry wolves, whose level of concentration was nail-bending.

The economics of the '50s, '60s and early '70s didn't rival the Depression years, but were nonetheless hard times for pool players. When I was coming up, a good *bite** from a fellow pool player was a buck ($1) or a deuce ($2). We missed many meals and some nights wound up *carrying the banner** in the bus station or an all-night movie. City buses were the standard mode of transportation. Only a few players had cars. If you had as much as three *barrels** to play someone with, you were a fortunate man.

We didn't care if we had a "good" game or not. Who might beat whom, was not a major concern. Arbitrary skill handicapping went out the window. Our real concern was that our opponent had money that he was willing to lose. A really "good" game was when you had ten dollars and your opponent had a hundred.

**shark*: Not to be confused with Pool-Shark — unethical gamesmanship. To distract your opponent while he is trying to shoot.

**tushhog*: A strong-arm, tough-guy, bully type.

**bite*: A loan that is seldom repaid.

**carry the banner*: To have no place to sleep. To wind up in an all night movie theater, a park bench, or a bus station.

**barrels:* Payoff units. i.e.., $30 would allow you to play 3 games for $10 each. The amount of games you can pay off measured against your bankroll.

Hubert "Daddy Warbucks" Cokes
photo courtesy Bill Bell

"Rags" Fitzpatrick
photo courtesy Bill Bell

John "Rags" Fitzpatrick
photo courtesy Bill Bell

Marcel Camp
photo courtesy J D Dolan

Top *Lemon* Men

"Brooklyn Jimmy" Cassas, Jack Cooney and **Bernard "Bunny" Rogoff** were the best. **Brooklyn Jimmy** had a better *lemon* than **Jack Cooney**, but it was for a lot less money. Cooney's scores were much higher. All Jimmy wanted to do was make enough to get to the racetrack every day.

A young Jimmy met **Eddie "Detroit Whitey" Beauchene** while on the road in Detroit. Whitey kept him up hustling pool for three days using pills. Jimmy had never taken pills before. Finally, Whitey brought Jimmy home with him, but still wouldn't let him go to sleep.

That was when Jimmy found out about Whitey's dark deed. Jimmy overheard a drunken Whitey and his wife arguing. Whitey woke Jimmy and asked him to agree that Whitey had done the right thing— selling his kids to play another pool session! After all, Whitey had had the *nuts.* (Whitey had lost the session and the kids).

The end of their brief partnership came when Whitey brought a fat, drunken black lady into the bedroom, woke Jimmy again and told him he had to screw her. When Jimmy refused, Whitey threw him out of the house.

Forced to wander the Detroit streets with no money, no sleep and no prospects, Jimmy hitchhiked back to NY swearing that he would kill Whitey the next time they met.

Months later, Whitey showed up at the legendary **7-11 Poolroom** in New York City. Jimmy did not kill him; instead he ended up *staking** Whitey for $300, which Whitey promptly lost. Jimmy swears it was a *dump.**

Jimmy's rationale for not strangling Whitey was the assertion that Whitey had a Svengali effect on people, and could sway anybody that came in range of his spell. I am almost ashamed to say that Whitey had the same effect on me.

Jack Cooney put the *lemon* on me and almost tricked me. He asked me to play some cheap One-Pocket at the Congress Bowl in Miami, FL. I was automatically suspicious and paranoid in those days, so I looked over his game very carefully.

**staking*: Putting up the money for a pool player to play, with a deal to split the winnings 50/50.

**dump*: To lose a backer's money on purpose, as a "business man" would do and later collect 50% of his losses from your opponent who was your co–conspirator.

ALL AROUND HUSTLERS TOURNAMENT
Johnston City, IL

Row 1— L - R "Cowboy" Jimmy Moore, Danny Gartner, Al Cozlowski, Pauly Jansco, George Jansco, Alton Whitlow, Eddie "Detroit Whitey" Beauchene, Danny DiLiberto, Norman "Jockey" Howard

Row 2— L - R William "Wienie Beanie" Staton, "St Louis Blackie" LeSeur, William "Cornbread Red" Burge, Eddie "Knoxville Bear" Taylor, Maurice "Tugboat" Whaley, "Portland Don" Watson, Luther "Wimpy" Lassiter, Joey Spaeth

Row 3 — L- R Bernard "Bunny" Rogoff, Lewis "Junior" Goff, Cisero Murphy, Earl Shriver, Jack "Jersey Red" Breit, Tom Cosmo

I quickly became convinced he was a genuine idiot and was planning to raise the bet as soon as possible. I was saved by a stool-pigeon, who *pulled my coat,** and informed me that Cooney was a top player while Jack was in the bathroom. If not for that, I would have fallen for his *lemon* act.

Jack Cooney

Greatest Bar Room "Lemon" Hustler:

Bernard "Bunny" Rogoff (aka Pots and Pans). I have seen Bunny spill a glass of wine on a sucker's chest to *lemon* him up. I later discovered that Bunny's drunk act wasn't really an act. One beer would put him into orbit. To quote the great Rogoff, "I finally figured out that I had a booze problem when I realized I was hustling pool in bars that didn't have any pool tables."

Bernard "Bunny" Rogoff was one of the most creative bar-hustlers of all time. Bunny invented most of today's standard bar hustling ploys. Rogoff was a pots-and-pans salesman. Selling cookware enabled him to survive on the road. Here's his famous cooking set gimmick explained in Rogoff's own words:

**pulls your coat*: Alerts you to something. Knocks somebody's action to you. Think of someone tugging on your coat because he wants to tell you something.

"I hustled pool all my life, but I always worked. I sold Mirro Cookware. I'd bring the cookware in and set it on a pool table and show everybody my business card. I'd tell them the stuff was left over from the home show and that we normally sold them for $60, but because they were left over we were letting them go for $40. I'd never say anything about playing pool. But most of the time someone would challenge me to play for the cookware. They'd put up $40 and the cookware only cost me $20. They were giving me 2-1 on the money, and hardly anyone can beat me that way. You'd be surprised at the people who couldn't even run three balls who tried to win that cookware set.

Occasionally, I ran into good players, but it didn't matter because they were giving me 2-1 on the money. But most of the time I'd catch people who couldn't play at all. I never mentioned gambling or anything. I would approach them, tell them what I had and start for the door if no one seemed interested. One of the guys would always say, "Hey, I'll play a game of pool for that cookware."

That was my gimmick to get people to play. I sold a lot of cookware too. I was underselling the stores. I was making my expenses with the pots and pans, but I made more on the pool tables. Selling cookware meant that I always had money in my pocket, so I was never under pressure. I didn't have to worry about going broke, because I always had merchandise to sell."

Bunny was the master at busting a joint in short order. When he happened upon a $5 or $10 money game in progress, Bunny immediately raised the bet to $100 a game.

Here's how he did it:

Bunny: [challenging the table] I'll play for a draft beer (25¢ in those days.).

Opponent: The player at the table inevitably complains — "We're playing for $10. You can't break up a money game to play for a two–bit draft beer."

Bunny: [acting scared and intimidated] "Oh, yeah! I'll play you for $110." Bunny then takes his quarter out of the slot, turns his back to the table and begins walking back to the bar.

Opponent: [thinking Bunny is bluffing, grabs Rogoff by the arm] We can play for $100 if you want to."

Bunny: Takes a $100 [which he already has in his hand] and throws it on the table. "There's my money! Where's yours?"

This is powerful psychology, because the player at the table must now play for $100 or lose face. ***He*** was the one who made an issue about playing for money, and now the player's ego is engaged and clear thinking vanishes for a while. Almost everyone goes for the $100 bet.

Of course, that wasn't the end of the hustle. Bunny offered bystanders side bets of $5, $10, $20 and $50, and these bets were added to the take. Within an hour or two the joint had been cleaned out.

Bunny was one of the best bar table Eight Ball players of all time, so opponents had no idea what they were getting into. Rogoff was so good on bar tables that he beat really good players while stalling. Bunny beat many big-table champions playing bar-table Eight Ball during his heyday. As Bunny puts it, "They cried like babies."

According to **"Iron Joe" Procita**, Rogoff was one of the very best at making "trick shots" in open play (*i.e.* tough multi-ball combos, mind-wrecking kiss shots and subtle moves). Many of Bunny's shots were so fantastic that suckers thought they were being beaten with "luck."

Great Straight-Pool Players

Willie Mosconi of Philadelphia was the greatest I ever saw. Willie gave three exhibitions at my neighborhood pool room, **The Dragon Cue**, in Chicago's Chinatown. It cost $1 to see Mosconi play and the crowds were sparse. Mosconi's deal with the owner, **Jimmy Wing**, was that they would split the admission proceeds 50/50. Mosconi played three 200-point games in a three-day period. Willie ran *200 and out** the first game he played. When Mosconi reached 200 points, he stopped shooting and gave a trick-shot exhibition. The next day Mosconi ran *200 and out* again, and again stopped shooting at 200. The third day, I was his opponent. Mosconi ran 160 and out. Then, more trick shots— which he never missed. The games were played on *4 1/2' x 9'* ***Brunswick Anniversary Tables*** with 5" pockets.

**200 and out*: Made 200 points consecutively, without a miss.

The climax of this story occurred about six weeks later. **The Dragon Cue** hosted another exhibition, this time with "**Minnesota Fats**." I asked Jimmy what deal had he made with Fatty. He excitedly told me he had made a terrific deal with Fats. All Jimmy had to do was give Fats **all** the money. Admission to see Fats was $2, twice the amount to see Mosconi.

The place was jammed. People were climbing on each other's shoulders to see the show. Fats missed and missed and missed. His trick-shot show was deplorable; he hardly ever made a shot on the first try. Fats had to finally give up shooting a particular *massé* * trick-shot after about 15 or 20 failed attempts.

Fats blamed the tables, he blamed the cloth, he blamed the cue ball, he blamed the chalk — Fats blamed anything — especially the air-conditioning. Fats periodically looked menacingly at Jimmy Wing as though it were all poor Jimmy's fault. Jimmy slunk over into a corner, worrying that the crowd might lynch him if Fatty gave the word.

Through it all, Fatty's confidence and cockiness suffered not a degree of loss. Fats was totally nonchalant about his miserable performance. It was at that point that I realized I was fortunate enough to be in the presence of real genius. I unashamedly became another Fats groupie from then on.

True story: Fats once claimed that a room owner couldn't afford to pay him his exhibition rate, so Fats did the guy a favor and charged him $40 just to walk into the joint, go into the bathroom and take a leak.

Baby-Face Story: When I was a kid in Johnston City, **Baby-Face (Alton Whitlow of Detroit)** told me a typical Fatty story. When Baby-Face was sixteen years old, Fatty, a year or two older, was living in Detroit and hanging and hustling with the Face. They decided to take a road trip to New York City.

Baby-Face's dad loved Fats so much he would let Face go anywhere just as long as Fatty was with him. So they boarded a train and headed East. Baby-Face brought his girl friend along. To while away the time on the train, Face and Fats played call-rummy (a long suit of Fatty's) and Fats quickly won all of Face's money. With Baby-Face now broke, Fats next moved on Whitlow's girl friend and took her from him too.

When they reached New York, a now steaming mad Baby-Face couldn't take it anymore and challenged Fatty to a fist fight. The outcome was predictable. Whitlow lost his money, his girl friend, and, of course, the fight.

**massé* : A fancy-shot, whereby the cue ball is made to curve.

Great Straight-Pool Players (continued)

In a 150-point straight pool game, **Luther "Wimpy" Lassiter** would make **Irving "The Deacon" Crane** *dog it** enough to beat him. However, in a long match of 1500 points or more, Crane could beat anybody from the year 1960 on. In the "short" game, Wimpy dominated the players of my era. Unfortunately, it wasn't until late in his career that Lassiter was allowed to compete in big tournaments. It was a very exclusive club. If you carried the stigma of a gambler, as Wimpy did, you were excluded from playing in big-time Straight-Pool tournaments.

My Favorite One-Pocket Players

Ronnie Allen was the greatest power mover.

The most telling description regarding Ronnie Allen's One-Pocket game comes from top player, **Bill Incardona**, who is also the voice of **Accu-Stats.** When Bill was asked to rate Ronnie's game against *One-Hole** champion, **Allen Hopkins** of NJ, Billy gave this account:

> "I played Hopkins for $1000 a game in his basement in Jersey. He spotted me 10 to 8. Even though we were in his house, on his own table, and he is a great player, his game is very conservative and predictable. I was totally comfortable and relaxed and was able to play my game, which allowed me to beat him.
>
> I later played Ronnie in Las Vegas, in ***my*** pool room, on ***my*** table, for the same bet and with the same spot, 10 to 8.
>
> The difference was, when I played Ronnie, the whole time I felt like I was in a very hot oven. I never had a clue as to what Ronnie was going to do next. He was crashing balls and running out and the cue ball was constantly flying around all over the table. I got to thinking the only safe place to leave the cue ball was in a bank vault."

Leonard "Bugs" Rucker was the greatest power banker, who literally made a shot for his life playing against **Eddie "the Knoxville Bear" Taylor**. Rucker's backer, **Melvin,** a big-time drug dealer who later went to prison for assassinating a narc, didn't want Bugs to shoot a ball that would decide the session.

**dog it:* To succumb to pressure and be unable to play your regular game.

**One-Hole:* Another name for One-Pocket.

Jersey Red & Me

Grady "The Professor" Mathews
photo courtesy Conrad Burkman

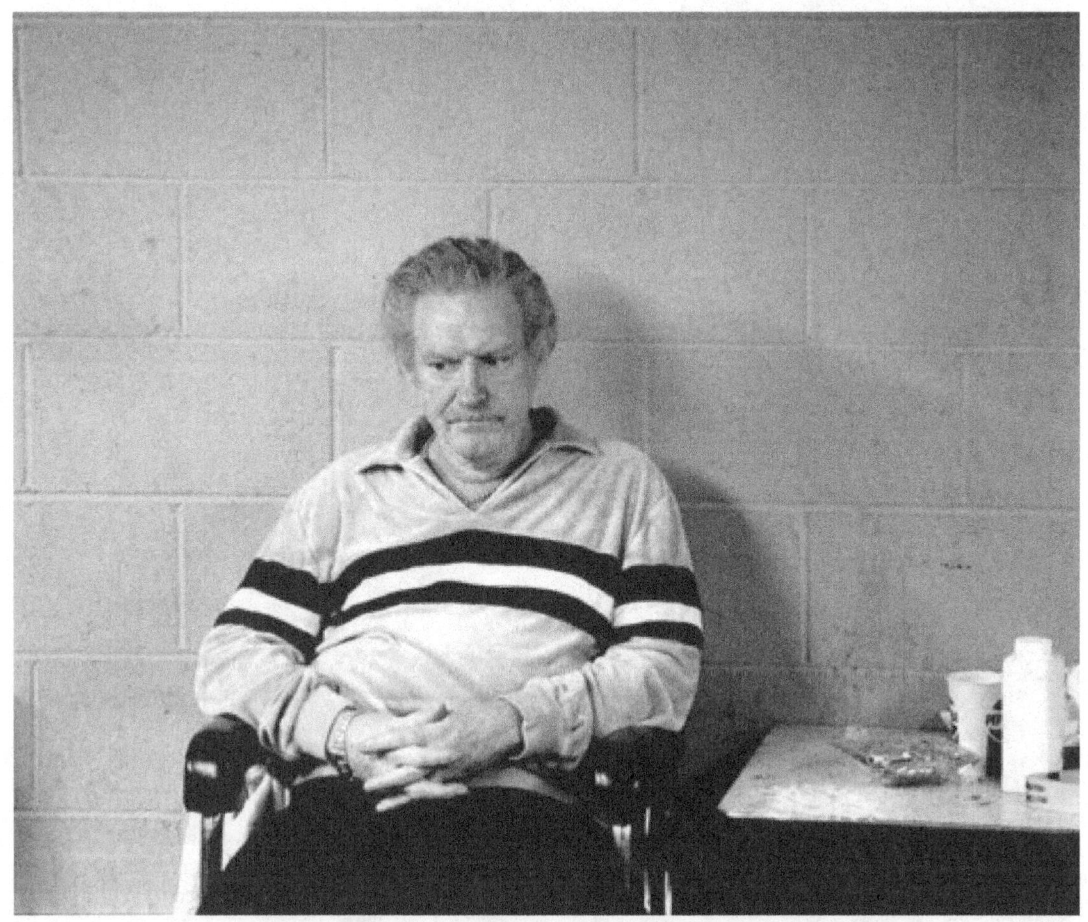

Cornbread Red Contemplates His Inner Cue Ball
photo courtesy Bill Porter and Mike Haines

He told Bugs that he had better not shoot at what he was thinking about shooting. **Melvin** wanted Bugs to play safe, and he took out two guns and laid them on a table. His backer would literally kill Bugs if he missed!

Bugs was in a hopeless One-Pocket trap, and knew he could only win the game and the session if he made the shot he was considering.

Needless to say, Bugs is still alive. He made the shot, ran out and won the set! The backer, who a minute before was going to shoot Bugs, did a 180-degree turn-around and started hugging and kissing Bugs. He even pulled off his diamond wrist-watch and gave it to Bugs as a bonus.

Efren Reyes has the most phenomenal cue-ball control, and is probably the greatest One-Pocket player of all time. Incidentally, Reyes learned how to play One-Pocket from Billy Incardona and myself when he was living in Chicago. While being interviewed by a pool magazine writer, Efren graciously gave Billy and me our *props*,* admitting he picked up the game from playing with us. Reyes can spot anybody alive. Efren could probably beat any of today's players 10 to 8.

Artie Bodendorfer was the most solid percentage shooter.

Once, Artie was pounding on Hall of Famer, **Nick Varner**, playing One-Pocket. It was just after Nick had returned from New York where he had just won the World's Straight Pool title at the **Commodore Hotel**. Nick's father, realizing the situation had become hopeless, tried in vain to get Nick to quit. He told Nick that he had no chance of winning anymore. Nick's rationale and reply were astounding: "I can't quit, I'm learning too much."
(*This story was also mentioned earlier in the interview with Steve Booth.)*

Jack "Jersey Red" Breit (nee Breitkov**).** Late in life, when he was no longer a favorite to win a tournament, "Jersey Red" stole a gaff from the movie **"The Producers."** Before going to a tournament, Red would secretly get ten or twelve guys to each stake him. He would then *bite* them for a few bucks more for expenses. Red would pay for one entry and after he got knocked out of the tourney and out of the money, Breit would pocket the leftover *cheese.**

**props*: Slang, short for slang word "propers." That which you have coming.

**cheese*: Money.

The only downside would be if Red finished in the money, since each backer would be then looking for his end. That never happened.

Eugene "Cincinnati Clem" Metz might have been the toughest safety player of them all. Jersey Red told the story of when Clem was playing **"Connecticut Johnny" Vives** (winner of the first Johnston City One-Pocket tournament). Clem and Vives had been playing for many hours. Vives had been on a starvation shot-diet, getting nothing good to shoot during the whole session. Clem was squeezing him like a python.

Finally, Vives spots Clem looking up-table at a long bank shot. It looked like Clem was finally going to leave Vives far-away, but at least leave a shot toward Johnny's pocket.

Vives nudged Jersey Red as if to say, "Lookie here, Clem is going to finally loosen up and give me a shot at my hole." Vives's hopes were soon dashed when Clem shot up-table at the long bank and drew the cue ball back into the stack!

Eddie "The Knoxville Bear" Taylor was another candidate for greatest of all time. Eddie could bank, move and shoot. Once, however, after days of playing Clem in Cincinnati, Clem's safe play finally shut The Bear's game down and Clem prevailed.

Larry "Boston Shorty" Johnson played all games well, including top-notch 3 Cushion billiards. Shorty won several of the One-Pocket tournaments held in Johnston City.

Shorty also won a national 3-cushion championship in Chicago in the early '70s. He beat **Bud Harris** pretty good and averaged over 1.00. Shorty played near-world-class 3-cushion; he was one of the greatest all-around players. He played 3-cushion better than Crane, Mosconi and Greenleaf put together. Shorty was a *real* billiard player, not a pool champion who wanted a romp in the 3-cushion game.

Legend has it that Mosconi, Procita, Crane and others did well when they competed in World 3 Cushion Tournaments in the 1940s. But legend is wrong! They didn't win a single game against the better billiard players. They established terrible records and averages. Hoppe and the real billiard pros beat the pool players about 50-30. Procita won one single game against a top billiard player (Arthur Rubin, 50-49 I think).

Benny "The Goose" Conway

Jose Parica

Marcel Camp: After he got old and fat, Marcel claimed he couldn't play because he couldn't shoot around his belly. **Minnesota Fats**, a gambling opponent of Camp's for many years, called him "Ma Barker" (*a la* the obese, shoot-em-up, desperado gang mother from the '30s). Whatever bankroll Camp had, it was all carried on his person. If Marcel had $25,000, the whole package was somewhere on his body. I learned plenty of One-Pocket watching Camp.

Grady "The Professor" Mathews gave up the biggest spots, made the hardest games, and probably gun-fought for big money with as many of the top players as anybody.

My Favorite Nine Ball Players

#1 Harold Worst, of Grand Rapids, MI. Nobody would play Worst even-up for big-money. Here is a typical story about Harold Worst:

It was in the '60s at the **Michigan State Pool, Snooker and Billiard Tournament** at the **State Fair Grounds** just outside Detroit. A lot of hustlers showed up. **Minnesota Fats** was there, so was "**Handsome Danny" Jones**, **Cornbread Red**, **Babyface**, **"Toledo Joe" Thomas** and a dozen others looking for action.

It was raining very hard during the tournament. Indeed, one table had to be covered with a tarp because of a leak in the roof.

Fats tried to impress the crowd by demonstrating some *massé* shots, but he missed every single one. Finally, after about 20 tries, Fatty gave up and said, "It's too wet to make *massé* shots!"

Harold Worst was in a corner watching the dismal performance, sucking on a half-pint of whiskey he had in his hip pocket. As usual, Worst was also openly expressing his contempt for the other players.

A few minutes later Worst had the PA system announce an exhibition of fancy *massé* shots on a 5 x 10 billiard table on the West side of the hall. As Worst set up the first shot, a monster 3/4 table full force *massé*, he stated loudly to the crowd, **"It may be too wet for some people, but it ain't too wet for the All–American Boy!"** The remark was obviously aimed dead center at Fats.

Efren Reyes Vs Jimmy Wetch

photos courtesy Bill Porter and Mike Haines

Efren Reyes & Nick Varner

Worst then proceeded to make 15 or 20 full-force *massés* without a single miss. He was hitting the shots so hard that the cue ball was bouncing 6 or 8 inches into the air.

Worst made the cue ball spin like a gyroscope. The cue ball went up-table at a good clip, then the furious backspin slowed the ball to a halt and began propelling the cue ball back; slowly at first; then with incredibly rapid acceleration, the wildly overspinning ball rocketed to its destination. On some shots, Worst made the cue ball hit a cushion dozens of times during the shot.

Observers had never seen such spectacular *massés*. The cue ball was still increasing in velocity when it reached the end rail coming back. Worst's inspired demonstration had a magical quality that reminded some onlookers of how early French peasants thought the cue ball was *demonized* when **Captain Mingaud*** first showed the world the *massé* shot in the early 1800s.

Worst put on a truly astounding performance, because Fats wasn't exaggerating about the poor table conditions — the cloth was playing slower than hell! Making full force *massés* on such wet cloth required a world-class stroke. No one else in the room would have dared to attempt any of Worst's mighty *massé* shots considering the conditions. In fact, no one else in the room could have made Worst's phenomenal *massé* shots under *ideal* conditions.

None of the other players put on any more exhibitions after Worst's knock 'em dead performance.

#2 Luther "Wimpy" Lassiter, of Elizabeth City, NC. Nobody would play Wimpy even-up either.

Predictably, Worst and Lassiter never gambled with each other. However, I witnessed a challenge made by Worst to Lassiter in Johnston City, IL., after Lassiter had beaten Worst in a tournament Nine Ball match, Worst was in heat after the loss and offered to play Wimpy Nine Ball for $200 a game after the tournament matches were over.

I and many others, swarmed to the gambling room after the last match see the big game. Neither player showed up.

**Captain Mingaud*: Inventor the leather tip, developer of english and creator of the *massé* shot.

It turned out that Worst would not play on the Sabbath — it was late Saturday night — and Lassiter, having heard that Worst had recently beaten the Canton, OH legend, **Don Willis**, wasn't eager to play either. (*I added some enhancement of this story that was introduced earlier in the Interview.*)

#3 Efren Reyes of the Philippine Islands. Worst and Lassiter played in the *pushout* era. Reyes plays in the *shoot to hit it* era. Nobody kicks at a ball better than Efren.

Cheapskate Award

The late **Mike Carella** of Miami, FL. After winning $25,000 in Detroit, Mike was obligated to tip the gamekeeper, **Bugs Rucker**, who refereed the game and racked the balls for 24 straight hours. Mike told Bugs that **Kenny "Romberg" Remus** owed him $200 and if Bugs could collect it, he could keep it.

"Blue Shirt" Art. After winning $3000 in Texas, Blue Shirt went into the parking lot and slept in his car rather than get a room. His penny-pinching went unrewarded. He got stuck-up for all his winnings by the guys he beat when they spotted him camped out on his back seat.

Three Greatest *Sharkers*

Ronnie Allen of OK, **Charles "Low Down Dirty Red" Jones**, Las Vegas (now departed) and **Alphonso "Fonzi" Daniels** of Chicago, IL.

The greatest *shark* move I ever saw was when Fonzi was playing One-Pocket on a *5' x10'* table with a high-roller named **Watusi.** Watusi was being spotted 8 to 7, and with two balls left on the table, he was frozen to the back rail with a long shot to his pocket and his game ball. Fonzi had *his* game ball also hanging in *his* pocket; but if Watusi made his shot he would win the game.

Sweat poured off Watusi's forehead as he stroked and stroked at the ball. They were betting very high, and this was a critical game to win. Watusi finally began to deliver the stick to the cue ball. At the exact instant the cue tip was about to make contact with the cue ball, Fonzi quietly remarked, "You better chalk up." Watusi miscued so badly that the cue ball didn't travel over a foot. Fonzi shot in the *hanger** to win and deadpanned, "I warned you."

**hanger:* An easy to make shot. Where the object ball is literally on the lip of the pocket where a strong breeze could knock it in.

Alphonse "Fonzi" Daniels
in *flagrante delicto*

Don Willis & Thomas "Amarillo Slim" Preston
photo courtesy Conrad Burkman

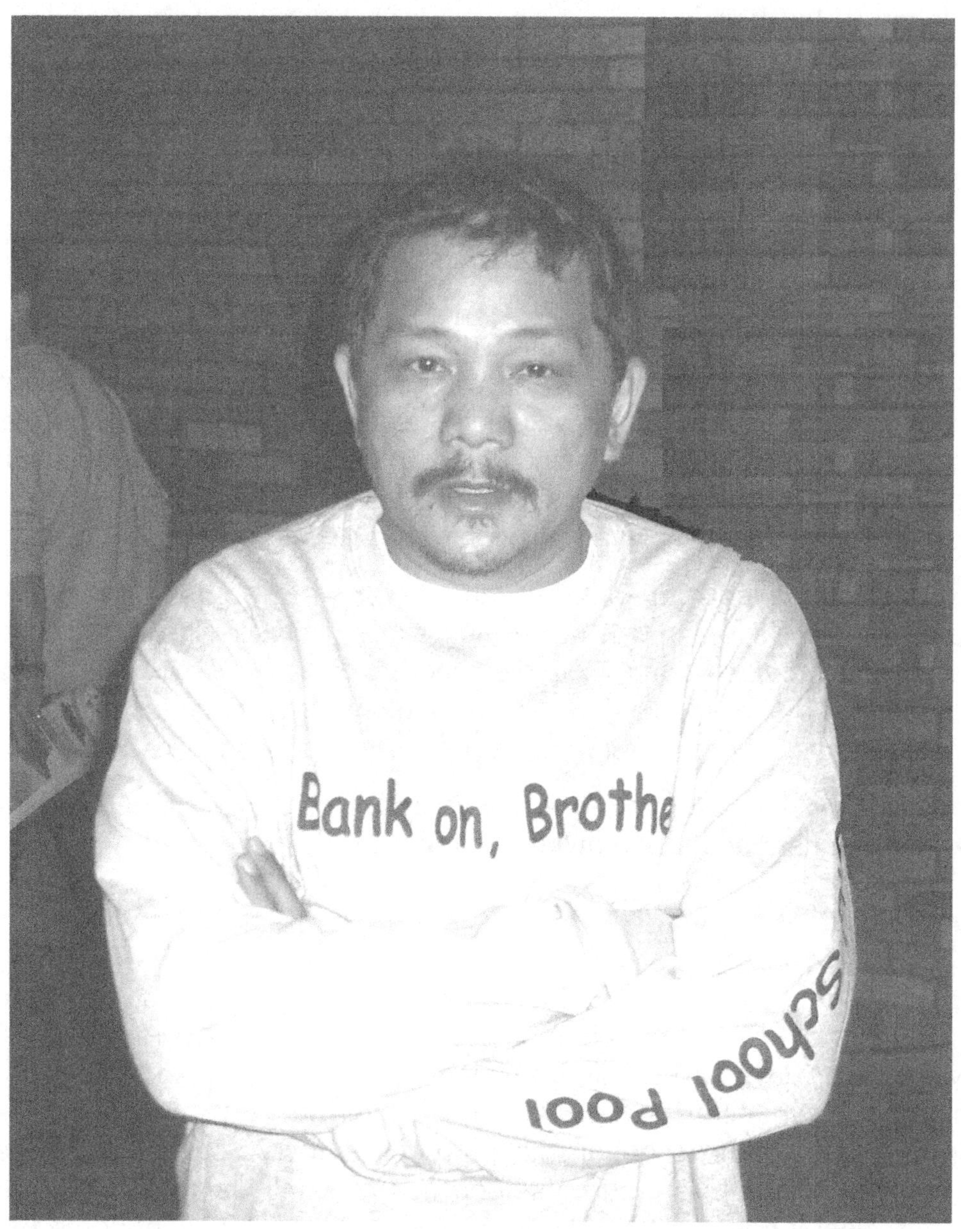

Efren "The Magician" Reyes

Most Pleasurable Shark

George Walker was a southern boy who owned a big-time action bar, **The Stardust Lounge** on North Avenue in Chicago in the 60s. Winning in George's bar was no mean feat. George would do anything he could to beat you when you played there. Besides *shark* you, he doctored up the chalk by soaking it in chemicals and baking it in an oven. He put pins under the cloth near a pocket to divert a softly hit ball. He would *tushhog* you and *jar** you if you drank anything, and he would move the table if you went to the bathroom.

But my favorite shark involved his wife **Chris**. George's country-girl wife was one of the sexiest creatures alive. She wore mini–skirts when there was no such thing. She would sit in a chair watching the game in her mini, *sans* panties. If you had a tough shot and were facing her, at the moment you were delivering the stroke, her legs would open and she would flash you. It may have bothered some players, but I actually played position to get hit with the flash.

There was a top player from Flint, MI named **Harry "Poochie" Sexton**. He had a pock-marked face and was no raving beauty. However, he was credited with having an oversized dong. Poochie lived with George for a while. It was rumored that he had gotten lucky with Chris after she became curious about the large member story. I was never more jealous of anybody in my whole life.

My chance with Chris never came. A few years later, George's lunatic brother Lonnie, in a drunken rage, put a bullet into her brain.

The Greatest *Stay-Up* Men

#1 Milborn "Gar" Frazier, AKA **"Gar The Iron Man"** of Chicago, nee South Carolina, was the uncontested champ. He set the world's record in the '70s by staying up 21 days and nights gambling. (Naturally, he used pills!) Gar approached his own record in the '80s at my place, **The North Shore Billiard Club** in Chicago, when he began playing pool January 1st (the place was closed for New Year's Eve) and continued nonstop until January 14th. Gar went home, slept 8 hours, returned and played until the 21st, went home for a day, came back and finished out the month.

**Jar, Jar someone, to be Jarred*: Similar to an old-fashioned "Mickey Finn." To put Hyacin or Scopalomine in someone's drink, seriously altering their vision and perceptions. Jar victims think they are playing great but can barely make a ball. It's a very dangerous drug. Many players have died from overdoses. The KGB and the CIA used it as truth serum.

Jerry "The Barber," C.J., & Gar Frazier *

In the course of his run, Gar pulled two of his own teeth with pliers and vomited twice into a garbage can. His feet swelled up so much that we had to cut the leather toe part off and turn the shoe into a sandal. He also never washed for the full 31 days. None of those events gave Gar cause for pause.

4 B's CLUB

Before **The North Shore Billiard Club**, I had a joint called the **4 B's Club**. The place was named after the four partners who each had a **B** in their name. The time was the early and middle '70s. Many top players came through the **4 B's Club** and gambled. The great Grady Mathews spent some time there and loved the joint.

Gar would stay in there 7,8,9,10 days at a time playing poker or pool or staking somebody. He was the only *stakehorse* I ever had who would not let me quit when I had a bad game. Gar would beg me to play, "Just one more set, one more set." A lot of rough and rowdy guys hung out in the **4 B's Club**, but you could win all you wanted and never have a problem.

* Only known picture of Gar Frazier

Harry Platis, One Of The "Great Men" In Pooldom? You Bet He Is!

photo courtesy Bill Porter and Mike Haines

Harry "Poochie" Sexton

photo courtesy Conrad Burkman

We managed to get stuck up twice, though. It was very scary getting tied up with bailing wire, and being forced face down onto the floor, as we were in our first heist. They were good heist men, because everybody in the joint was usually packing. Unfortunately, the shotguns the stickup guys carried trumped our pistols.

The main attraction for these robberies was probably Gar, because he always carried a huge bankroll. I semi-missed the second robbery because I was sleeping on a cot in the back room. The robbers rushed in through the back door and ran right by me (the lights were off in the room). I was terrified they would see me on the way out, so I got under the cot and waited them out.

I need to mention that it was a metal fold-up cot and there was a bar in the middle that I had to squeeze under. To get under the cot I had to lift it a few inches off the ground. When I finally got under it, the cot wasn't touching the floor! I was supporting it on my back. Thank God they never noticed.

During the robbery they told everybody to drop their pants. Gar, The Iron Man, asked if he could be excused from that drill since he didn't want everybody to see his shorts, considering he hadn't changed them in about a month. The heist-men sadistically refused his request.

Gar was a unique, fabulous personality. More of his adventures need to be told. Gar was a battle hardened, old **WW II** vet (he served the entire length of the war in actual combat, from Africa to Italy, from 1942 to 1945), but at heart he was a softie, an easy mark for the *bite* and a true friend of the unfortunate.

I was at Gar's house once when I noticed he had a barrel of peanuts along with a barrel of bird seed in his hallway. "What the hell are these for, Gar?" I innocently inquired. "They're for the squirrels and the pigeons, you dumb-ass!" Gar took care of everybody, friend or fowl.

Gar had a house in the old Uptown area in Chicago. It was definitely not a high-rent district, being filled with whores, dopers and white-trash hillbillies. Every Christmas, Gar would fill an old supermarket cart with toys and mosey up and down his street passing out toys to the underprivileged kids on the block.

One Christmas, Gar ran into trouble when an old hooker took an attitude with his offer and refused to send her kids down from her second-floor apartment to get the presents. "We don't need no charity from you, you old bastard!" She ungratefully shouted.

Gar persisted and yelled, "C'mon down and get these toys for yer kids, you goddamn whore!" The lady was unmoved by his generosity and dumped a pan of water out the window on him.

Another night, while walking home from the store in his seedy neighborhood, he was accosted by a big mugger with a long knife. The mugger demanded Gar's bankroll, but Gar pushed him away and took off running with the now-angry mugger hot on his heels. Gar had a plan, though. He was running to his car parked in front of his house. While on the way, he fumbled his trunk key out. He got to the car, quickly popped the trunk and removed a large hammer. Now he turned and faced his oncoming adversary who skidded in his tracks, did an about-face and took off running in the opposite direction with Gar now hot on *his* heels!

The avenging Gar cut a formidable figure flying down Wilson Avenue waving that hammer high above his head. "Don't trip now, mutherfucker, ‘cause I'm dead on your ass!" he shouted, providing strong incentive for the mugger to keep on keeping on.

At 70 Gar became diabetic, but he never took care of himself, resulting in his right leg being cut off at the knee. Gar refused rehab and amputee counseling, citing that he was on the Anzio beachhead for two months and was plenty familiar with missing limbs. He stayed in the hospital a total of two days after the operation before he released himself! He immediately went to a card game and played poker all night. I know all this happened because Gar stopped by my bar for coffee the morning after the card game.

Things got worse for Gar; next he lost the left leg at the knee. Then the thigh of the right and left leg. Finally, he had a stoke that paralyzed his left side. All this never slowed him a step. He became a beggar in a wheelchair and was out working the street every day.

A friend spotted him on a busy corner begging and playfully asked what Gar would do if he just snatched up the money in the beggar's cup? Gar had a newspaper in his lap with his hand under the newspaper. When he pushed the paper aside Gar was holding a 7" switchblade knife and told the guy, "Go for it!"

Operating with 1/4 of a body, Gar had more balls than a squad of US Navy SEALs.

After a morning of begging, Gar loved to go to the racetrack. In those days the track was not handicap-accessible and people had to go up a long ramp to the admissions booth, which posed a serious problem for the wheelchair-bound Gar.

He solved the dilemma by hiring someone to push him around in the wheelchair. Gar probably should have used a higher set of hiring qualifications, because the guy that wound up pushing him was totally blind! They were a hilarious duo, with Gar cursing, shouting orders and directions at the blind guy and urging him to go faster. Between the two of them, they didn't have a full contingent of body parts.

More Stay Up Men

#2 Greg Steven's weekly schedule at **Le Cue** in Houston, TX was to sleep Monday, Tuesday and Wednesday, eat one gigantic meal Thursday, then appear in the poolroom and play nonstop through Sunday. Stevens did this every week for at least a year.

#3 Jimmy "Fly Boy" Spears of OH**.** Although he was light-years away from competing with the top two, Spears could perform 3,4,5,6 days on a regular basis, high-rolling the whole time. Fly Boy preferred chemicals to booze.

Greatest Stay Up Man— No Chemical Assistance

Artie Bodendorfer, Chicago, IL.

After playing **Artie** for 24 hours, nobody had a chance. He would rob anybody after a day of play. As the match progressed, Bodendorfer's percentage shooting really started to matter. Plus, Artie could play for two or three days on coffee only with no food, and he would never sit down. He would pee about once every 24 hours.

After a three-day One-Pocket match with **Grady Mathews**, even though Grady came out a few games ahead, Grady's *backers,* **"Fat T.R." McIntosh** from Tampa FL and **Monroe Brock** from Richmond, KY, vowed to never again *stake anybody* against Artie.

Grady's *backers* pulled him up two or three games ahead, but after 72 hours, Grady was finally starting to wear thin and Artie seemed to be getting into better and better stroke. Monroe lamented, "How can you play against somebody who doesn't sit down, eat or piss?"

Able To Consume Different Combinations And Still Play Good
This category requires two different provisos:

Booze:
The nod goes to the great, **Ronnie Allen**. In his younger days, Ronnie liked to keep at least four different combos within arm's reach: beer, scotch and either champagne cocktails, or vodka screwdrivers. On a good day, Ronnie downed all four.

Chemicals:
#1 "St. Louie Louie" Roberts, St. Louis, MO. While living with a hypochondriac Chicago cue maker, Louie once emptied the cue maker's medicine cabinet. The cue maker routinely had shelves of assorted medicines that could bring you up, take you down or eliminate all pain.

Louie (no pharmacist he), would just take potluck and play Pill-Russian–Roulette. He'd say, "I'll try two of those white ones with three of those pinkies and seal the deal with one of those red babies. I'll save these brown stripers for later." Louie would chase them all down with a few six–packs of beer, then play for days and never miss a ball.

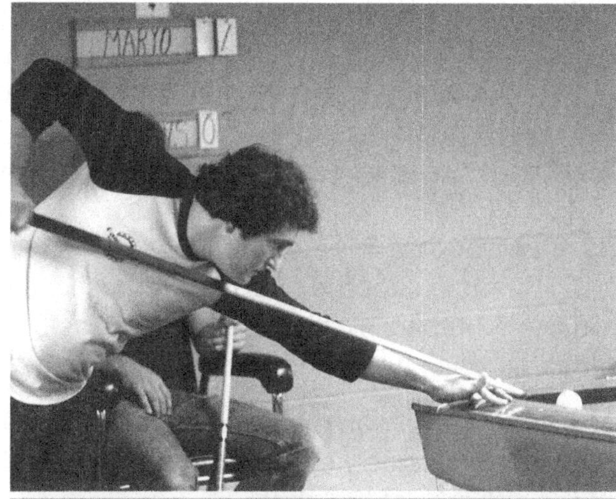

"St. Louie Louie" Roberts
photos courtesy Bill Porter and Mike Haines

CHEMICALS (Continued)
#2 Leonard "Bugs" Rucker. When he was just coming up, Bugs liked to start off with *Terps** cough syrup, kick it up with a few *"xmas trees,"* * while taking periodic pulls out of a flask full of gin, intermittently smoking joints and then snorting all the coke he could beg from *backers* and sideliners. Whereupon Rucker proceeded to run-out from everywhere.

A pharmacologist commented, "If you fed that mixture to an elephant, it would fall over dead in minutes."

Top Ten Rogues Gallery

#1 Eddie "Detroit Whitey" Beuchene. When he went broke, Whitey and his German Shepherd named **Windy** used to go out begging together. Whitey would wear dark glasses and brandish a tin cup and pencils. As mentioned earlier in the Interview, It was rumored (I use words like ***rumored***, to keep the risk of getting sued to a minimum) that Whitey sold his two kids to black-marketeers to raise money to play a pool session.

#2 Ray "Boots" Maples, long deceased, of Atlanta, GA, became famous for hitting people over the head with cue sticks and beer bottles when they weren't looking. Maples was a double-tough street bully known to engage in *spike fights** in back alleys for money.

Maple's favorite game was Alabama 8-ball where the 1-ball and the 15-ball are played in a designated side pocket. He rarely missed a money ball regardless of the difficulty of the shot.

Maples cut a very dashing figure when he was sober. He was handsome, well–groomed and spiffily dressed. When Maples was drunk, he was a hideous slob, urinating in the spittoons in the poolroom.

Maples *dumped* his own father to Detroit Whitey in a pool game, but wanted a bigger cut for his part in the deed. To quote Maples, "Gawd damn, Whitey, after all, he is my fathah!" When his truth or honor came into question, Maples would raise his right hand and solemnly swear to his most infamous line, "I take an oath on my dead mother's pussy."

**terps:* An old brand of cough syrup that was laced with codeine.

**xmas trees:* Barbiturates.

**spike fight:* A duel where opponents wear sharpened baseball spikes and fight in a confined area like a narrow alley.

A MUGGING ON CICERO AVENUE AND 83rd Street:
There were few tushhogs that Ray Maples stepped back from; but when he got into a beef with former welterweight contender **Jimmy Cox**, Maples knew he had no chance in a fair fight. Cox was a trained gladiator with a hair trigger temper and a punch like a heavyweight. Cox would knock Maple's lights out in any direct confrontation, because the difference between a professionally trained boxer and a street tough is a gulf that few untrained *tushhogs* can navigate. Maples knew this and so did Cox. Maples wanted no part of a fight he was doomed to lose.

When tempers began to flare between Cox and Maples, as was certain to happen with so much untamed testosterone in the same proximity, Maples resorted to preemptive action. Without warning, Maples hit Cox squarely in the middle of his forehead with a beer mug, leaving an ugly five inch circular scar that Jimmy wore for the rest of his life.

Fortunately for Maples, the blow knocked Cox out colder than a snowdrift in Alaska. Maples hurriedly took his leave from the joint before Cox revived.

A BEEF JOLT IN JOHNSTON CITY
It was several years before Cox and Maples crossed paths again at **The All Around Hustler's Tournament in Johnston City**. Word that both Cox and Maples were in town spread like wildfire among people who knew about the blood feud between the two hooligans.

Gamblers offered odds on who would kill whom. Voyeurs were eagerly anticipating the coming bloodbath. There might be gunplay; for sure there would be an epic battle between two notorious tushhogs. The possible showdown electrified the pool players in Johnston City.

When word of the beef reached the ears of tournament promoters, George and Paulie Jansco, two dangerous dudes themselves, they took immediate and decisive action. Maples and Cox were warned, "If there is so much as a bad word between the two of you while you are here, we'll send both of you home in boxes." Both Cox and Maples left Johnston City the next day, possibly because of learning that the deadly **Hubert "Daddy Warbucks" Cokes** was a personal friend of the Janscos.

George Jansco
photo courtesy Bill Bell

George Jansco, Luther Lassiter & Paulie Jansco

photos courtesy Conrad Burkman

Norman Hitchcock and Paulie Jansco

Cox became a career criminal after his boxing days, and spent several well-deserved stretches in various prisons. Rumor has it that Jimmy Cox was killed in a gunfight with an **Alabama State Trooper** after a failed armed robbery in the 1960s.

Maples, as is sometimes the case with such a contentious personality, had a small upside. He was deadly shooting off the game ball and he coined two of the great lines in hustler patter.

One night after he uncharacteristically missed several game balls and went broke in a *bar spot*,* Ray's partner, **James "Peaches" Rochford**, asked him what the heck had gone wrong. Maples, replied, "I was shooting good until those bastards **"put the Hamlet on me."** Ray was telling Peaches, in his own original way, that he had been jarred. Citing "Hamlet" was a reference to the Shakespeare play where almost everybody winds up getting poisoned.

The second great line produced by Maples occurred one day in **Bensinger's** when all the hustlers, including Maples, were sitting around bemoaning their collective *broke* status. At that point one of Maple's "customers" (*i.e.,* personal sucker) came through the front door, looking around the room for his playmate, Maples.

A nice score now imminent, Maples crossed his fingers, placed them over his chest, looked upward as if to acknowledge God's benevolence, sighing, **..."and in the window flew a dove."**

COMEUPPANCE FOR A BULLY

Maples got paid back for his bully behavior in a hillbilly bar on Sheridan Road and Wilson Avenue on Chicago's North side. Unhappy with Maple's malevolent personality and fed up with his aggravating, exasperating, disgusting and threatening behavior, a gang of patrons dragged a drunken Maples out into the street, only instead of breaking Ray's thumbs *ala* **The Hustler**, they put his leg across a curb and jumped on it until it was broken.

Maples died of a heart attack at **Campus Billiards** across from **Loyola University** in Chicago, while hustling a college kid playing Eight Ball. Ray's heart gave out while he was shooting at the game ball.

bar spot: An action bar with money games.

"Brooklyn Johnny" Ervolino & Me

#3 "Brooklyn Johnny" Ervolino (now departed; a great player and an old friend). I once tried to *bite* him in Los Angeles. Johnny turned me down, citing that he was broke. I ran into him next in Las Vegas, where on a roll I won about $15,000 on the dice tables. He bit me for $900!

Johnny's compelling justification for the *bite* was this original line: "When you were broke and desperate in LA and you came to me asking for money, what did I say to you?" My reply was a dumb, blank, inquisitive stare. Johnny continued, "I told you if I had it, you could get anything you want, right? Now, how are you going to treat me?" Behind that seemingly, flawless logic, I eagerly *un-assed** the $900.

It wasn't until later, when I finally came to my senses, that I realized that Ervolino had never actually given me anything but a promise. In reality, *he turned me down*! I did learn something, though. What a wonderful way to duck the incoming *bite* and also pave the way for a future *bite* for yourself.

#4 Vince "Pancho" Corelli, one of Brooklyn's finest**,** *dumped* the famous record mogul billionaire **Phil Spector**.

Vince was playing black pool champ **Marvin Henderson**. Pancho ran 80 balls while attempting to dump! Marvin got so shook-up that he couldn't make a ball. Marvin finally won the game *in the one-hole** 125 to 124! The actor **James Caan** was in attendance, watching the game.

**un-assed*: Gave it up. Turned it loose. Released.

**in the one-hole*: To need one more point to win the game.

#5 The Crew From Kentucky

A collective award goes to all the boys from Hazard and Corbin, KY, where they produce, per capita, more card-sharks, dice-hustlers and pool players than the law allows.

It is rumored that they have classes in the local high school on how to deal *bottoms and seconds.** "Mechanics Shop 101" has a different meaning in a Hazard high school.

A Kentucky crew set a record for greed when they worked over a sucker in Chicago. The *egg** had just received a huge injury settlement. With some of the money, he bought new furniture— TVs, stereos, etc. With the remainder he began playing poker with the Kentucky boys, who now made the South Side of Chicago their hustling headquarters.

The Kentucky boys quickly won all the settlement cash, but they were far from done with their victim. Next, they began working on the new furniture. They would bring the mark home, usually at 2 or 3 in the morning and he'd tell his wife, "Don't get up, Hon, it's okay." The Kentucky boys would then cart away the new TVs, stereos, sofas, etc.

The *egg's* wife took it like a good trooper— hubby losing all the money, losing all the furniture, leaving her with no TV to watch, etc— but the greedy bastards went too far. One night, hubby came home about 3 am and said, "Hon, you're gonna have to get up out of bed. I lost the bedroom set. It's okay, it's okay."

But it finally wasn't okay. The next morning "Hon" went to the police station and filed a complaint. The windup was, the Hazard boys got arrested and were made to give back the furniture and whatever money was left or face a federal gambling charge. They shouldn't have made such gluttons of themselves.

#6 Billy "Cornbread Red" Burge. Some of Red's backers jarred Ronnie Allen so badly in Johnston City that Ronnie fell to the floor writhing, foaming at the mouth with his eyes rolled back in his head. Red went over and kicked Allen, finishing with the remark, "Get up, muthafuckah, it's yo' shot!"

Fortunately, the Janscos intervened and rescued Allen and made them return his money. After the Janscos found out what had been going on, there was no more jarring in Johnston City. Ronnie was definitely not an innocent victim, since his own backers had jarred Red two days previously.

**bottoms and seconds*: Cards that are dealt off the bottom of the deck or to deal the second card from the top.

**egg*: A mark, a sucker.

#7 Billy Incardona — Laid more traps than the Orkin Man.

#8 Ronnie Allen — Was raised in a carnival. Need I say more?

#9 Leonard "Bugs" Rucker — One of the world's greatest bite-men. On Chicago's South Side they call it "begging." Bugs begged enough money in his career to maybe finance the first Gulf War. I speak from personal experience, as I have suffered the T-Rex type teeth marks from his ferocious bite on all too many an occasion.

photo courtesy OnePocket.

 # 10 Bill "Wienie Beanie" Staton — I have tried very hard to keep my big mouth shut regarding the departed "Wienie Beanie." But I can't hold back anymore, and hopefully enough time has elapsed since his passing so that I have at least shown some amount of respect. It's in bad taste, I know, to speak ill of the dead, but words like "Southern gentleman" and "Wonderful old man stuff" does not at all describe "Wienie Beanie." He was a good player, a good gambler, and basically a charming fellow, but "Wienie Beanie" would steal the laces off your shoes and then tell you how much better you looked in sandals.

I had plenty of larceny myself, we all did in that cut-throat era had, but I looked like Pope Paul next to "Beanie." Beanie flew no flags, and if he could have, he would have set a trap to bust Little Orphan Annie.

Steadiest And Most Consistent

Cecil "Buddy" Hall. He was like Michael Jordan. Buddy hardly ever had a bad day.

Artie Bodendorfer. The only time I ever saw Bodendorfer play really badly was one Saturday afternoon when he got trounced by Kentucky's **Clyde Childress.** Artie took me down with him. I was betting on the side and I was stuck badly. Attempting to recover my investment, I secretly slipped speed pills into Artie's coffee. (He would never take pills voluntarily). It didn't work. Later, I learned Artie had lost 15 football bets in a row while playing Clyde. He kept going to the phone for results. At day's end, Bodendorfer was down $70,000! Artie's pool game suffered commensurately. His slump was short-lived. He came back the next day and annihilated Clyde. I missed getting even because I was out partying all night. (Tragically, Clyde died soon afterwards in a car crash).

Best Shooting At The *Money Ball* For The *Big Cheese*

A close tie between **Artie Bodendorfer, Leonard "Bugs" Rucker, Ronnie Allen, Billy Joe "Corn-Bread Red" Burge, Luther "Wimpy" Lassiter**, **Harold Worst** and **Cecil "Buddy" Hall**.

Artie's face on the *cheese* shot would look like somebody was squeezing his privates with a pliers. Then he would uncork his straight-through "jerk" stroke and the big-money ball would drizzle into the pocket.

Bugs Rucker would stare and stare at the shot, while taking many warm-up strokes. Suddenly he would jump up, turn his cap around backwards, get back down, take one quick stroke and whack the ball home.

Ronnie Allen would bring his *stake-horse's** tension to a mind-crushing fever pitch by making sure his *backer* knew just how tough the shot really was. Then he would get back down on the shot, take a last look at the trembling *stakehorse* and laughingly shout out, "Here we go!", before finally pounding the ball home. It was not easy to play high-stakes pool with Ronnie.

**stake-horse*: A pool backer. He who puts up the money for you to play.

Luther "Wimpy" Lassiter would study the key shot, look and look, powder up with talc, and look some more. Then Lassiter would then spend some time removing specks of chalk and dirt from the line of his shot. Once he was sure that no debris on the table would interfere with his shot, Wimpy would *shoot his cuffs,** (reminiscent of Ed Norton's unnerving antics while playing against Bensonhurst poolhall champ and best buddy Ralph Kramden — from the TV comedy classic, "The Honeymooners") get down and naturally bring the shot. Knowledgeable observers said that Lassiter was the best shot maker since Ralph Greenleaf.

Harold Worst would look around disdainfully, trying to make eye contact with anybody in the room who had the slightest doubt that he would bring the shot. Everyone usually looked away. Then Worst would get down on the table, his bald forehead a shade of beet red, give the object ball a laser-look as if daring it to stay out of the pocket, and then blast it home. Nobody hit the game-ball harder than Harold Worst.

This depiction first appeared in my other book, ***Banking With The Beard****.*

"**Cornbread Red**" liked to bet so high it put a "tremble" in his opponents stroke. Red was one of my heroes. Whenever I ran into him, I hung onto him the whole time. He had me totally fascinated. I followed him everywhere but into the bathroom. Red was another master at shooting off the game ball. When confronted with the big-cheese-money-ball, Red would derisively snort, "Haw, haw," in his inimitable style, then he would increase his normally long back-stroke about another foot, and slip-stroke the shot in, with dust flying out of the back of the pocket.

Red was unbeatable playing One-Pocket on a 5' x 10' snooker table. He was a great hustler, a great player, and a joy to watch — almost as funny as Minnesota Fats — a scandalous, shameless rogue, and I dearly miss him so.

WHAT'S YO' NEXT BEST GAME?

Cornbread Red was a folk hero around Detroit in the 1960s. Red's ability as a topflight pool hustler, his outrageous high-rolling behavior and his fearless spirit won the admiration of people in Motor City. Red was one of their own and the locals loved hearing about his escapades.

**shoot his cuffs*: To quickly extend your arms straight out as if preparing to start some sort of project.

One night Red was hustling in a joint that he had been sent to by **Detroit Whitey**. Whitey told Red that the sucker was an easy score, a mark who loved to play snooker and paid off like a broken slot machine. What Red didn't know, was that Whitey had already sent a slew of players in to beat the guy, and it was now a "heat" spot, a very dangerous place to hustle in.

A drunken Cornbread (as he was apt to be back then, before he got on the wagon for the next 40 years) immediately approached the fellow and started revving him up to play. Red slapped the guy lightly on the back and asked him, "What's yo' best game?" The mark began a slow burn.

When Red persisted with the same question and the same back slap, the mark violently declared, "Boxing!" and hit Red so hard that he knocked him backward onto his ass two full table lengths from where the blow was delivered. The *sweators** got a bucket of bilge water from behind the bar loaded with beer labels, dregs, debris and swill and dumped it on Red.

Undaunted, Cornbread jumped to his feet and said, "Alright, muthafuckah, what's yo' *next* best game?" The mark could only laugh at Red's bravado and finally said, "Snooker!" So they played snooker and Red wound up making a decent score. Cornbread did not give Whitey his end for steering him to the game.

Cecil "Buddy" Hall's concentration would melt the paint on a wall. His slow, methodical, deliberate style was nerve-wracking. Buddy was never careless with a shot. If you were betting on him and he was shooting at the game ball — however hard it might be — you knew you were going to get your money's worth from Buddy's effort.

Most Perfect Nine Ball Patterns

"Portland Don" Watson. When Don got to the Nine Ball, his position was so perfect that dapper-dressed, legendary gunfighter **Bat Masterson** could have tapped the ball in with his cane. When he wasn't in action Watson whiled away the time reading paperbacks.

On one memorable occasion, an unknown player came into the back room in Johnston City asking to play the Florida State Nine Ball Champion (who just so happened to be Portland Don) for $600. Don's reputation wasn't known to everyone, so he was reluctant to openly claim the title of "Florida State Nine Ball Champion" and remained silent for a while. When the "Florida State Champion" did not come forward (no one else was going to meddle with Don's action), Don said, "I'll play you some."

**sweator:* AKA, Eye-baller, Eye-fucker, sideliner, a pool-game-watcher with no vested interest in the match, except to root for both players to somehow lose. Sweaters have zero gamble.

The challenger wasn't much of a threat and Don quickly busted the fellow, who left without learning that he had accomplished his mission of playing the Florida State Champion.

After the challenger left a bystander remarked, "Shouldn't someone go out and tell the poor guy that he got to play who he wanted?"

Biggest Small-time Sucker I Ever Knew (non-pool player)

Gerard. An unknown card player from South America. Gerard loved to play Gin Rummy and was probably the greatest gin player of all time. He had coke-bottle-lens glasses and couldn't see a foot in front of him, so he never took his eyes off his own cards. Over the years he paid the rent (mine included) for many a hustler.

Everybody who played Gerard held out two or three extra cards to play with. You would need at least that many to beat him. Gerard was that good. Always up against the *nuts*, Gerard never won a session in four years. He finally broke his losing streak in a Chicago card room when he landed on an overconfident champion gin-player.

The gin champion was so confident of his game that he thought he could beat anybody if they just let him play *location** on them. However, a player needed to go much stronger than that on Gerard, who was used to playing against the *Hungarian nuts* every time he sat down to play. The outcome was predictable. Gerard quickly broke the gin champion. On his way out of the card room, the lady who ran the card room told Gerard that he owed for the table time.

Gerard, blank-faced, replied, "Time? What is time?" Since he had never won the whole time he was in the US, he had never had to pay for the table time; the hustler who broke him would always pay.

Most Powerful *Stroke*

Harold Worst— U.J. Puckett had a five-rail power draw shot he would shoot for the crowd's delight at the yearly tournament in Johnston City IL. One night, Worst asked Puckett if he could try his hand at the shot. Worst got seven rails the first try and Puckett never played that shot again.

**location*: The dealer unethically keeps track of several cards that he has secretly moved to the bottom of the deck.

Pool's Best Story Tellers
"Minnesota Fats," "Jersey Red," "Brooklyn Jimmy," Danny DiLiberto, "Pancho" Corelli, "Hippie Jimmy" Reid and then **me**.

The *Greatest Men In Pool**
"Jew Paul" Bruslov of Detroit was a top character in pooldom. Paul had made millions selling imported oven ware sets all around the country. He was a pool hustler in his early years, and when he became wealthy the only thing that having money changed about Paul was that now he wanted to bet more of it.

Jew Paul still loved the poolroom and the players. His favorite was Cornbread Red. He loved breaking Red. Red always gave Paul the *nuts* — spotting Paul 10 to 8 or 11 to 8, playing One-Pocket on a snooker table. Paul would win five out of every six sessions they played. However, when Red won a session, it'd be a doozy. Since Paul was a *straight ticket,** Red would charge Paul a huge chunk of cash on those rare times when he managed to win. Cornbread and Jew Paul were both colorful characters and their matches were a joy to watch.

Me & "Jew Paul"

**Great men*: A *"Great"* man in hustling vernacular, is someone with unlimited bankroll who loves to play, loves to bet and has a bottomless capacity for punishment.

**straight ticket*: A gambler who never quits until he is broke.

Lori Shampo
photo courtesy Bill Bell

Best Female Player For The *Big Cheese*
Lori Shampo from Detroit. She was a raving beauty, too. She routinely played $5,000 and $10,000 Nine Ball sets.

Rosey, The Airplane Man of Detroit.
Rosey *went off* for about a zillion dollars playing pool over a few years' time because he could barely run three balls. Rosey also liked bowling and bet on the matches occurring on different alleys. What he didn't know was that the local boys would have the whole bowling alley filled with their guys, so that just about any game Rosey bet on was controlled by them.

Biggest Drop-Off in Ability
Eddie Robin of Las Vegas. Robin went from winning four games of Nine Ball on extremely tricky equipment — the old Harold Worst pool table— for $10 a game against the great **Don Willis,** to getting odds of 8 to 5 playing One-Pocket from every *short-stop* around.

Best Writer in the Pool World
George Fels. In this I am unashamedly biased. The fact that I have known and hung with him for over 40 years is secondary and unimportant. George once wrote an eulogy in **Billiards Digest** for one of our favorite pool buddies, **Jack Gunne** from New York, who died at the very early age of 46. It was one of the most moving and beautiful pieces that I have ever read in my life. It broke me up then and if I look at it now, it will bring tears again. At Gunne's wake, George had left 2 new pieces of chalk in the casket. The last few lines in the article were, "So long, buddy. Thanks for the game. Take care of these two *cubes.** I'll come around when it's my shot, and we can play forever." Red Smith or Jimmy Cannon never said it better.

Kudos go to **R.A. Dyer** and **Thomas Shaw.** They play the word game pretty good too.

Greatest Single *Lemon Spread*
I immodestly assign myself that distinction. I achieved as I stated earlier when I posed as a billionaire industrialist from Pennsylvania in order to trap the highest rolling gambler who ever lived, **Archie Karas** of Las Vegas. We beat Archie for a bundle with that *spread.*

Greatest Woman *Sweater*
Barbara Cooney. She could sit in a chair and *sweat* her husband Jack's play for 3 to 5 days without food or water.

Best Looking Man Player
If I were a broad, I would have to pick **Jimmy "Pretty Boy Floyd" Mataya**, from Lansing, MI. Remember, he was once married to one of the top three most beautiful pool players, **Eva Mataya Lawrence.** A virtual tie for the 2nd and 3rd spots between **Robert Redford** look-alike, **Kim Davenport** of CA, and the tragically departed, legendary "**St. Louie Louie" Roberts**.

Worst Bathroom In Any Bar I Ever Hustled In
Chicago mobster and loan shark **Al Milstein's** all-night hillbilly bar on Roosevelt and Cicero Avenue in Cicero, IL takes the prize. You needed galoshes and a gas mask just to take a leak. Since I had neither, when I had to go I would take a deep breath, hold it, run into the toilet on my tippy toes and get the work done as quickly as possible, hopefully before I had to take another breath. I used to marvel at the hillbilly drunks who were able to lollygag and carry on lengthy conversations while in there.

**cubes*: Pool chalk.

Minnesota Fats
&
Hubert "Daddy Warbucks" Cokes

Jim "Pretty Boy Floyd" Mataya

Best *Tushhog*, My Era

"Sugar Shack Johnny" Novak from Port Chester, NY. He loved it when his opponents were 250 pounds and up. Novak's specialty was hustling bars that were famous for not letting the hustlers get out with the money. Places where if a stranger won, the locals would take the money back.

About halfway through the evening, Sugar Shack would be ahead and the bar's tough guys would start grumbling and threatening. At that point, Sugar Shack would put both hands on the pool table and announce, "If you can't afford to lose, you had better quit now, because if I win, I *am* going home with the money! If anyone thinks differently, he and I can settle that right now!" Somehow his "inner child" would get through to them — there were seldom any takers — and the suckers would quietly *go off** to the Shack.

**go off*: To keep playing and lose all your money.

"Big Henry Duke" Baker of Fort. Lauderdale, FL. **Dick Hall**, a decently-rated tough-guy from KY, was playing in the **Crossroads Bar** in Fort Lauderdale. It was a high action spot because it was the only bar open on Sunday mornings for miles around. Dick got into an argument with Big Henry and when things heated up sufficiently, Dick backed up against the wall with a lead pipe in his hand and invited Henry forward. Henry nonchalantly approached, looked Dick in the eye and said, "I think I'm gonna break your back." At this point (this is the version Dick told me personally), Dick said he felt the air go out of his body, his muscles went limp, his knees buckled and the pipe slid harmlessly out of his hand to the floor. That was the kind of frightening aura that surrounded Big Henry.

I had a similar experience with Big Henry at the same place. Big Henry once threatened me and I suddenly felt like I was under water. He was going to hit me and I froze up. I could barely move a muscle. Luckily, **"Sugar Shack" Johnny Novak** was with me and spotted the situation.

Johnny called out to Henry, holding a cue stick in his hand. Henry wasn't afraid of Sugar Shack but he wasn't crazy enough to spot Sugar Shack a cue stick. It was at least five minutes before the feeling in my legs came back to me.

Big Henry and Sugar Shack had many close encounters, but they never actually fought. If they had ever decided to, they could have sold out the Miami Auditorium with the number of people who would have paid to see them battle.

Toughest *Tushhog*, All-Time

Hubert "Daddy Warbucks" Cokes. He stood six foot three, long, lean and mean. He may have been the toughest son-of-a-bitch alive for the first 50 years of the twentieth century.

Minnesota Fats claimed Hubert once "bitch-slapped" **Baby-Face Nelson**. I knew Hubert well and I certainly wouldn't bet against Fatty's story. It was "rumored" that Hubert's hustling crew, which included **"Titanic" Thompson,** were the guys who had whacked New York mobster, **Arnold Rothstein** (the man who fixed the 1919 World Series) when he refused to pay a poker debt.

Keep in mind that **"Lucky" Luciano** and **Vito Genovese**, among others, worked for Rothstein at the time. That knowledge intimidated those country boys not a bit. I guess they figured that the most dangerous guys in New York were themselves.

Hubert had already had a gun battle with the sheriff of Hot Springs, AR over a woman. They both drew their weapons, Hubert shot the sheriff and had to flee the state.

When the IRS raided the Johnston City **All-Around Hustler's Tournament** in the early '70s, the agents who frisked Hubert were awestruck to discover that he had three pistols on his person: one in an ankle holster, one in his back pocket and a spring–action derringer strapped to his wrist. Hubert's explanation was that he carried a lot of cash and had a few enemies. Cokes was in his seventies at the time!

Tough as Cokes was, he had a soft spot for pool players. He was an easy *bite* and put plenty of pool players in action by *staking* them to play. He played pretty good, too. I watched him in Johnston City play weak players *8-or-no-count** One-Pocket.

In the 1930s, while playing in **Bensingers Billiard Academy** on Monroe and Wabash Street in Chicago, a *sweator* stuck his nose in Hubert's game and offered a decision that Hubert didn't like. Cokes hung the *sweator* by his overcoat collar on the wall coat hanger and left him there for the remainder of the session. He instructed the rest of the room that if anyone took the guy down, they would take his place.

Biggest Set Of *Cohones**

Detroit Whitey again. Once, Whitey sold **Sugar Shack Johnny** $2000 worth of phony gold chains. When Johnny caught up with Whitey about a year later, Johnny was so impressed with Whitey's moxie that he didn't beat him up.
Instead, Johnny took Whitey out drinking. While both were in a drunken stupor, they called me long distance to tell me the story. Sugar Shack figured anybody with enough nerve to do that to him deserved a night of free drinking.

Another time Whitey won a lot of money in a small town in Mexico; the guys he beat took him for a ride into the desert. Their aim was to rob and kill him. Whitey not only talked the Mexicans out of killing him, but he talked them into *staking* him to play pool in Mexico City, where he promptly *dumped* them to tougher guys!

**8-or-no-coun*t: A powerful handicap in One-Pocket, whereas the spotter has to run 8 balls consecutively in his pocket in order to win.

**cohones*: Balls, testicles, courage.

Greatest One-Handed One-Pocket Player

Ronnie Allen. With a little luck and a weak field, Ronnie could have won a One-Pocket tournament playing one-handed. Ronnie Allen will always be remembered for having a beer in one hand and a cue stick in the other while fearlessly popping in one impossible shot after another one-handed and simultaneously carrying on a constant patter with the *sweators.*

Great *Business Men**

Detroit Whitey. Once, while shooting at the Nine Ball, he was so drunk that he couldn't remember if he was supposed to make it or miss it.

Cornbread Red. In his early hustling days, Cornbread was getting *staked* in the **Stardust Lounge**, an action bar on North Avenue in Chicago. Every time his *backer,* **George Walker**, looked away, a drunken Red would slap the Nine Ball in the pocket with his bare hand and howl, "Gawd damn, he done *shit it in** again!"

"Jew Paul" Bruslov was the only human crazy enough to *stake* both Whitey and Red against each other! He did it just to be entertained. Paul would purposely leave before the session was over. Upon his return, both players would claim to have lost.

Best Player, *Pay-Ball On A Snooker Table**

My money is on **"Hippie Jimmy" Reid**. Jimmy loved shooting hard shots. He specialized in long, off-angle combinations that were a goodly distance apart. Jimmy usually kept a silly smile on his face the whole session. Reid enjoyed himself so much in those games that after many hours of play his enthusiasm began to demoralize opponents who were tiring of having to make tough shots and tough run-outs. Rumors that Reid used artificial stimulants have been greatly underestimated.

**business men*: A business game is when a player gets staked and loses on purpose

**shit it in*: Made a lucky shot to score a ball.

**Pay-Ball*: The game is multi-handed Six-Ball, but you get paid on every ball you make. The balls must be run in rotation from one to six.

"Hippie Jimmy" Reid Indulging In His Favorite Refreshment

Keith
photo courtesy Bill Porter and Mike Haines

Keith "Earthquake" McReady
Keith was stomping the continuous pay-ball game at Vern Peterson's old **Palace Billiards** in Bellflower, CA when he was just a tyke. McReady was all of twelve years old and he won so much money playing pay-ball that he got himself thrown out of school after innocently asking his Gym teacher to hold his bankroll for him during Gym class. When he handed the astounded teacher $14,000 in a big cash lump, Keith was immediately carted down to the principal's office and suspended from school.

Denny Searcy from San Francisco, CA.
Denny was a threat to break any pay-ball game. At Joe Burns' tourney in Dayton, OH, in a 5-day, non-stop pay-ball game on Burns' snooker table, Searcy won a suitcase full of money (at least 30k) beating the best pay-ballers in the world.

Best Acquirer And Handler of *Backers*
For big money games, **Ronnie Allen**. Ronnie hired and fired *backers* like Donald Trump organizing a monster deal.

For small to moderate action, Philadelphia's **"Peter Rabbit" Linhardt**. *Backers* would line up to give Rabbit their money to lose for them. Rabbit had been known to wear out as many as 10 *backers* in a single day.

Greatest All-Time Win Percentage Playing Tough Action
Artie Bodendorfer. He played all champions, gave out ridiculous handicaps to suckers, and was next to impossible to beat. However, I must add a footnote:

Ninety-eight percent of his wins came on his home court, **Bensinger's Billiard Academy**, which was in a damp basement and was a very difficult place for anyone to win. The air there had a very low oxygen content. Even *short-stops* that hung out there had batting averages of eighty percent. Road players usually avoided the place as if they might catch malaria down there. In reality, the place was dark, dirty, and smelly, and malaria may have been a possibility.

Greatest Bar Table Eight Ball Player With The *Big Cue Ball**
"Surfer Rod" Curry was the best I ever saw. He could do magical things with the oversized bar-table cue ball.

Keith "Earthquake" McReady. Keith is another worthy candidate for best Nine Ball player on the bar box. I had half of his bet when McReady played Nine Ball on a bar table with Cesar Morales (later to become Efren Reyes) at **Red's Poolroom** in Houston, TX. Keith won the first set and lost the next. Efren caromed in the Nine Ball some kind of way 25% of the games he won.

Greatest Bar Table Eight Ball Player
Artie Bodendorfer. There is no telling how good he played bar Eight Ball because he never lost at it! He didn't play a lot of bar pool and he was always selective about whom he played, but the truth is, he never did get beat at that game. On a big table the only guy to beat him playing Eight Ball was the Mexican champion, **Cannella**.

David Matlock
photo courtesy Bill Porter and Mike Haines

Greatest Bar Table Nine Ball Player
David Matlock. One of the greatest bar table players of all-time, Matlock took 'em all on and got the *cheese.*

**big cue ball*: An oversized cue ball, no longer in vogue, once used on many bar tables.

"Three Fingered" Ronnie Sypher

Greatest Bar Table Nine Ball Player With The *Big Cue Ball*
"Three- fingered" Ronnie Sypher from Ocean City, Md. I was on the road with him in Los Angeles. **Ronnie** took on all the great Mexican players that dominated the bar-pool scene at that time. **Sugar Shack Johnny** was with us. Some of the joints we played in were a little scary. Johnny made sure we were able to leave with the money we won.

Greatest Ten-Ball Players
Efren Reyes, "Hippie Jimmy" Reid, Cecil "Buddy" Hall and Allen Hopkins are my choices.

Never Paid A Restaurant Check
Sammy Eubank and **Dale Smith**. They were famous for having never paid a restaurant check in 18 years on the road. The technique was called *scooting the check.** A restaurant that was easy to beat was called a *scoot spot.* I have been the recipient of several free meals with them, and I must say that the food digests just a little better after a successful *scoot.*

Sammy Eubank

Dale Smith

Never Paid a Motel Bill

"Detroit Whitey," then Sammy and Dale again. Whitey was # 1 not because he beat more motels then Sammy and Dale, but because he was able to talk the motel managers into letting other pool players also stay at the spot without putting up any money. Then Whitey and the other pool players would beat the spot *en masse*. You can blame Whitey for today's Inns requiring you to put cash up in front.

**scooting the check*: To illegally eat in a restaurant and not pay your check.

Most Talented Pool Player

Probably **Danny Diliberto** from Buffalo, NY. Danny could run over 200 balls and was undefeated in 14 pro fights (12-0-2). Diliberto was an AA minor-league baseball player and a 200 average bowler who once bowled a perfect 300 game. Danny had a phenomenal throwing arm. He could throw a golf ball farther than anybody in the world. Danny could make a field goal on a football field with a golf ball by throwing it 100 yards through the goal-post uprights. He won the money doing that at Johnston City, IL. in the '60s.

Danny DiLiberto

photo courtesy Bill Porter and Mike Haines

Later, he trapped the late Roger Maris and Mickey Mantle at a Fort Lauderdale bar during Yankee spring training. Danny bet Maris he could throw a golf ball farther than Roger could.

Diliberto won the bet from an amazed Maris by throwing the ball all the way across the waters of the **Fort Lauderdale Causeway** on Highway A1A. If I remember right, Roger didn't even take his turn and tried to renege and call off the bet. Danny, who had a punch that could down an elephant, stood his ground and finally got paid.

Pooldom's Believe It Or Not

James Justice, of WV, and later Chicago, would bet he could jump up onto a pool table, backwards and flatfooted! Then he would break everybody, when he bet he would do it on one leg, but not backwards. James was also the fastest pool player in a short sprint race. He was the running champion in every prison he was ever confined in. He was probably the only guy who could beat Chicago's **Paul Jones** in a race where they both had to run backwards.

Paul Jones could walk for blocks on his hands, but he had many other talents. On a bet, Paul reached orgasm at the **Rack and Cue** in Detroit without touching himself. He had his pants and shorts down at his ankles, while 30 pool players were howling and catcalling, trying to shark him. The bet was 10 minutes. Paul only took 5. He could have compounded the score and doubled up if he would have revealed what it was that he was thinking about.

Worst One-Pocket Players Ever

Howard Henken and **"Lefty Bob,"** both from Chicago. When "Lefty Bob" played Artie Bodendorfer, Artie would lay Bob 200 to 1 on the money plus the break, for $2 a game. Howard was an even worse player, because Bob robbed him when they played each other. Bob even thought he could give Howard a ball. When I played Bob, I gave him 16 to 1 on the money, plus the break. I could only run two balls and had to stop and play a safety. I would only play him if I was dead broke. Several times he won the first game and I had to put up 16 beads on the scoring string. I would have to win 16 in a row to keep him from discovering that I was playing without money. He never caught me.

Tommy "The Sailor" Kramer & Artie

Most Obnoxious Drunk

Tommy 'The Sailor" Kramer was so brutal and disgusting that a reprobate like **Detroit Whitey** called him "Tommy the Toilet."

Howard Henken
& Little Pup

Notables Include The Beard, Grady Matthews, Mike "Shoes" Gambony, Efren Reyes, & Mike LeBron
photo courtesy Bill Porter and Mike Haines

Dayton Tournament: Joe Kerr, Steve Cook, Joe Burns and Cecil "Buddy" Hall
photo courtesy Bill Porter and Mike Haines

Cole Dickson, Gunfighter Deluxe

Buddy "The Rifleman" Hall
photo courtesy Bill Porter and Mike Haines

That's Me After Being Inducted Into The Bank Pool Legends Hall Of Fame

Cross-Side Pass-Over Reference Angles

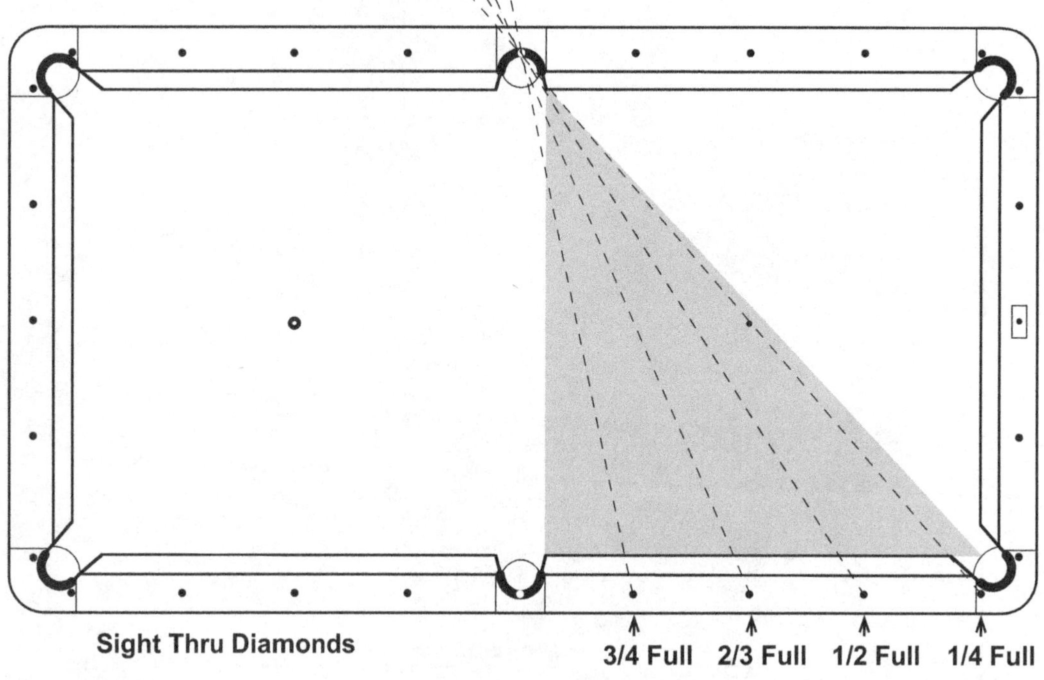

When the Cue Ball and Object Ball lie on, or are parallel to, a reference angle; this is the amount of cut to use on the object ball with firm speed.

3/4 Passover Track

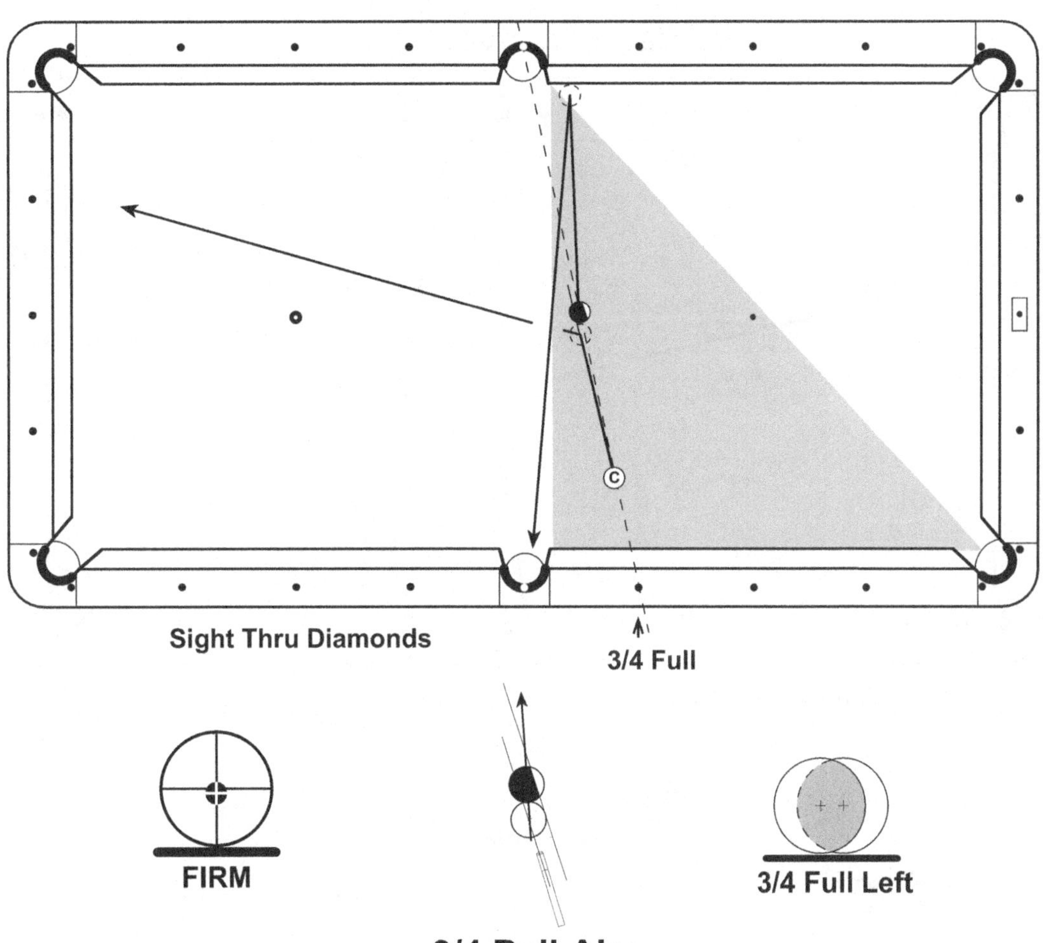

3/4 Ball Aim

2/3 Ball Passover Track

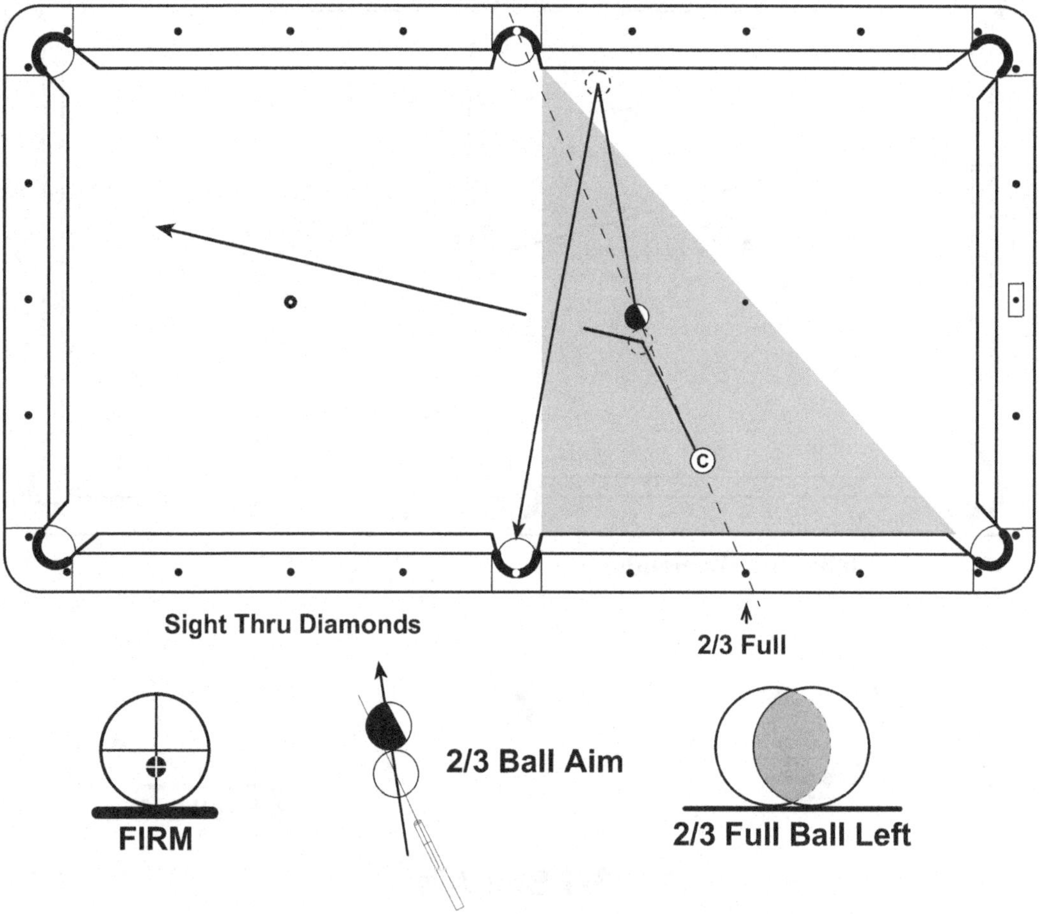

Sight Thru Diamonds

2/3 Full

FIRM

2/3 Ball Aim

2/3 Full Ball Left

1/2 Passover Track

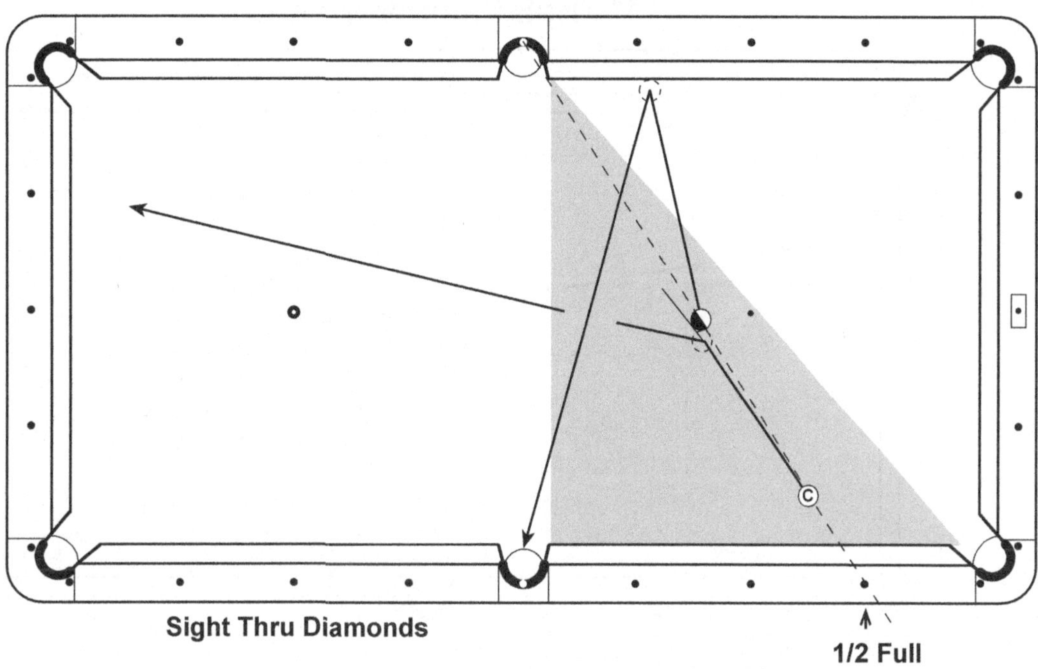

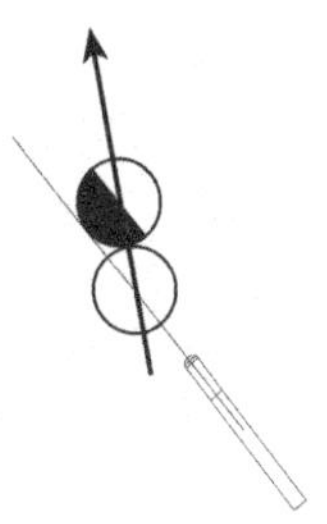

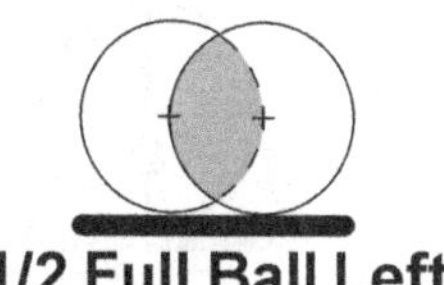

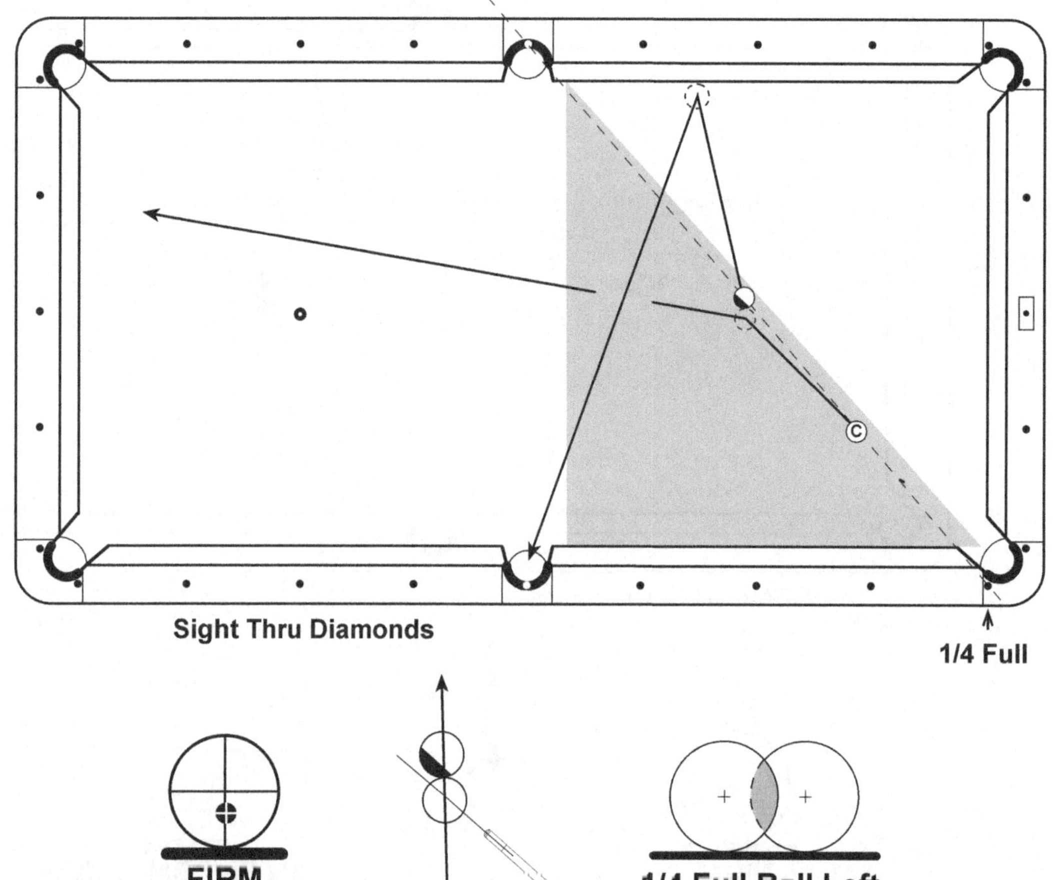
1/4 Ball Passover Track
C
Sight Thru Diamonds
1/4 Full
FIRM
1/4 Full Ball Left

Parallel Tracks

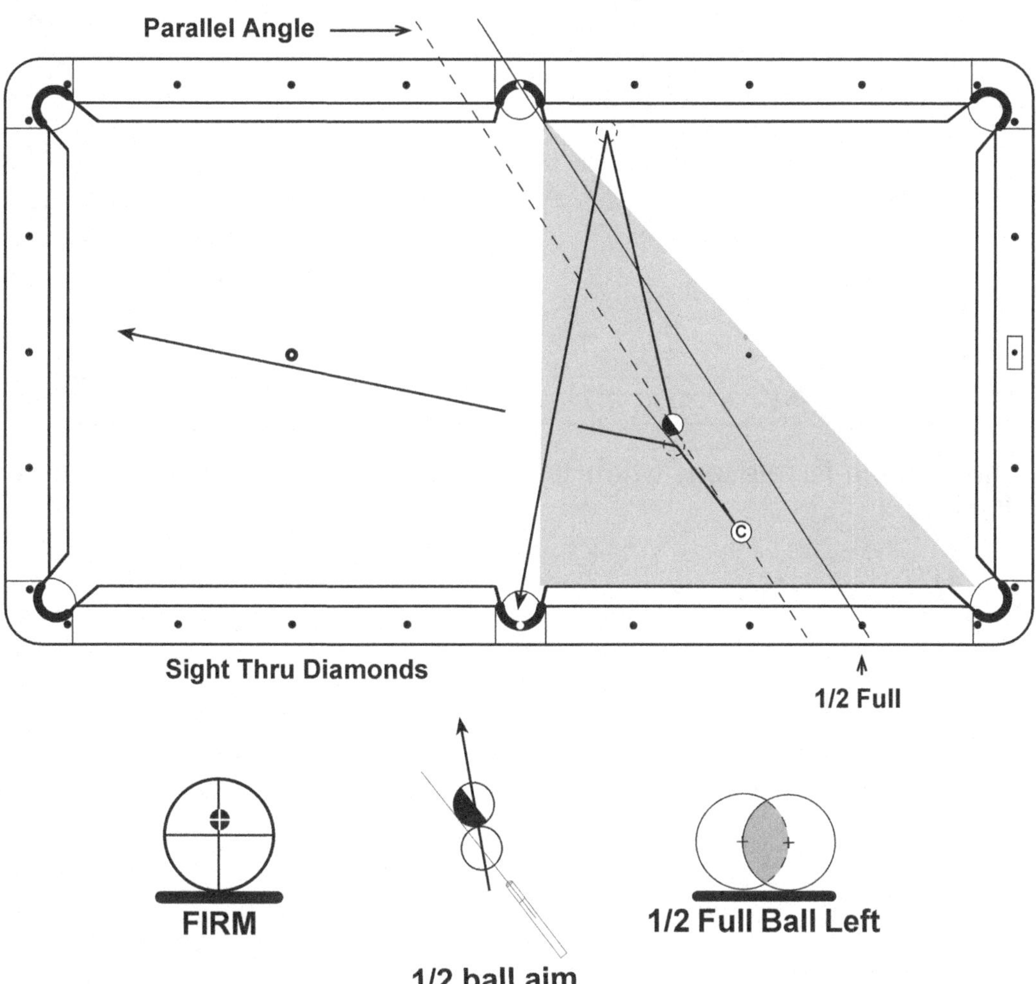

When the cue ball and object ball lie on, or are parallel to, a reference angle; this is the amount of cut to use on the object ball with firm speed.

This system is relevant when the shot occurs in the darkened area of the table.

Pass-over Reference Angles Off The Short Rail

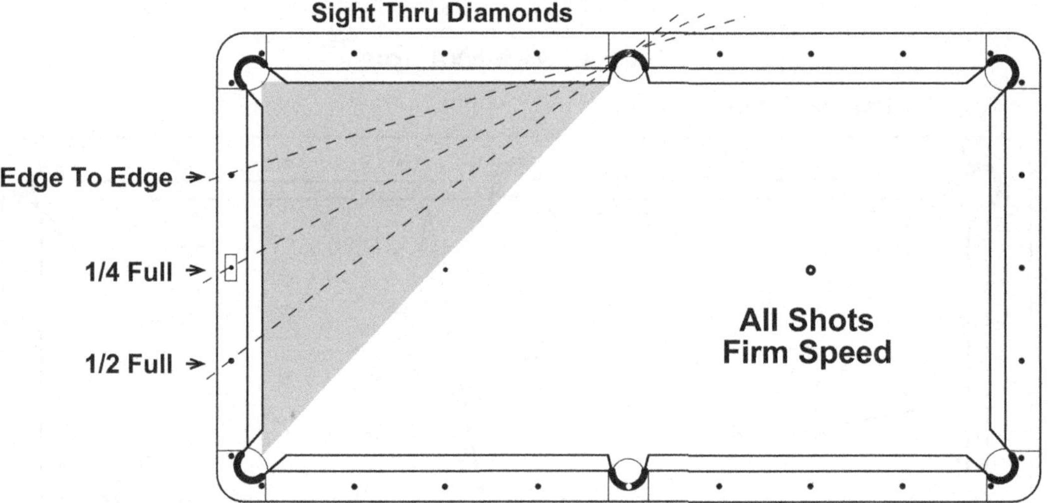

This system is relevant when the shot occurs in the darkened area of the table.

Pass-over Reference Angles Off The Short Rail

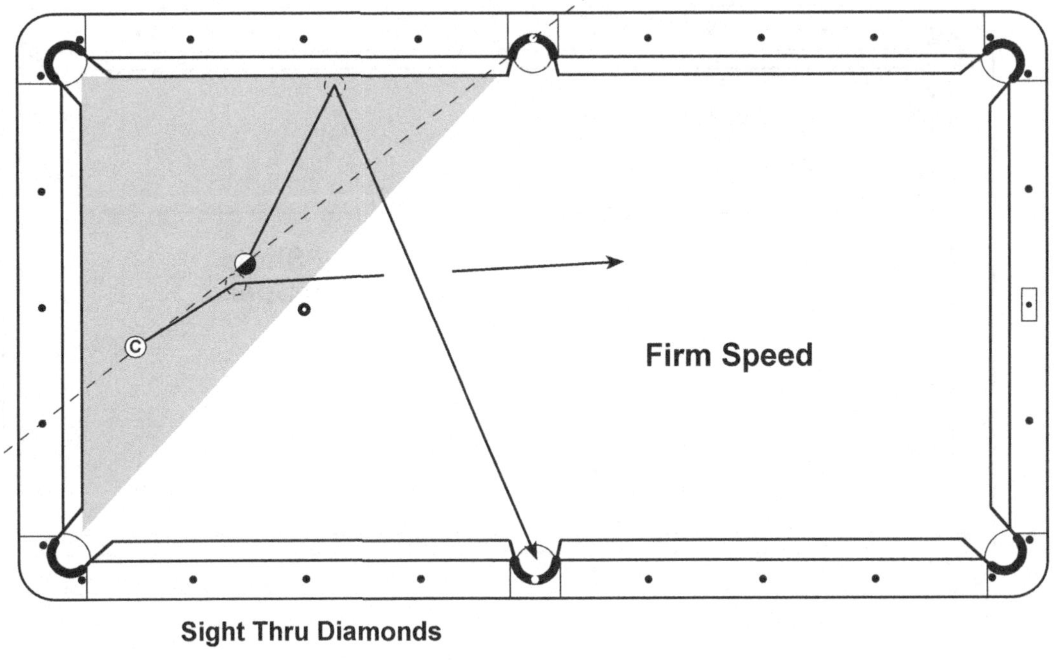

This system is relevant when the bank occurs in the darkened area of the table.

Pass-over Reference Angles Off The Short Rail

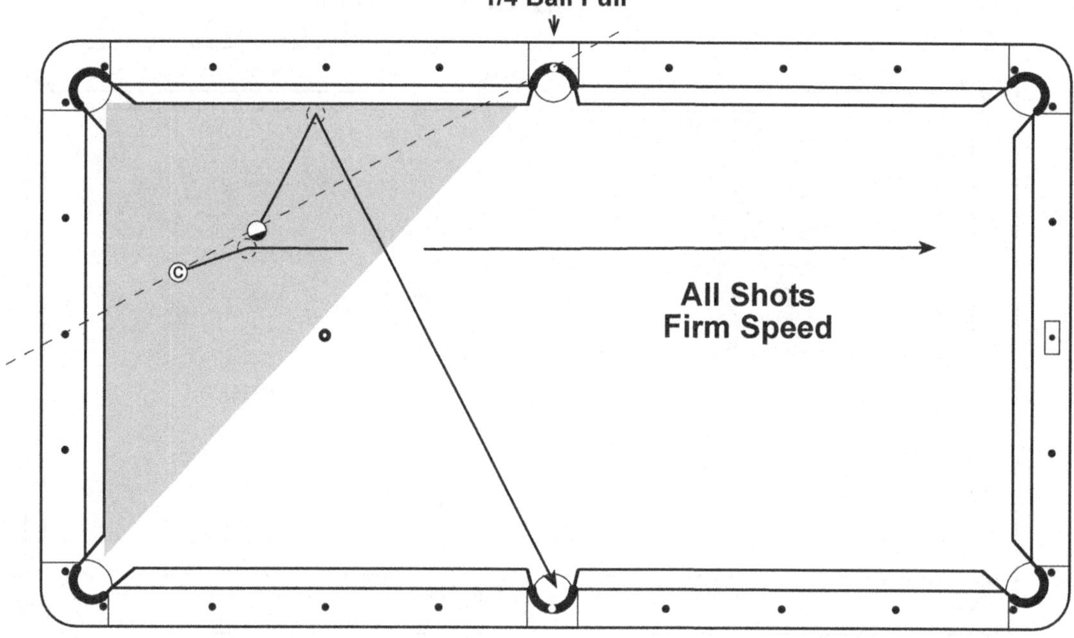

Thinnest Cut — Edge to Edge Aim

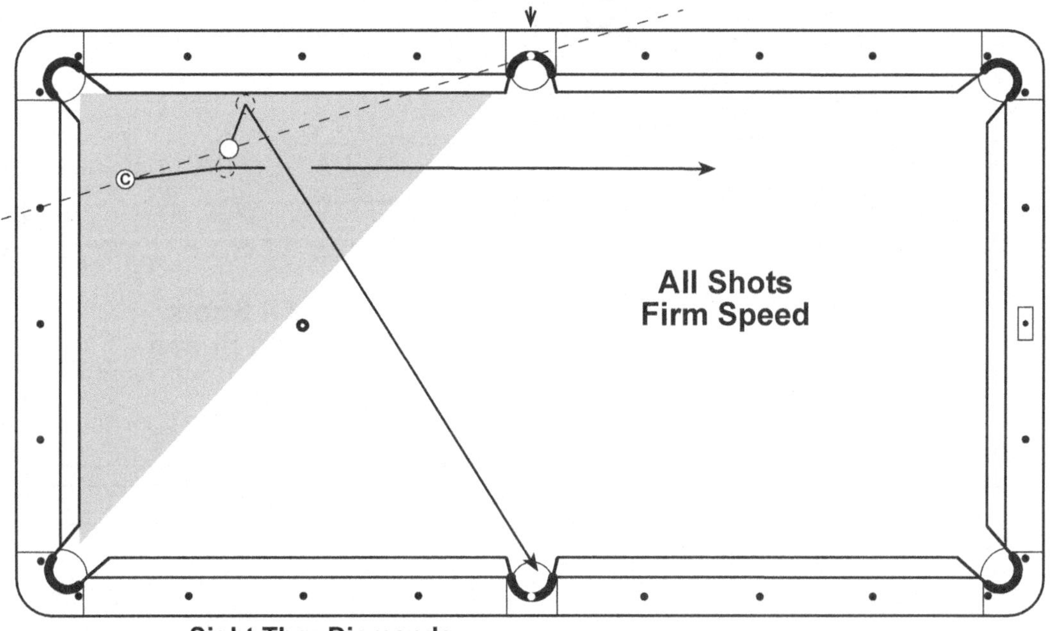

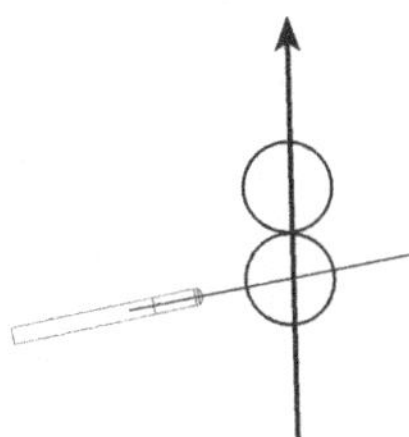

Edge To Edge

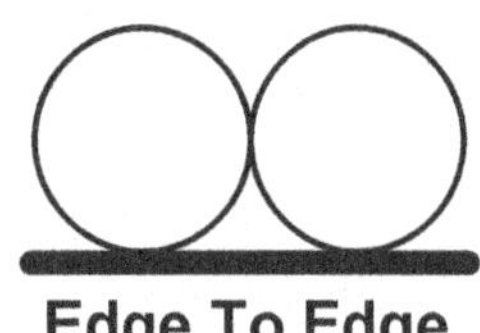

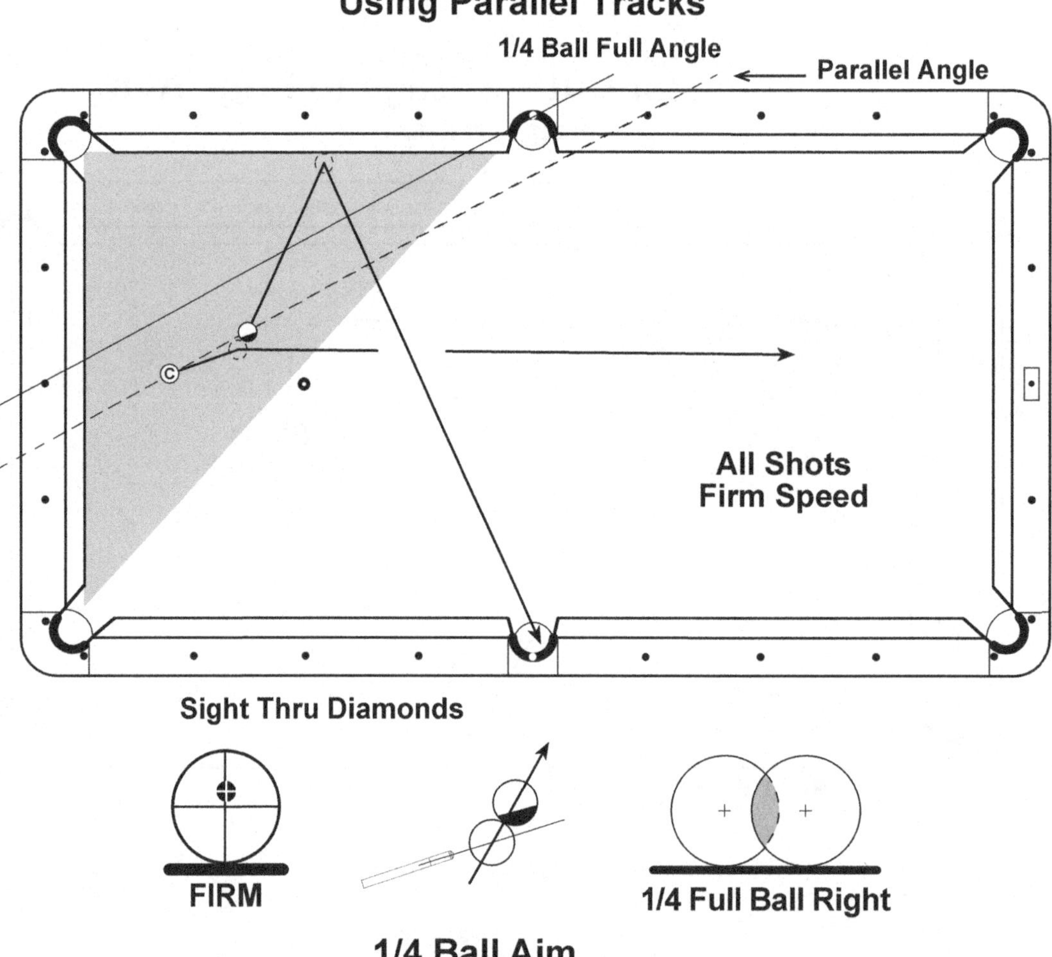

This system is relevant when the shot occurs in the darkened area of the table.

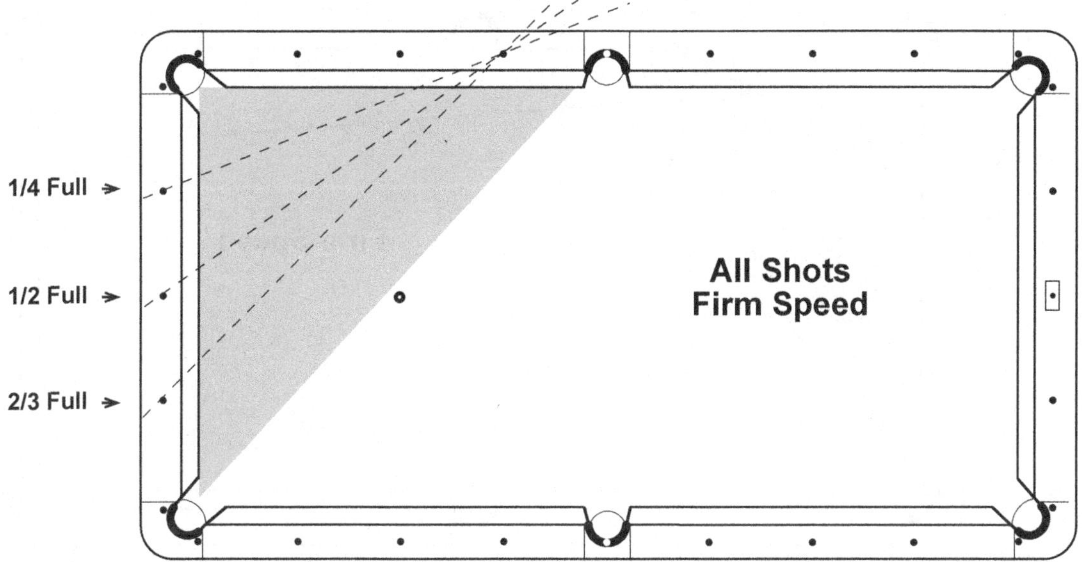
Pass-over Reference Angles Off The Short Rail
Short Rail Angles Thru Diamond 3
1/4 Full
1/2 Full
2/3 Full
All Shots
Firm Speed

Short Rail Reference Angles Thru Diamond 3

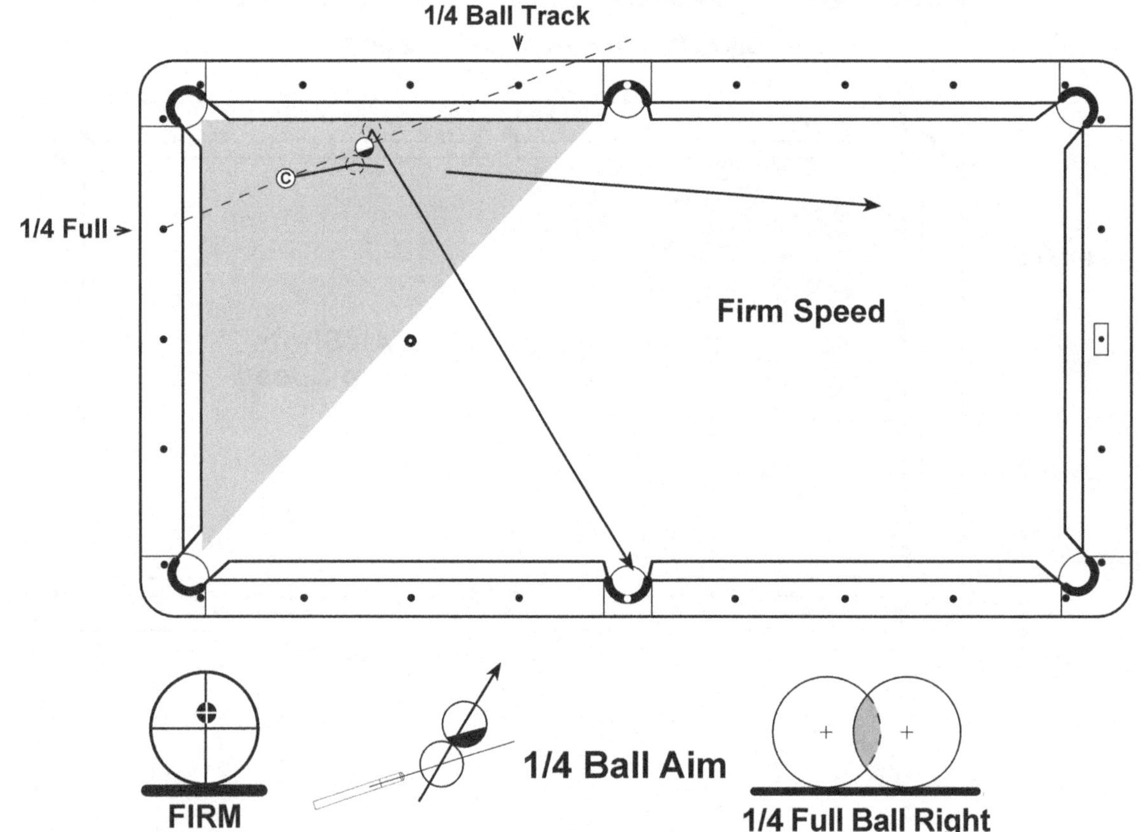

Short Rail Reference Angles Thru Diamond 3

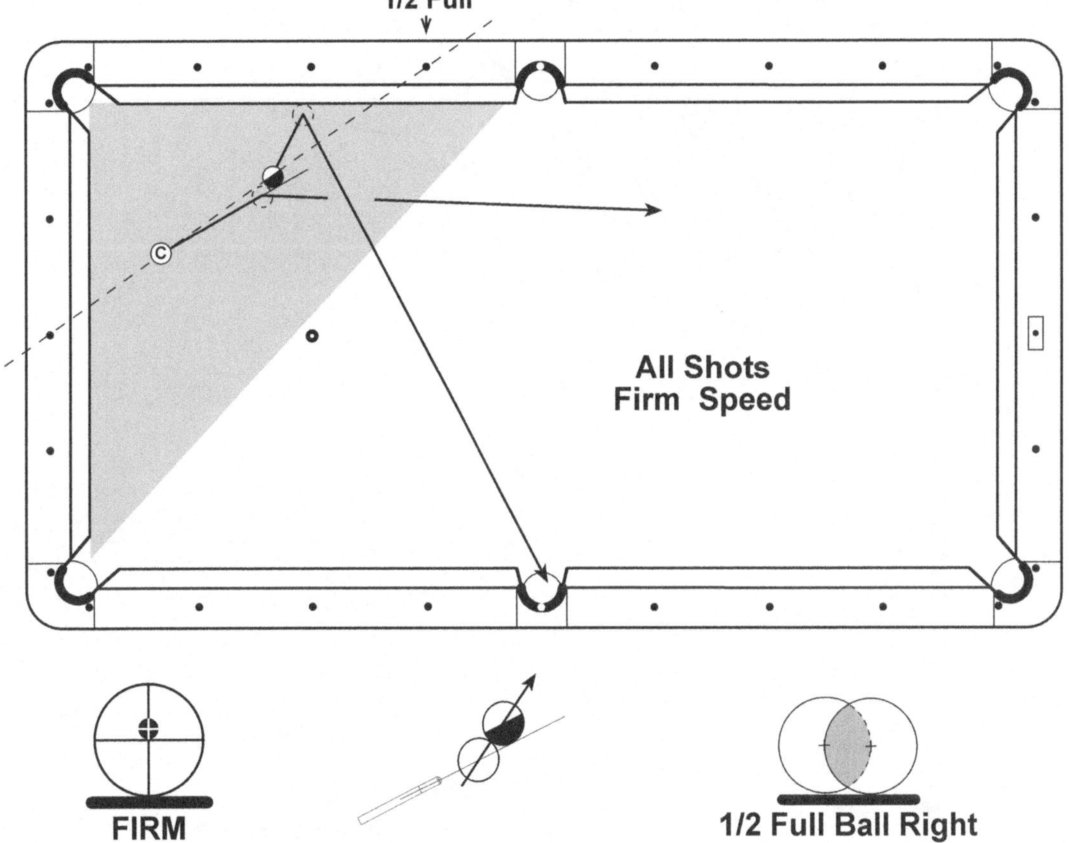

1/2 Ball Aim

Short Rail Reference Angles Thru Diamond 3

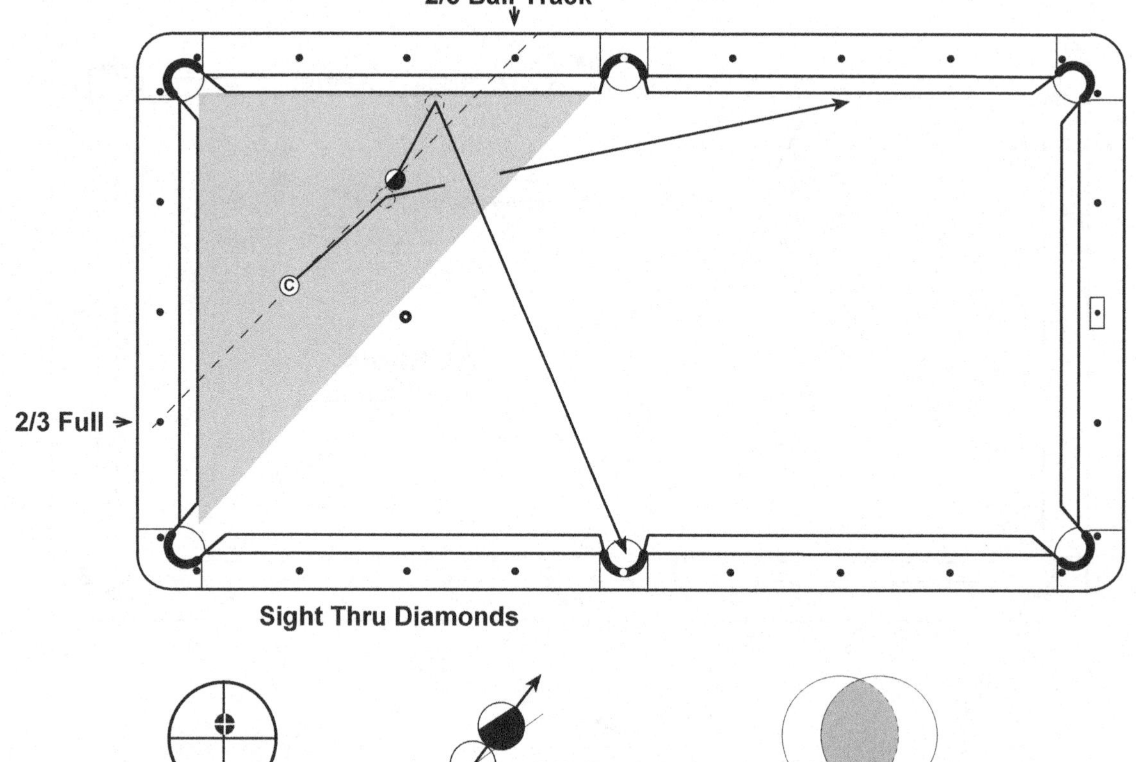

Parallel Tracks

2/3 Ball Track Example

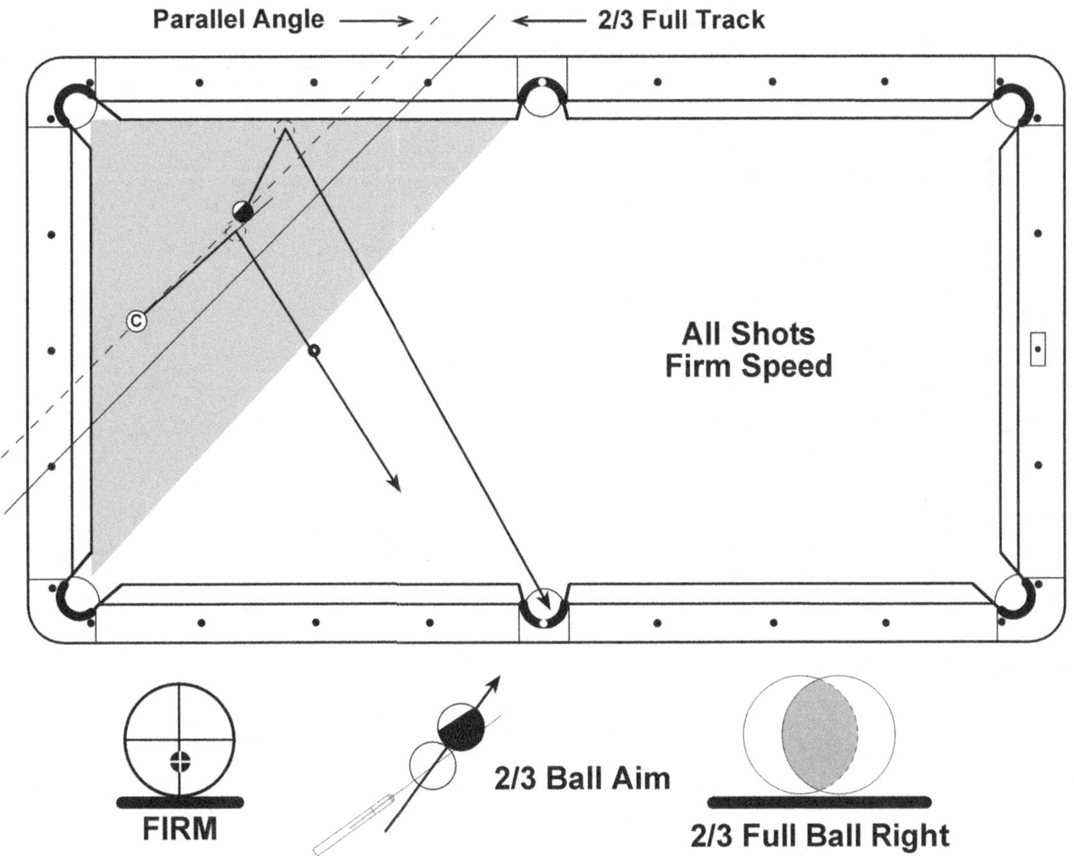

Cross-Side Pass-Over Reference Angles

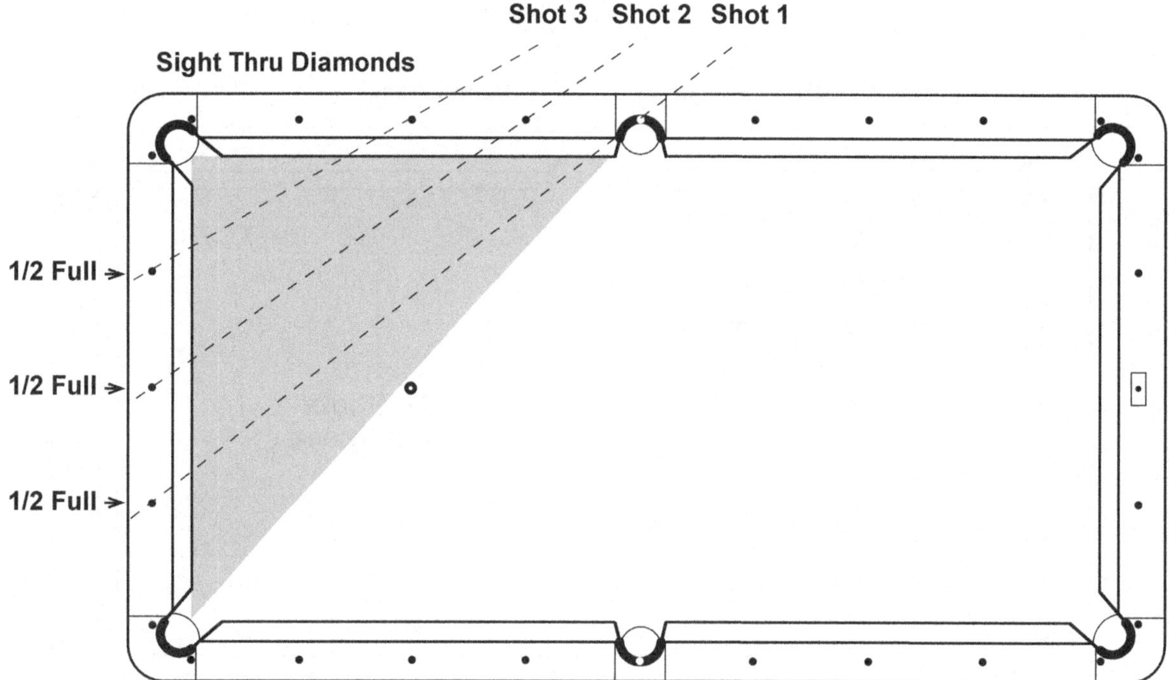

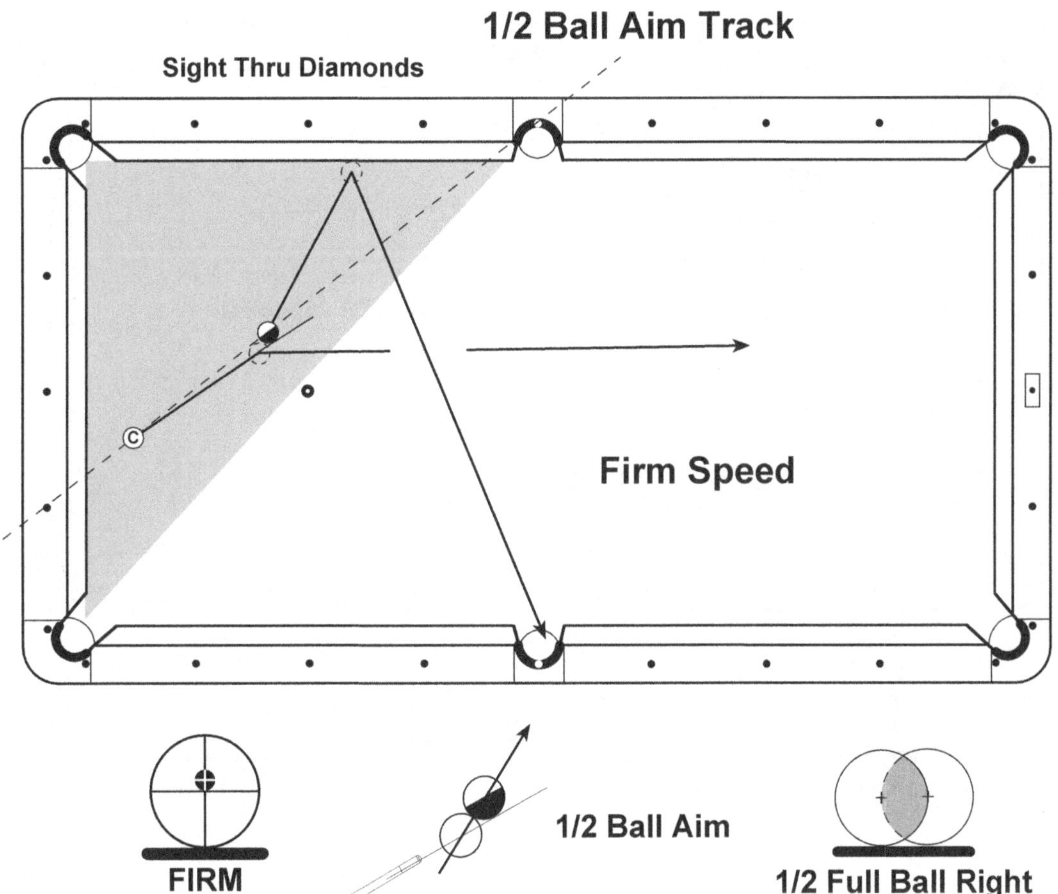
1/2 Ball Aim Track
Sight Thru Diamonds
Firm Speed
FIRM
1/2 Ball Aim
1/2 Full Ball Right

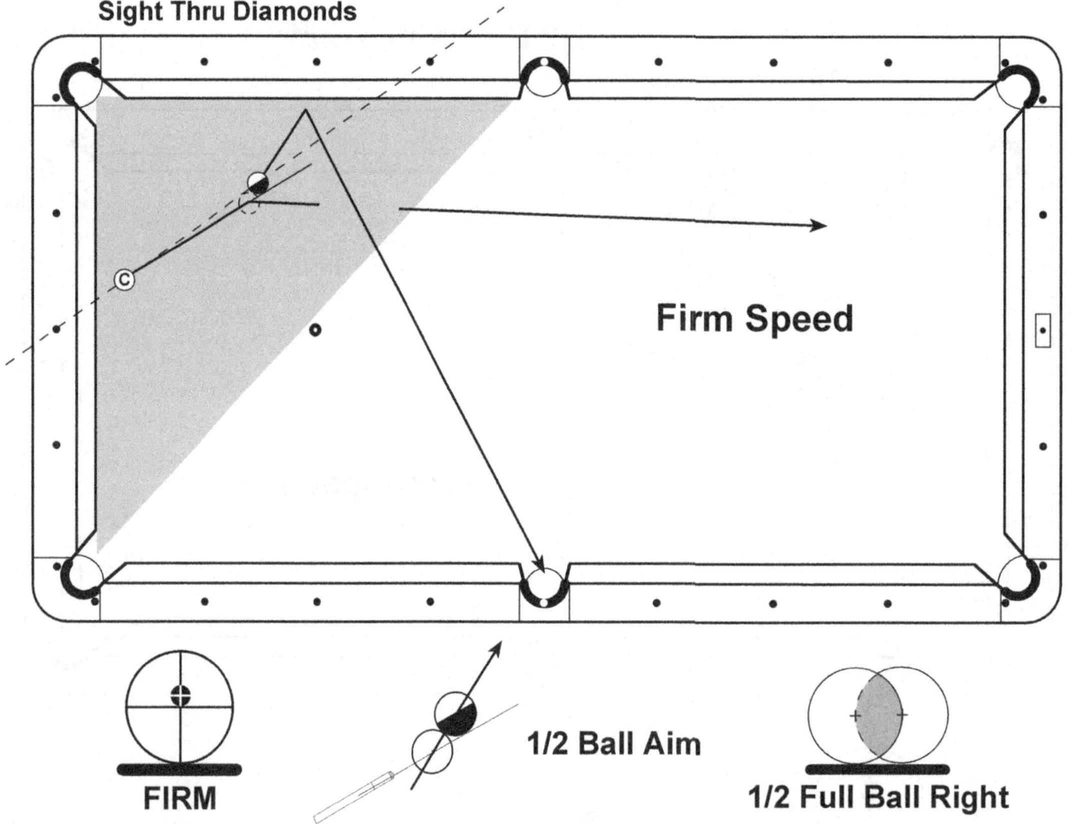
Sight Thru Diamonds
Firm Speed
FIRM
1/2 Ball Aim
1/2 Full Ball Right

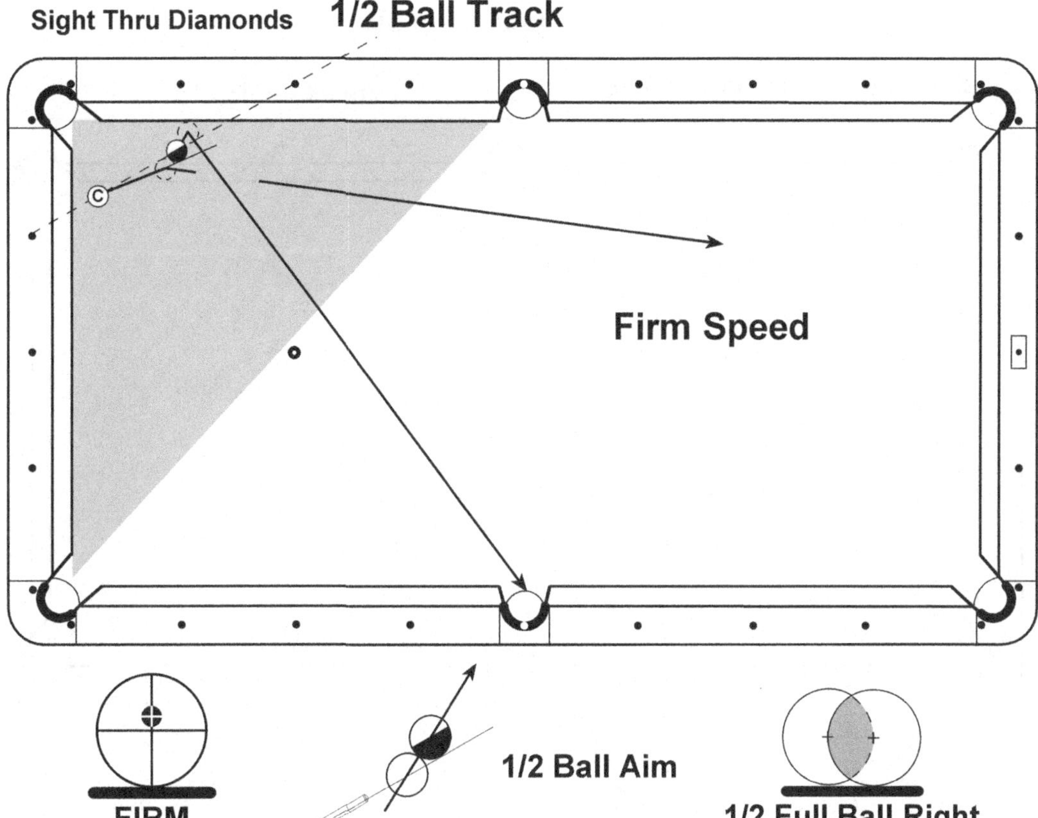
Sight Thru Diamonds
1/2 Ball Track
Firm Speed
FIRM
1/2 Ball Aim
1/2 Full Ball Right

Parallel Tracks

1/2 Ball Track Example

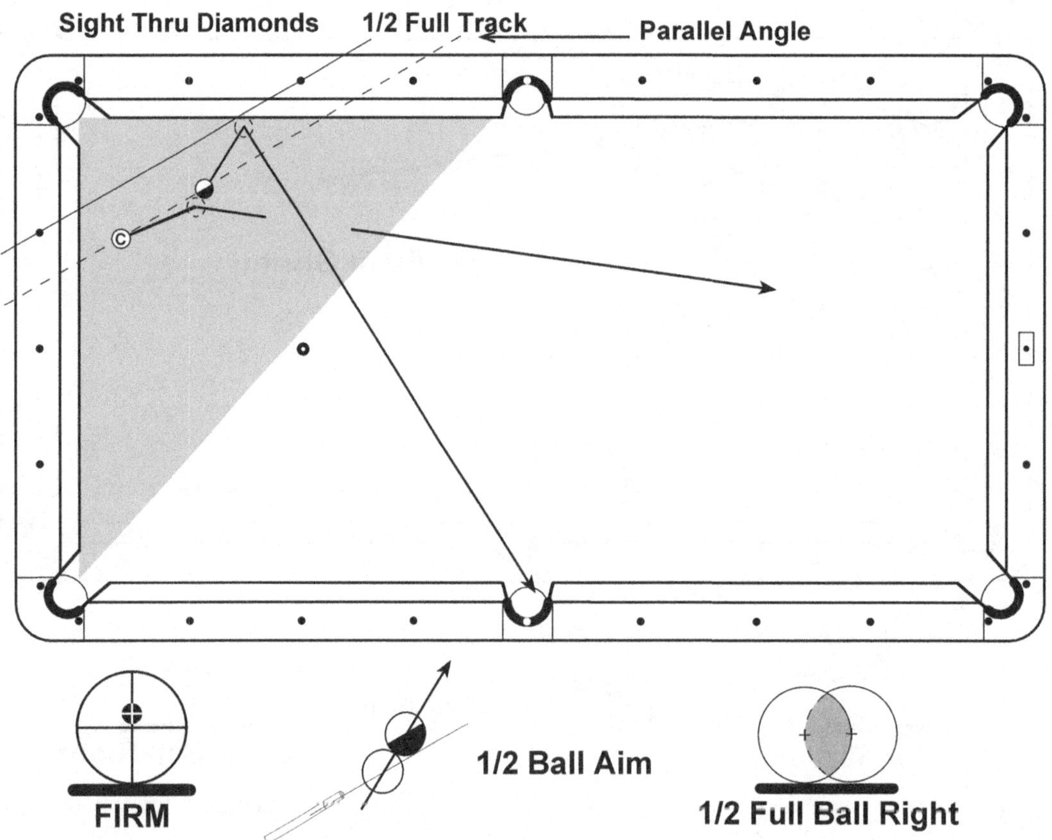

Cross-Corner Pass-Over Reference Angles

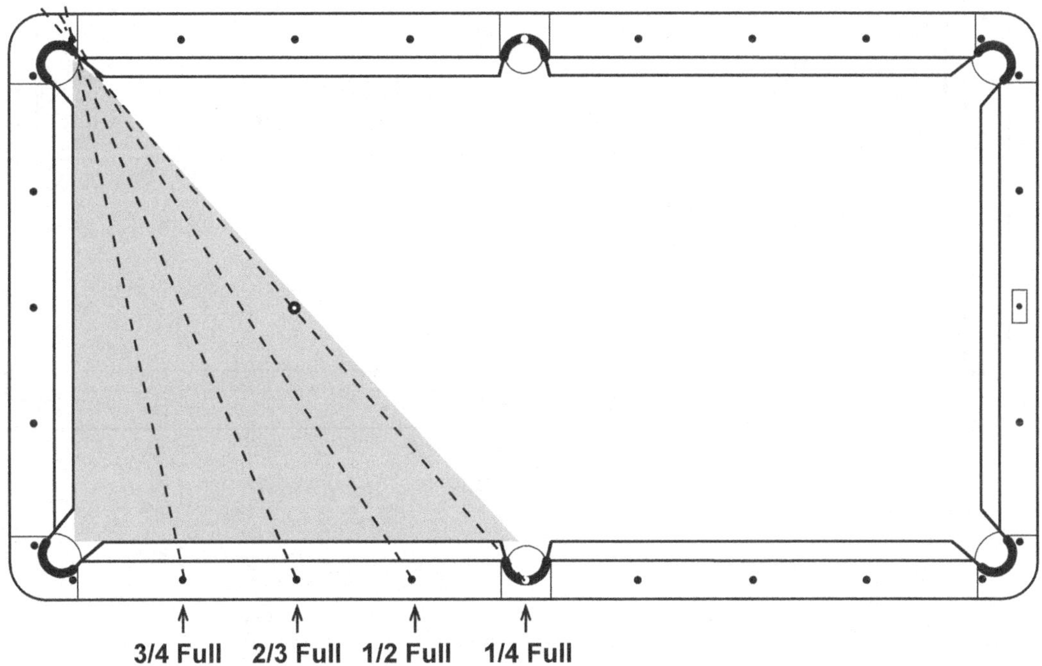

When the Cue Ball and Object Ball lie on, or are parallel to, a reference angle, this is the amount of cut to use on the Object Ball with firm speed.

Cross-corner reference systems operate the same as the cross-side systems, except you must make allowances for possible kisses.

Cross-Corner Pass-Over Angles

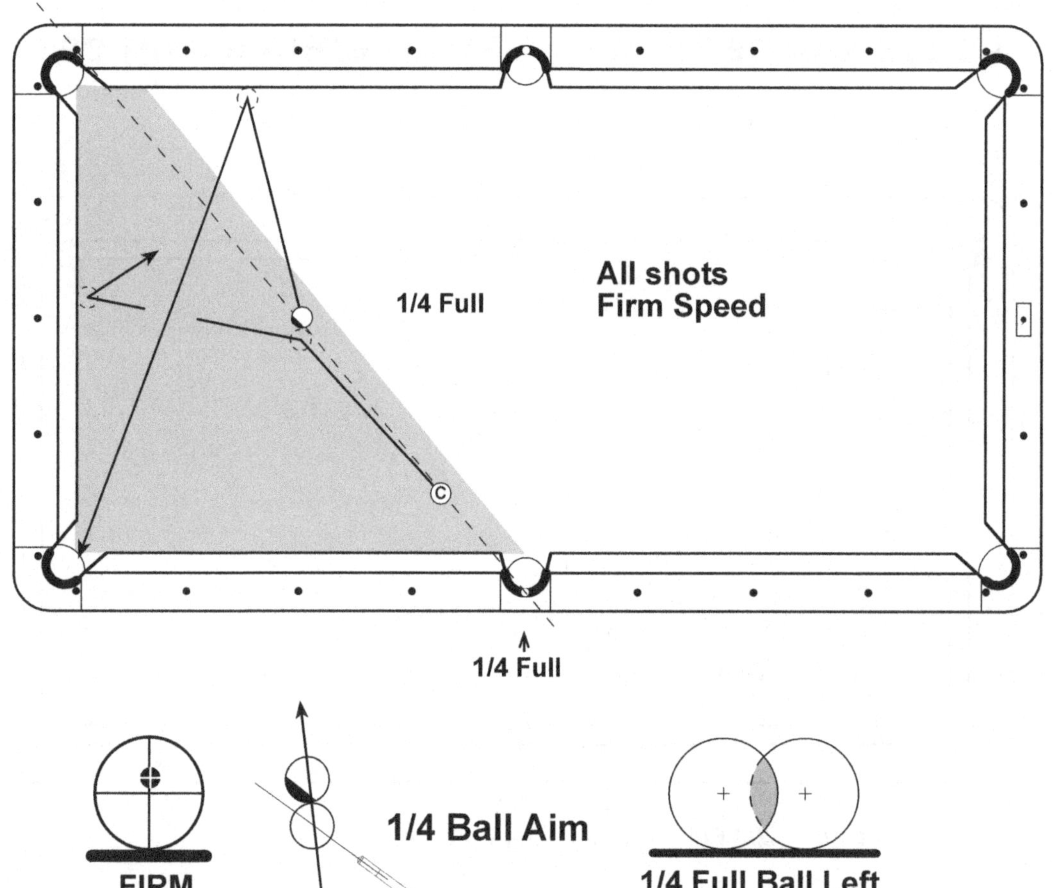

Cross-Corner Pass-Over Angles

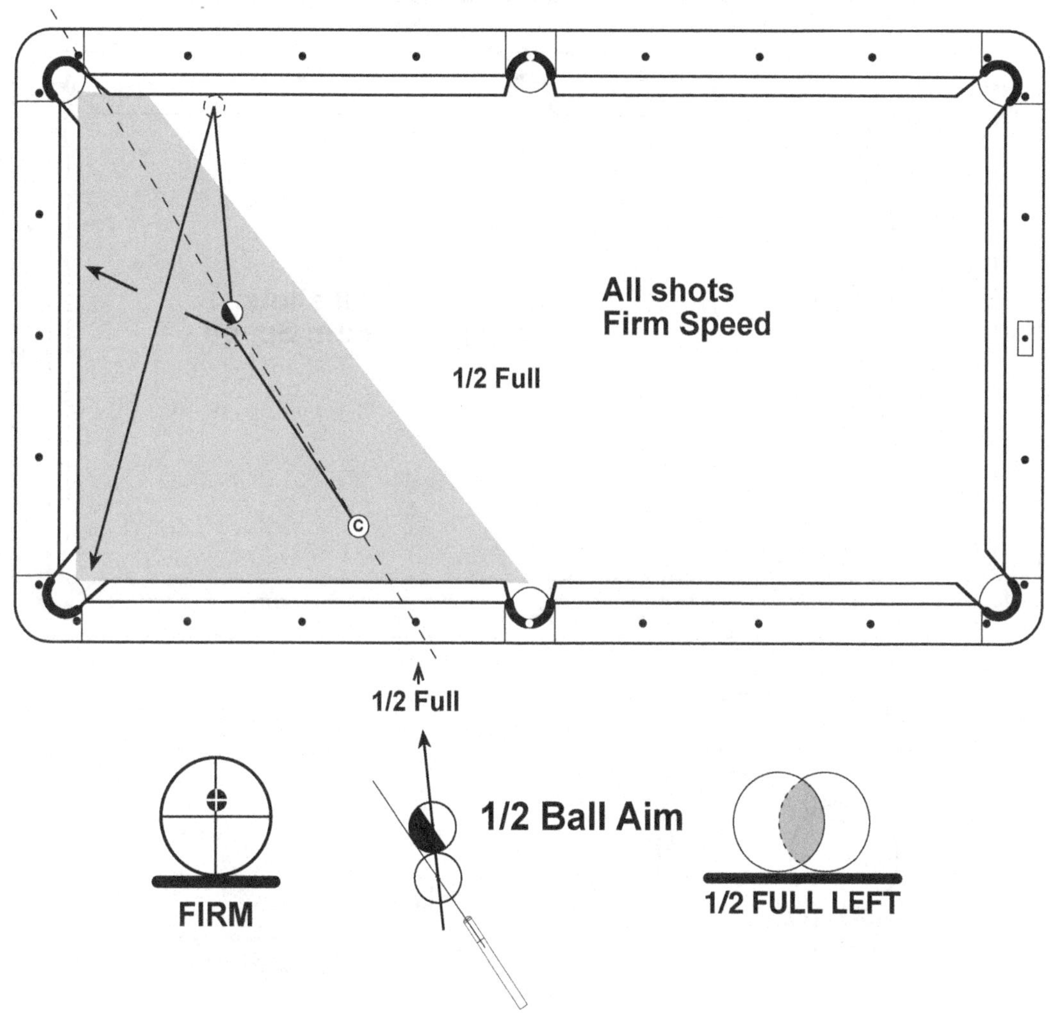

Cross-Corner Pass-Over Angles

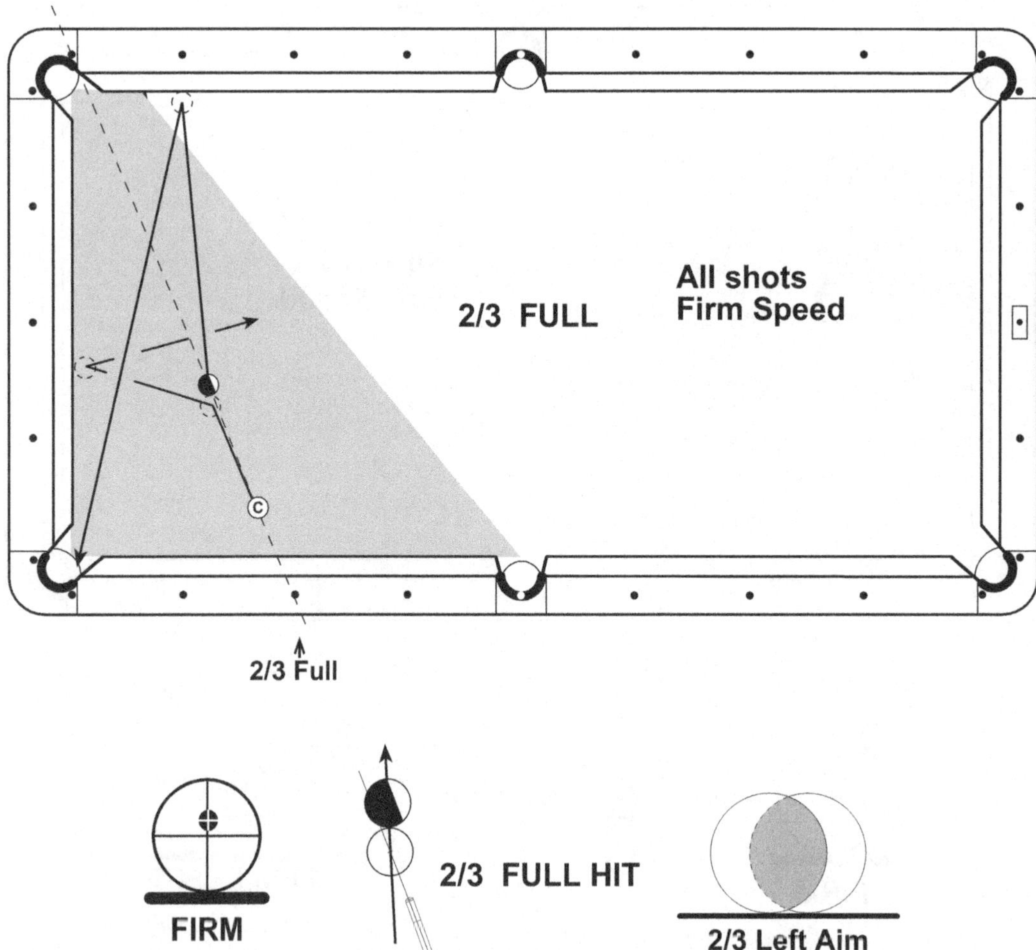

Cross-corner reference systems operate the same as the cross-side systems, except you must make allowances for possible kisses.

Cross-Corner Pass-Over Angles

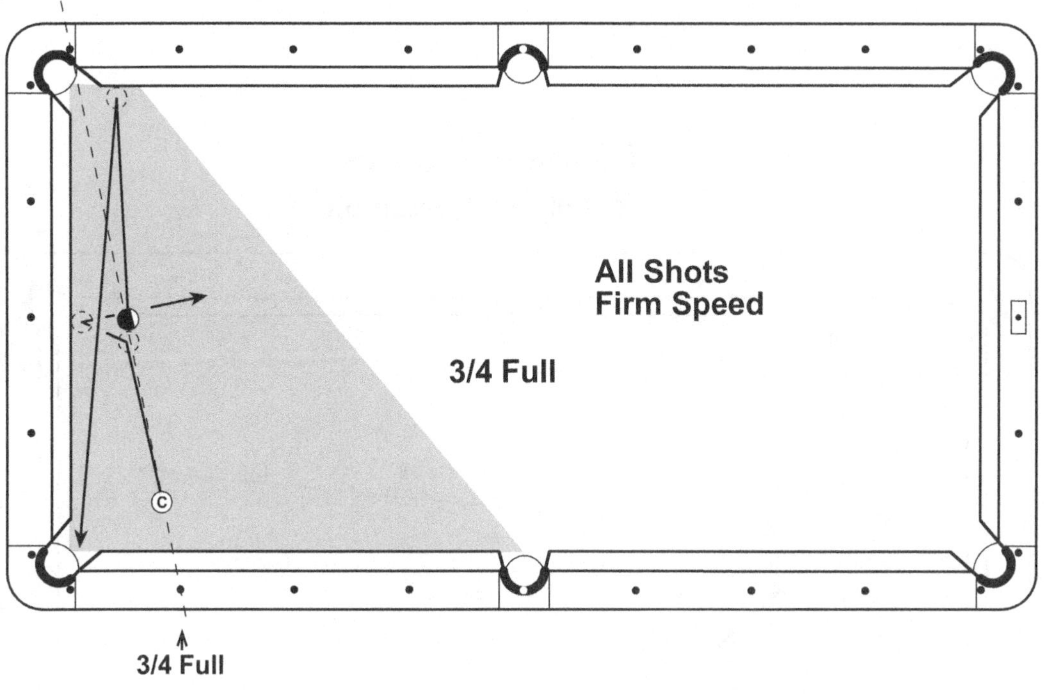

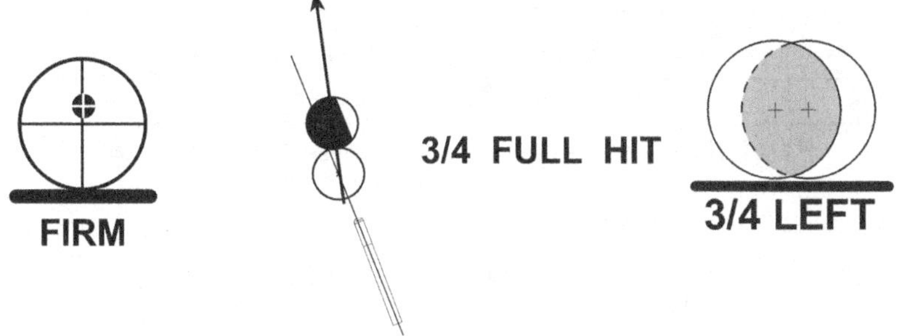

Parallel Tracks

1/4 Ball Track Example

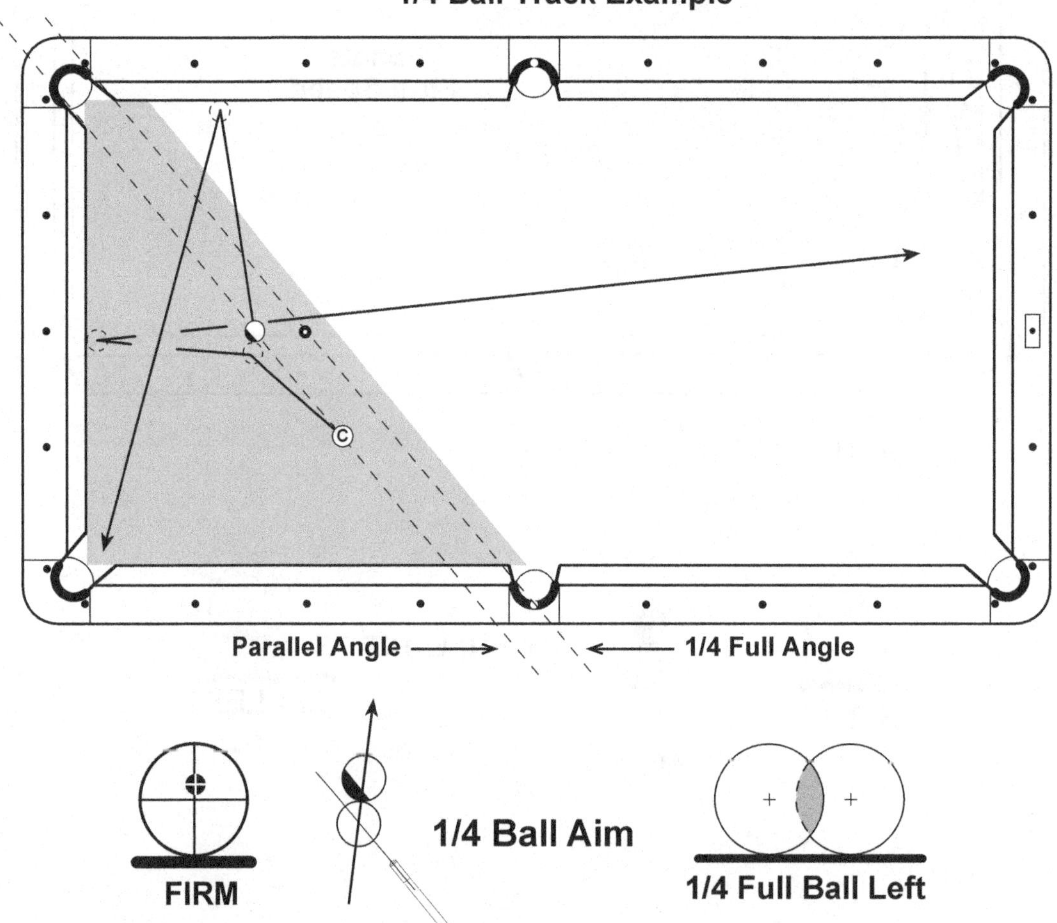

Cross-corner reference systems operate the same as the cross-side systems, except you must make allowances for possible kisses.

Reference Points Between The Side Pockets

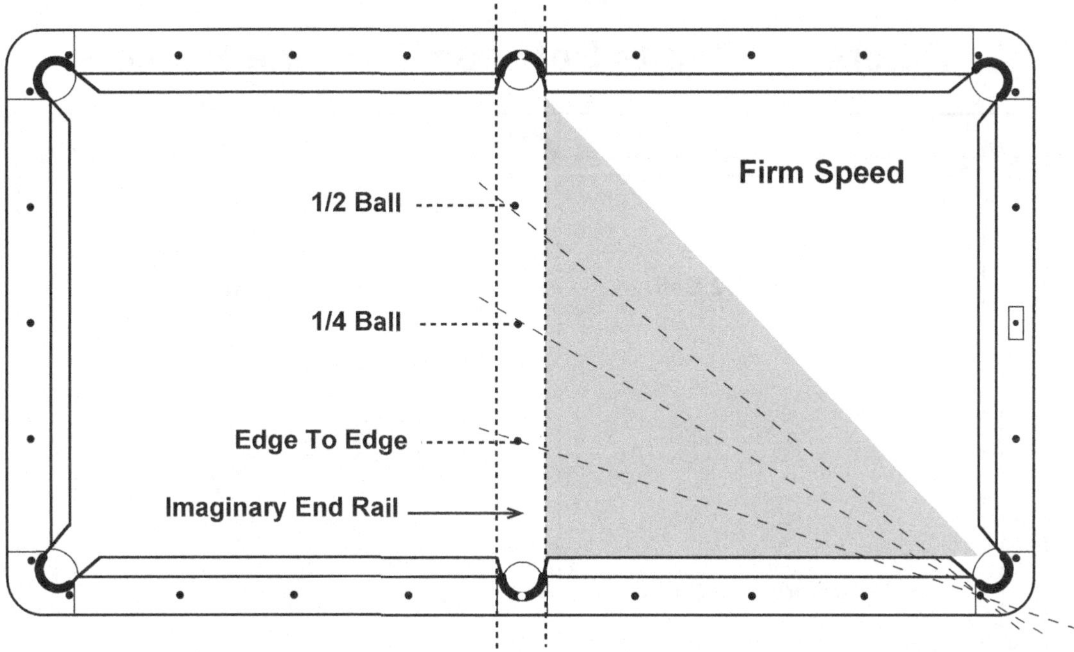

This system is relevant when the shot occurs in the darkened area of the table.

Reference Points Between The Side Pockets

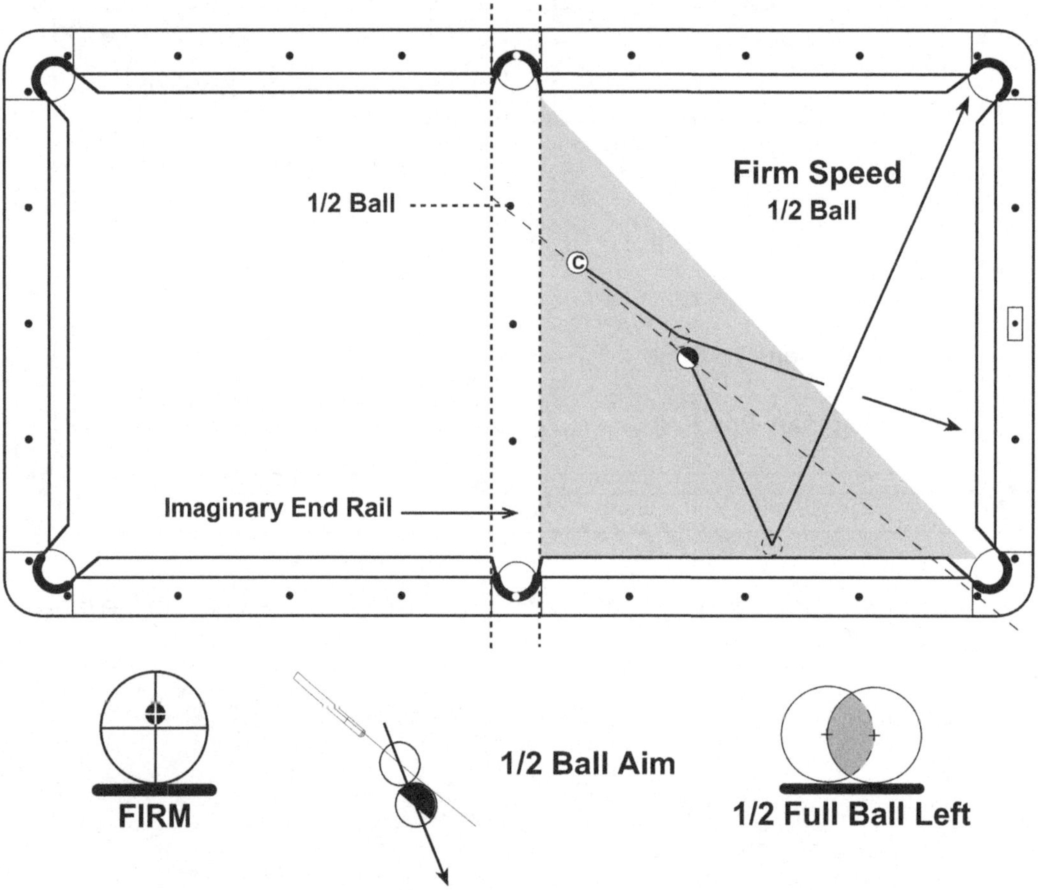

1/2 Ball

Firm Speed
1/2 Ball

Imaginary End Rail

FIRM

1/2 Ball Aim

1/2 Full Ball Left

Reference Points Between The Side Pockets

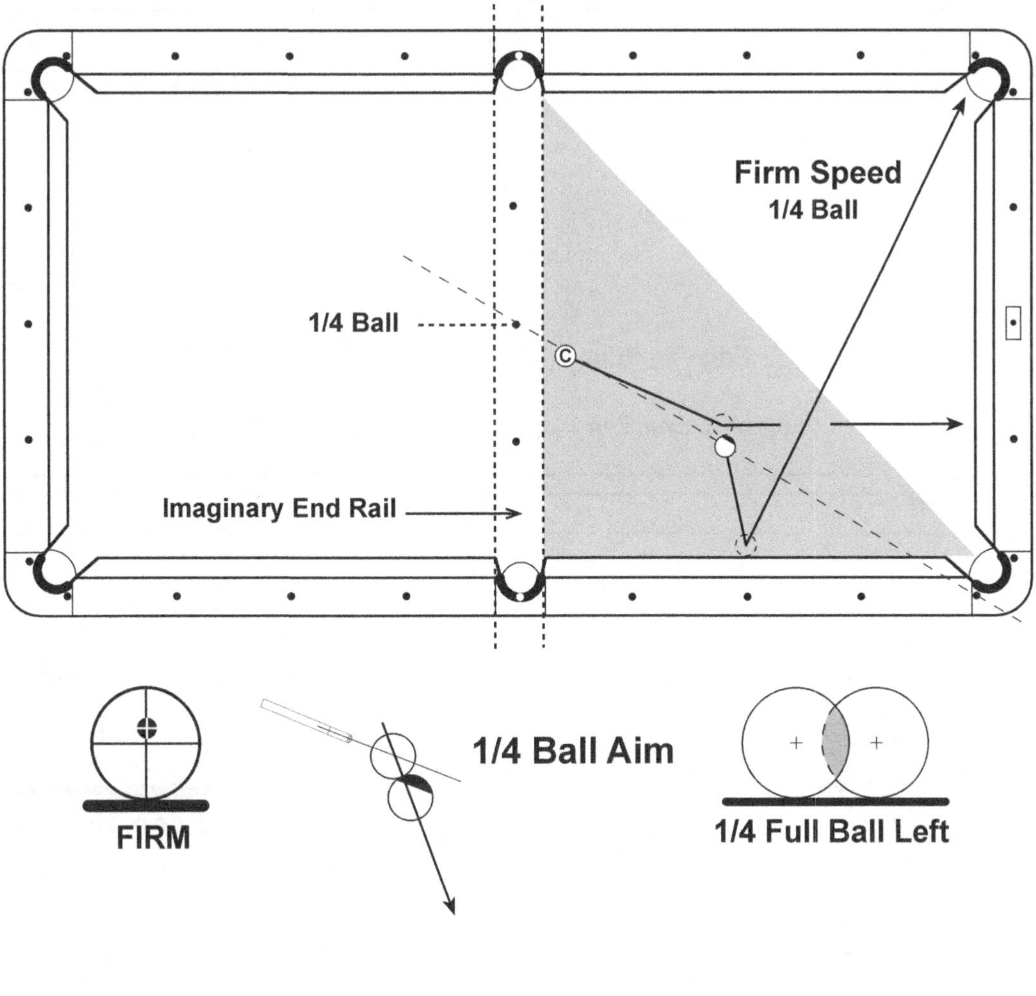

Firm Speed
1/4 Ball

1/4 Ball

Imaginary End Rail

FIRM

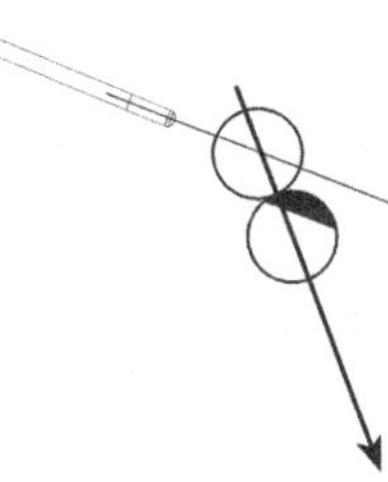

1/4 Ball Aim

1/4 Full Ball Left

Reference Points Between The Side Pockets

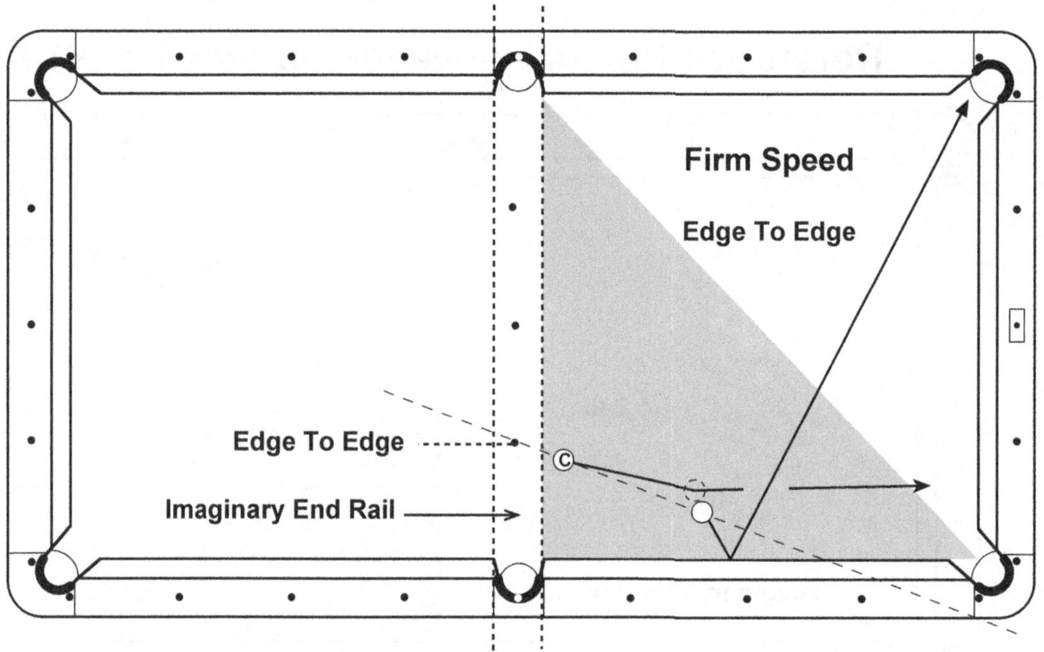

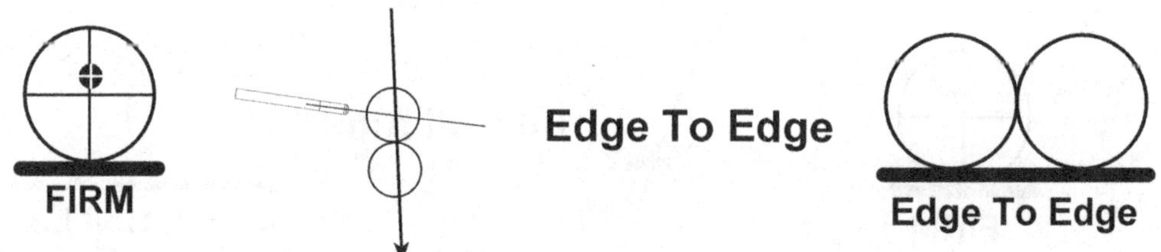

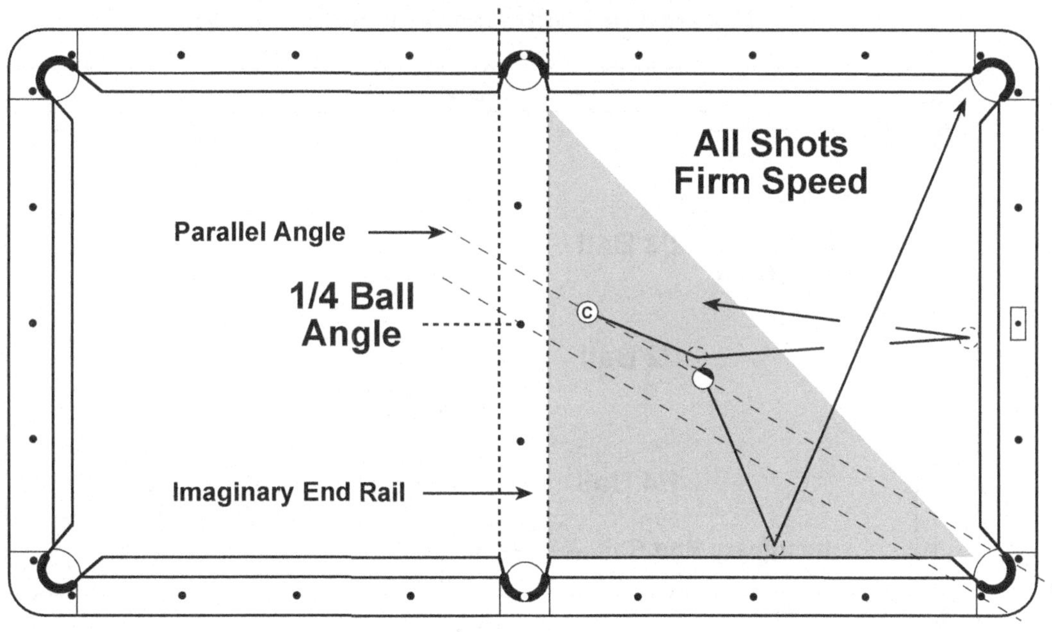
Parallel Tracks
1/4 Ball Track Example
Reference Point Between Side Pockets
All Shots
Firm Speed
Parallel Angle
1/4 Ball
Angle
Imaginary End Rail

FIRM

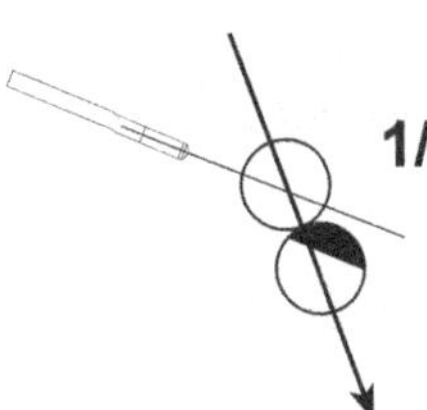
1/4 Ball Aim

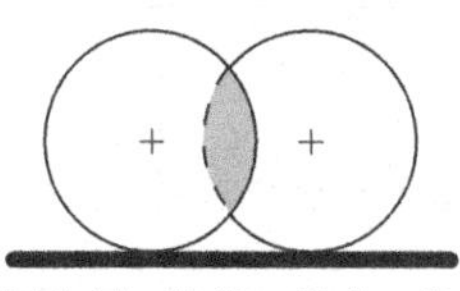
1/4 Full Ball Left

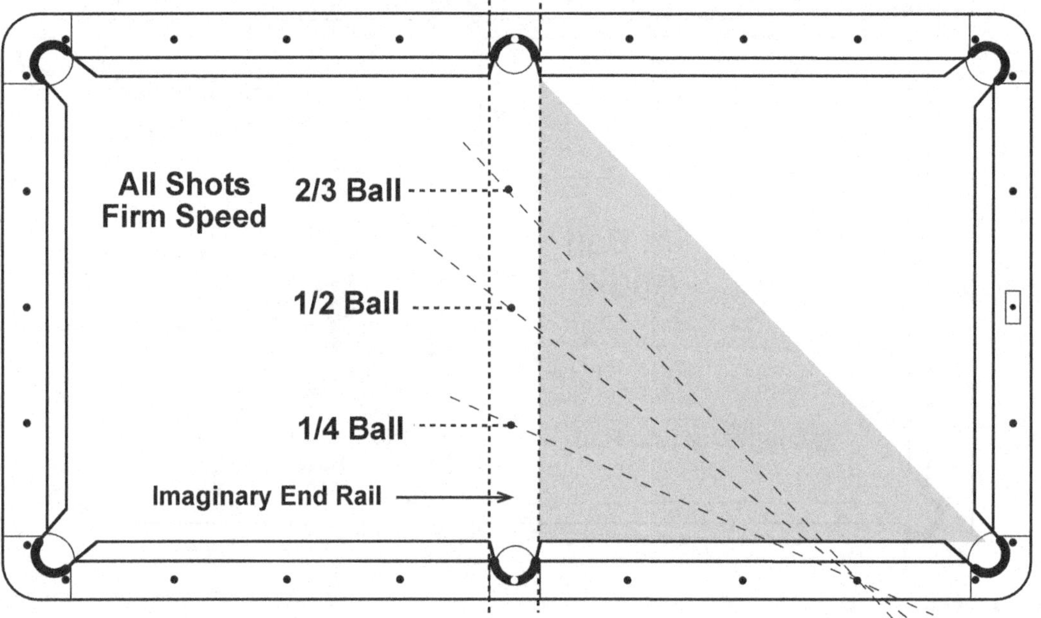

This system is relevant when the shot occurs in the darkened area of the table.

Cross-Corner Pass-Over Reference Angles

Reference Point Between Side Pockets

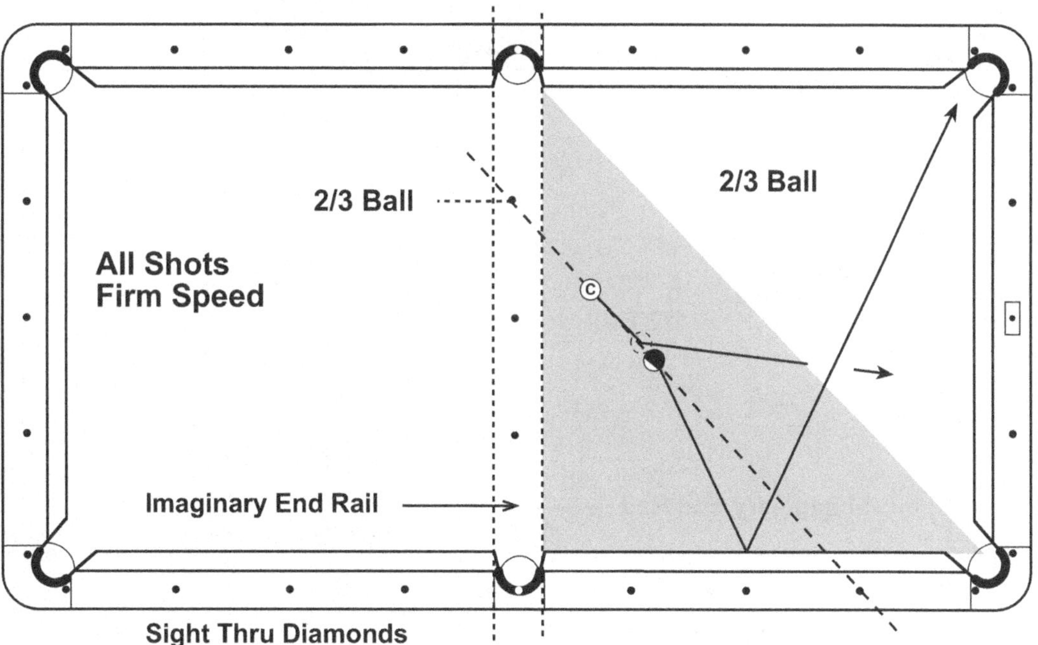

Cross-Corner Pass-Over Reference Angles

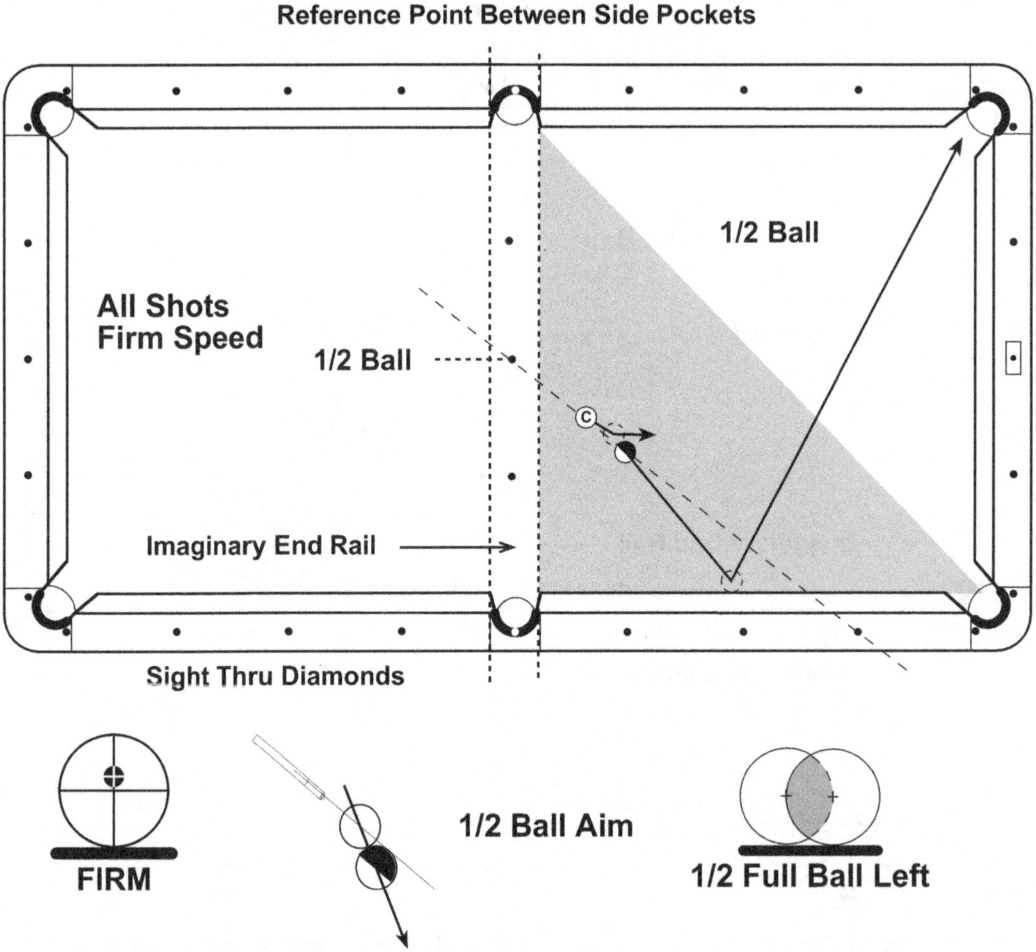

Reference Point Between Side Pockets

FIRM

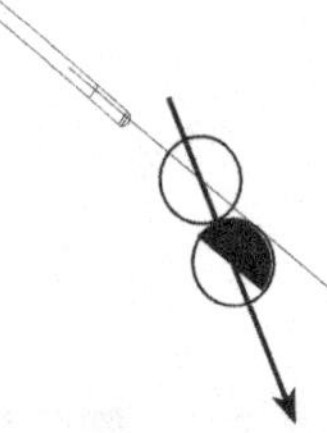

1/2 Ball Aim

1/2 Full Ball Left

Cross-Corner Pass-Over Reference Angles

Reference Point Between Side Pockets

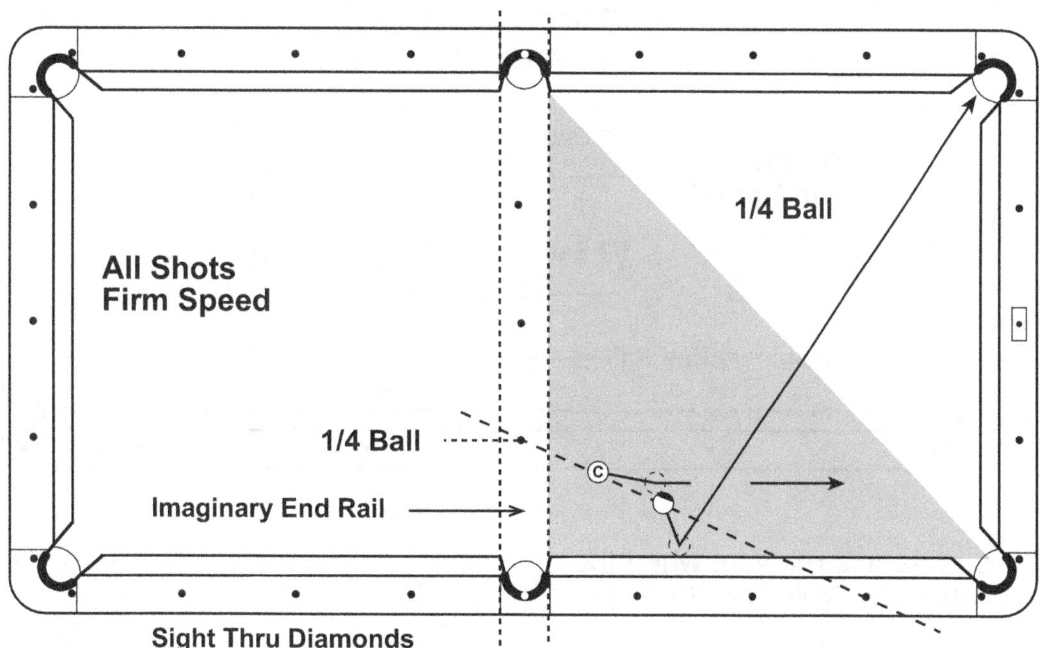

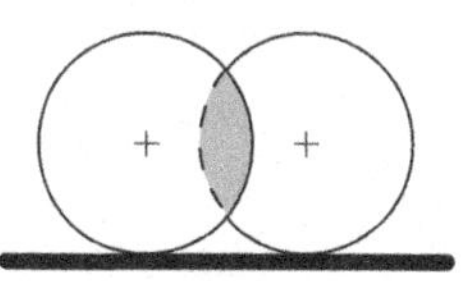

Cross-Corner Pass-Over Reference Angles

Reference point betweeen the side pockets

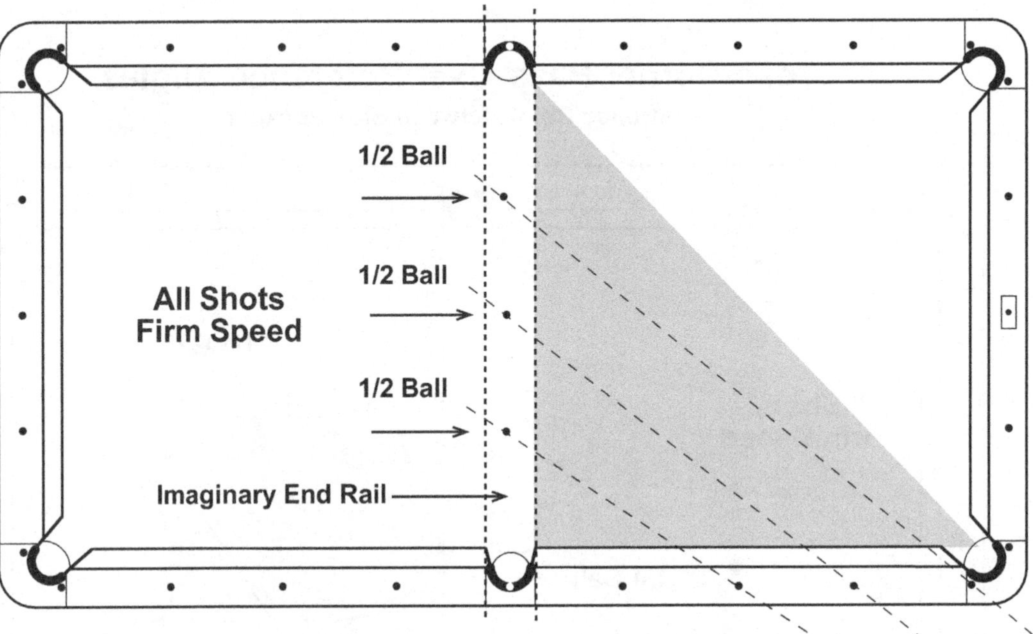

This system is relevant when the shot occurs in the darkened area of the table. Beware of possible kisses on Cross-Corner Banks.

Cross-Corner Pass-Over Reference Angles

Reference point betweeen the side pockets

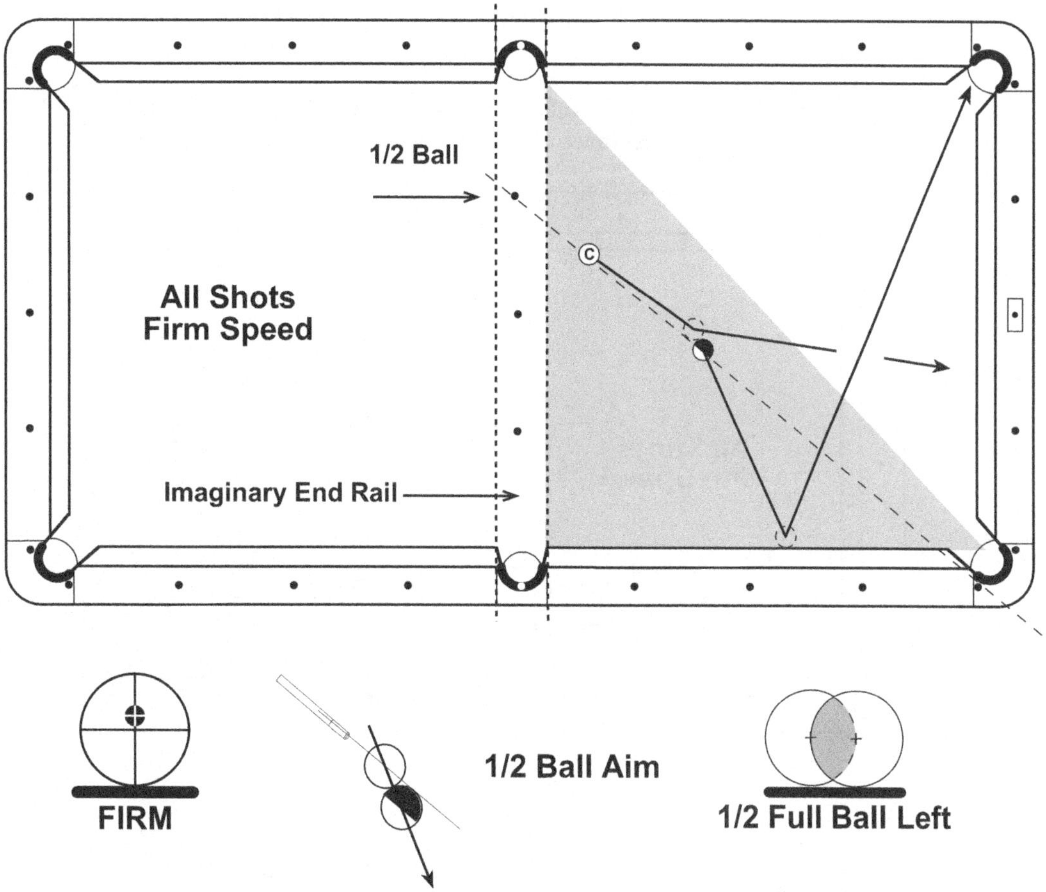

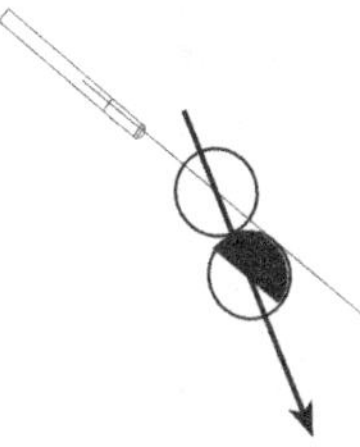

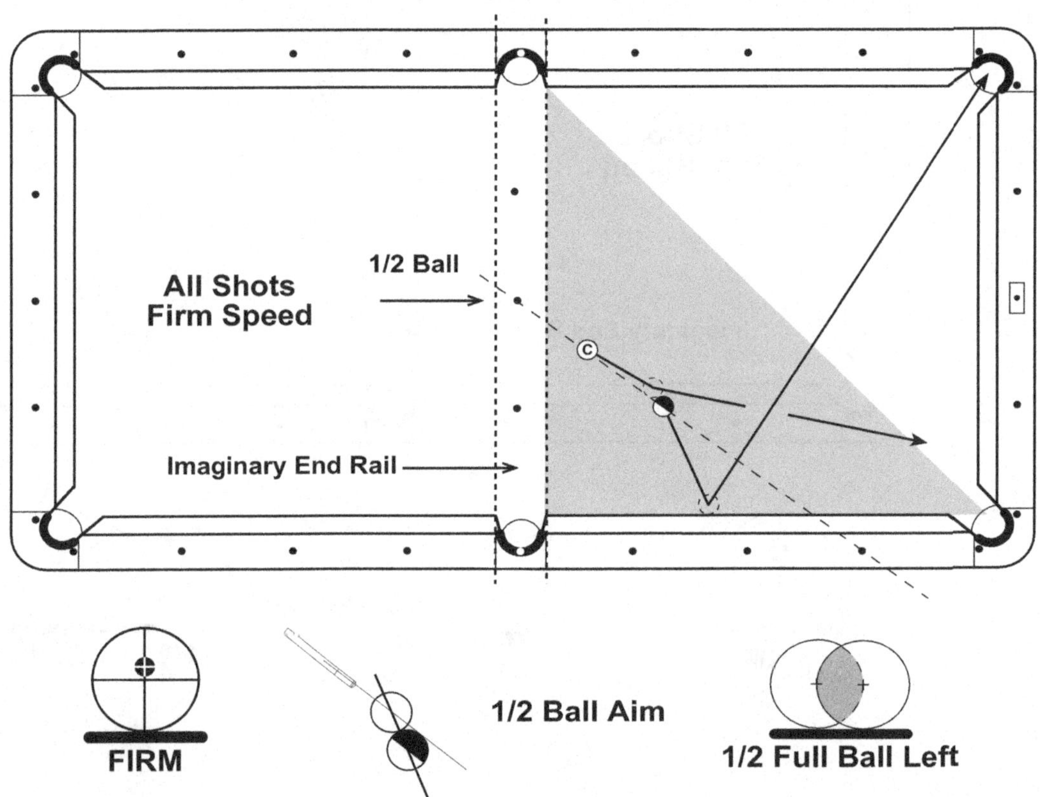
Cross-Corner Pass-Over Reference Angles
Reference point betweeen the side pockets
1/2 Ball
All Shots
Firm Speed
C
Imaginary End Rail
FIRM
1/2 Ball Aim
1/2 Full Ball Left

Cross-Corner Pass-Over Reference Angles

Reference point betweeen the side pockets

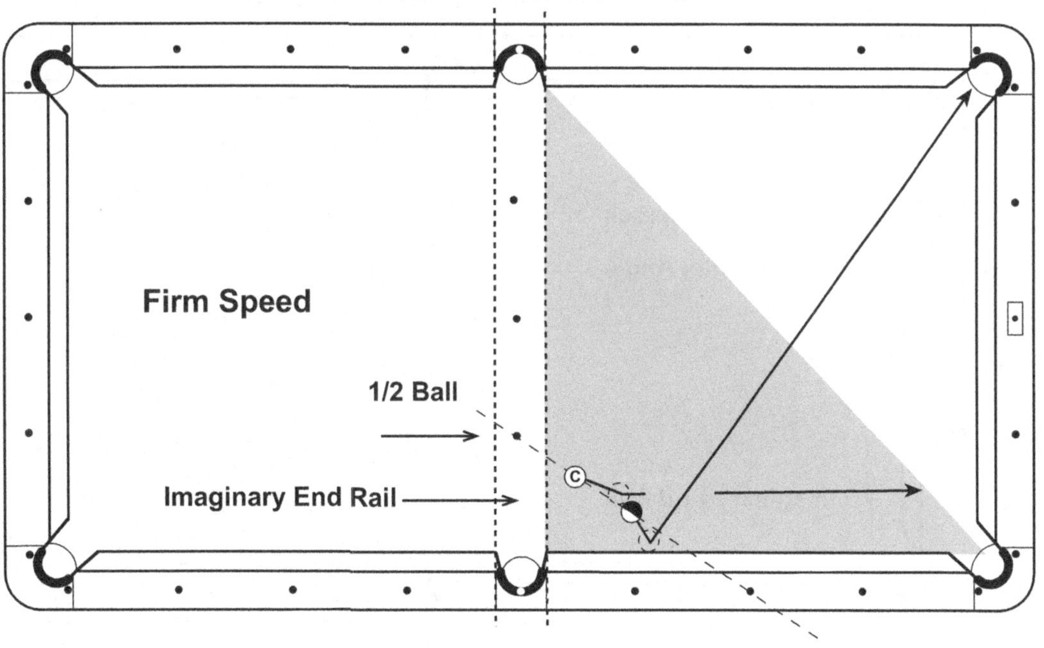

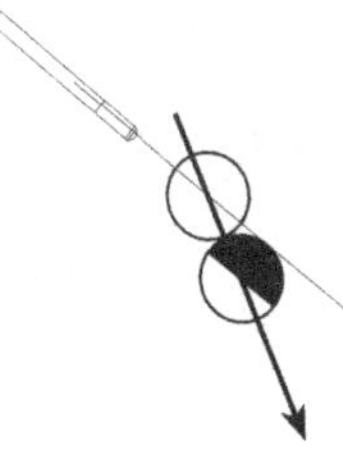

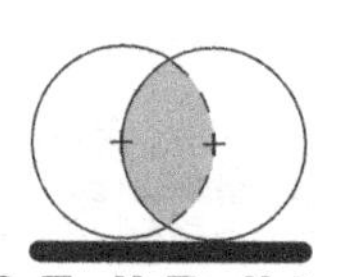

Parallel Tracks

1/2 Ball Aim Track Example

Reference point between side pockets

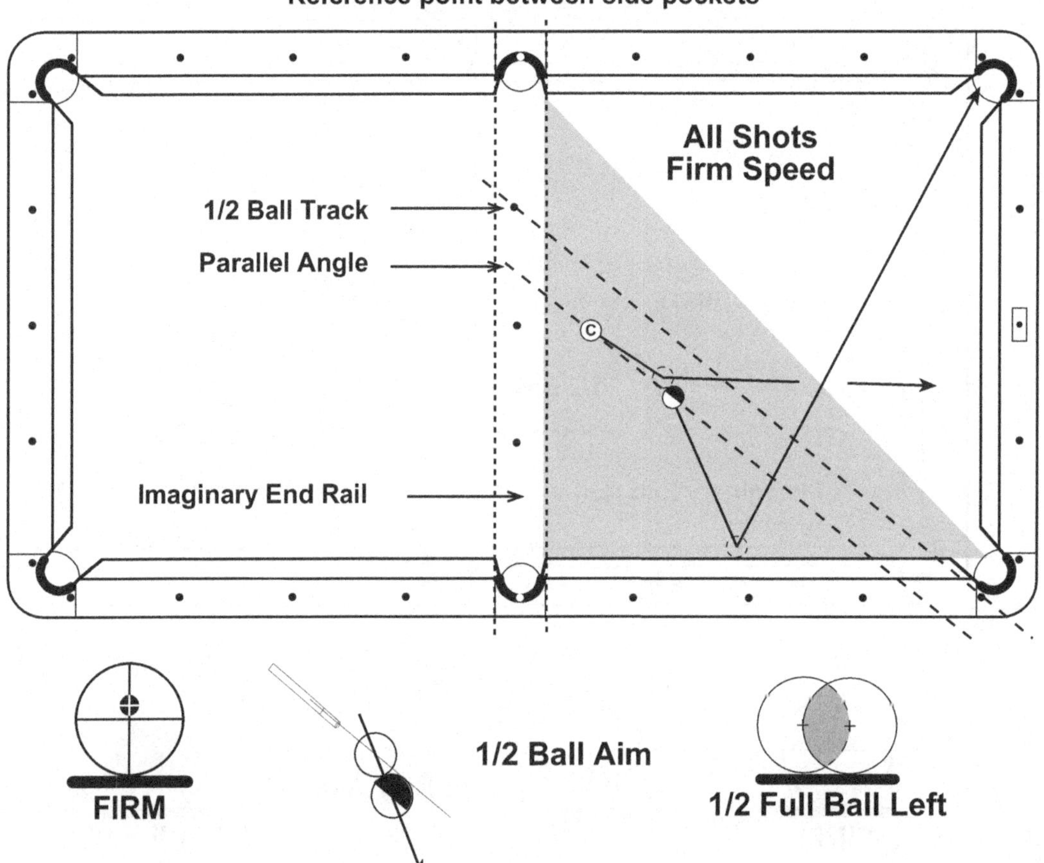

Straight-Backs

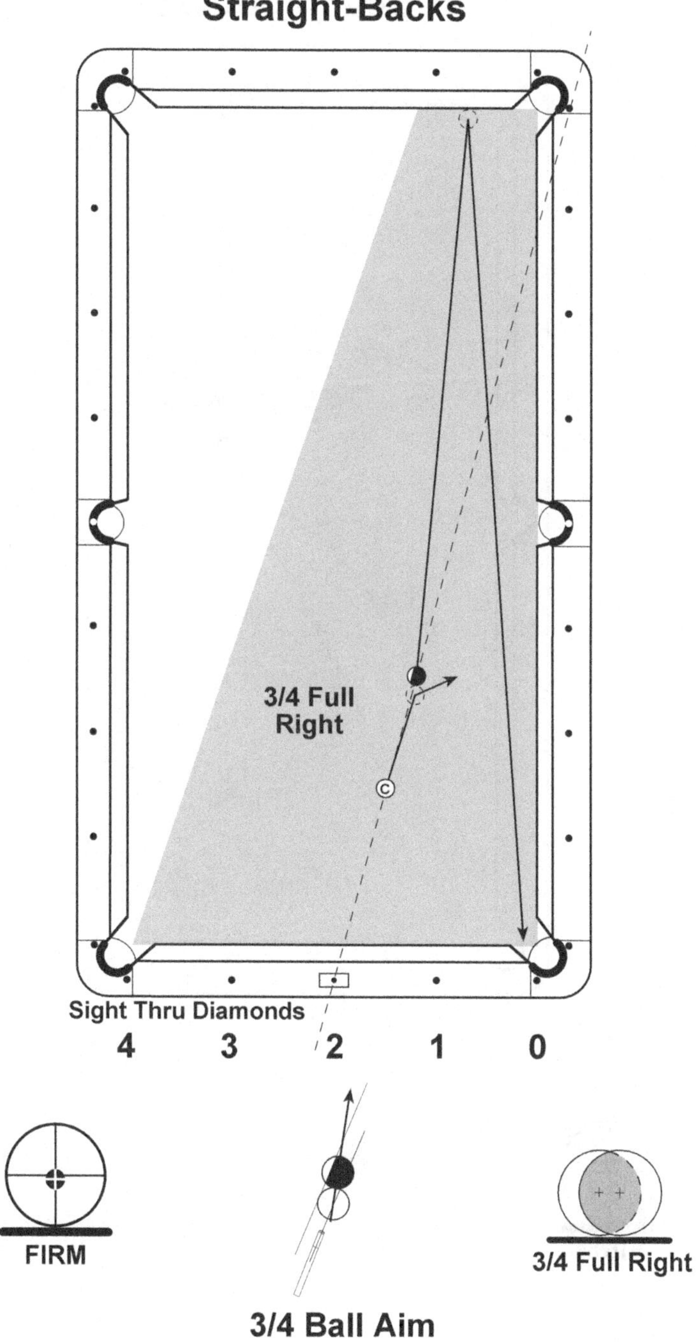

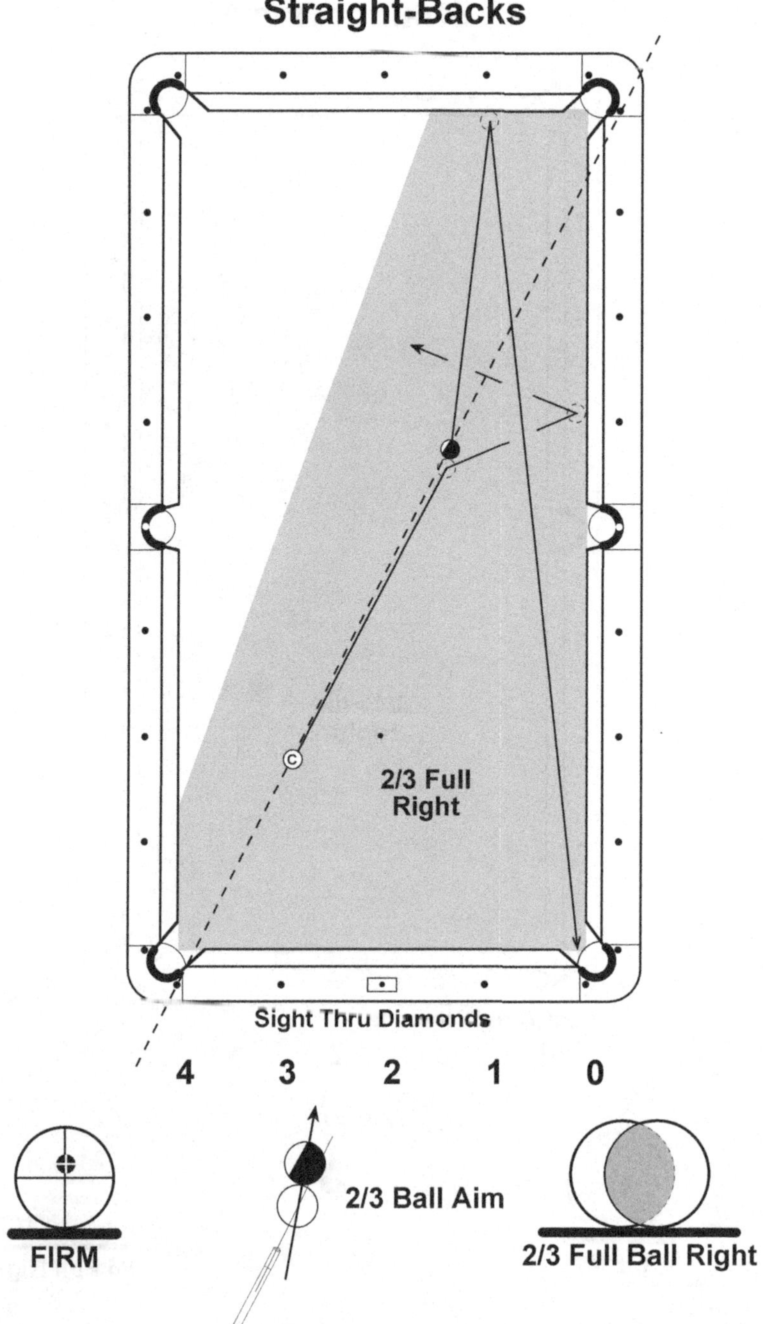
Straight-Backs
2/3 Full
Right
Sight Thru Diamonds
4 3 2 1 0
FIRM
2/3 Ball Aim
2/3 Full Ball Right

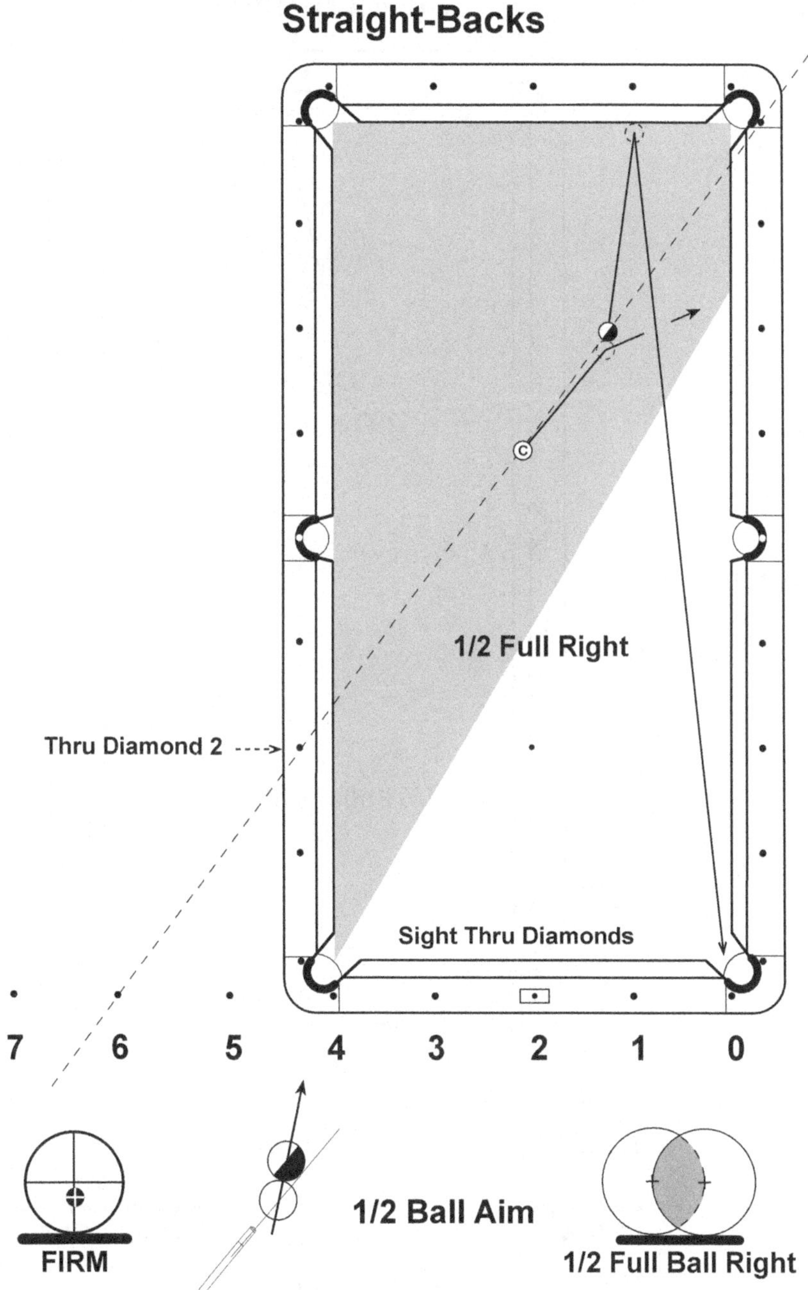

These straight-back reference systems operate the same as the cross-side systems, except you must make allowances for possible kisses.

Straight-Backs

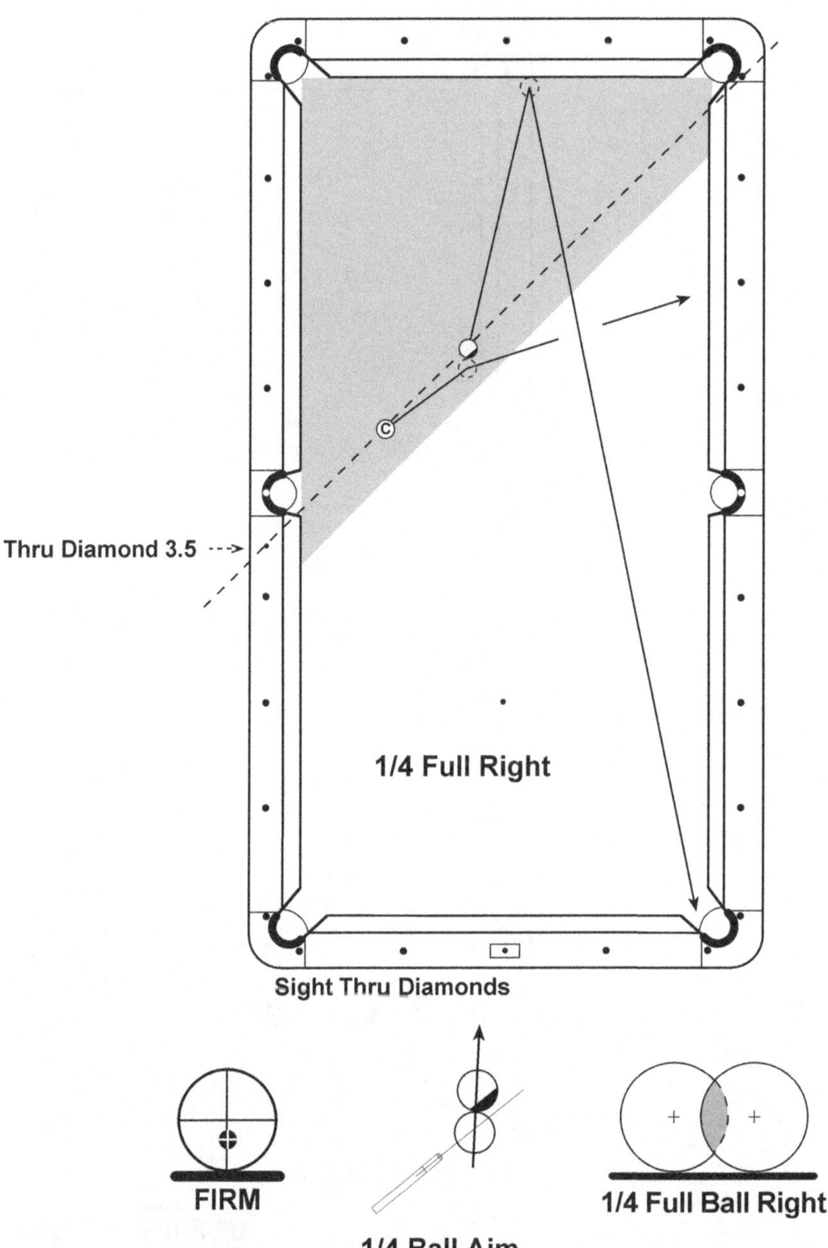

FIRM

1/4 Ball Aim

1/4 Full Ball Right

Straight-Back reference systems operate the same as the cross-side systems, except you must allow for possible kisses.

Legends of
Bank Pool
'Freddie the Beard'
Bentivegna
One Pocket Hall of Fame
Elected into the Legends of Bank Pool 2005
OnePocket.org

MORE PONTIFICATING

Oldest Hustler

Tom Smith, of OH, at 100 years was the oldest pool hustler. He didn't start playing pool until he arrived in America from Yugoslavia when he was in his 60s! **Walter Tevis**, who wrote **The Hustler**, probably based a pool character in that book on old Tom (the first guy Fast Eddie played when his thumbs healed). Tom, at 100, could still run 2 racks in Straight Pool. He stood ramrod straight, was strong as a bull and always wore a suit and tie. While in his 90s, he was a gigolo to 70-and 80-year old widows. At age 90, Tom fought off a stick-up man in Miami, FL and refused to give up the money. Even though he caught a gun butt to the head, Smith did not release the *cheese*.

Thinking on your feet award

I was in an all-black poolroom in Detroit, at Courtland and Lynwood St., with **James "Youngblood" Brown**. He had just finished telling me how well regarded he was in the place, when somebody called **Cadillac Willy** came in and demanded the money James owed him. When James gave alibi after alibi about being broke, Willy pulled a gun and started shooting. I dove under a pool table. James grabbed the biggest guy he could find and hoisted him up as a human shield to hide behind while Willy was trying to shoot him. James ended the assault by throwing his (and my) bankroll in the air (about $640). People diving for the money interrupted the attack, and we were able to get out alive.

Great Black Players

John "Cannonball Lefty" Chapman from Chicago's West Side. Cannonball played all games, including a smattering of 3-Cushion Billiards.

This is how "Cannonball" warmed up before a match: He had such a supple body he would roll up into a ball on the floor; knees up against his chest, head between his legs, arms around his ankles. You could have rolled him down a hill.

"Mexican Johnny" Vasquez used to go to the West Side and play Chapman bank pool. I once asked how Lefty played him and what kind of handicap was involved. Johnny replied that Lefty spotted him 14 to 8 playing banks on a *4' x 8'* pool table.

I gasped. I couldn't believe anybody on earth could give a journeyman player like Johnny that much of a spot. I asked him, "How the hell could you possibly lose getting that much weight? "Johnny replied in his inimitable style, "Sheet, man, dat ain't sucha good game. Lefty git a shot, he bank leben, bank twelve, bank ten."

Javenley "Youngblood" Washington from Chicago's South Side—the original Youngblood. Washington was one of the all-time great bank-pool players.

Besides his fabulous pool skills, Youngblood had some mental problems. Javenley was periodically institutionalized at **Manteno's** mental center in Chicago. Youngblood's *backers* helped him escape over the wall of the mental institution and go to the West Side to play "Cannonball Lefty" Chapman bank pool. Youngblood was still wearing the hospital bracelet on his wrist.

The battles between Youngblood and Chapman brought *sweators* in from everywhere. It was like the World Series. The poolroom was packed wall–to–wall. When the session was over, the *backers* would return Youngblood to the asylum and hoist him over the wall to resume a dreary life as a mental patient.

Javenley"Youngblood" Washington

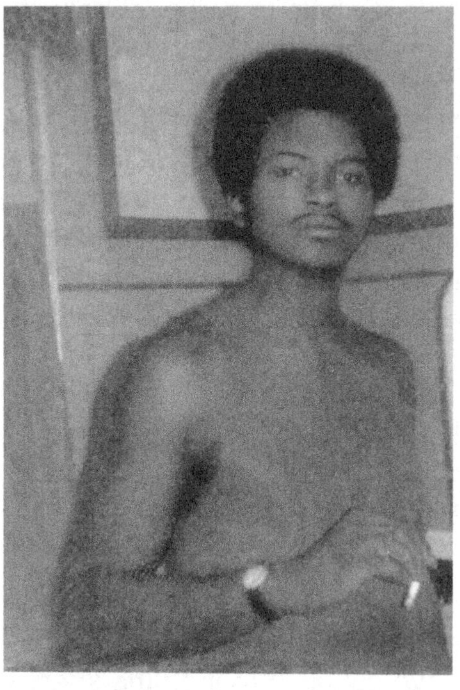

Kenny "Romberg" Remus

photos courtesy Glen "Piggy Bank" Rogers

Worst-Looking Strokes

Isadore "Pony" Rosen from Chicago. At the apex of his backswing, it looked like Pony was going to miss the whole cue ball by at least 3 or 4 inches.

Cisero Murphy from Brooklyn. Murphy's stroking arm made left-and right-hand turns on his backstroke. Murphy's grip hand looked like he was shaking dice during his preliminary swings. Somehow his delivery retraced those same paths and miraculously straightened out just before he hit the cue ball.

Cisero played a challenge match with **Luther "Wimpy" Lassiter** in Lassiter's home poolroom in Elizabeth City, NC. and beat him. At that time Wimpy was rated the #1 straight pool player in the world. Cisero ran over 200 balls during the match.

Artie Bodendorfer stroked like he was cutting cordwood with a rusty saw.

Most Brutal Self-Punishers

"Mountain" Mullenex, from Lincoln Town, NC. When he lost, Mountain would take a whole tray of pool balls, throw them up in the air and then stand under them while they crashed down on his head.

"Cigar Bob" from Philly put on such a great show when he missed a ball or lost that the only way he could get *staked* was when he had a game that he couldn't possibly win. If he missed a ball Bob might punch himself in the jaw, then stagger a few feet and remark, "Oh, tough guy, huh? Won't go down, eh? How about this!" He'd blast himself with another shot, more brutal then the last, and collapse to the floor.

Cigar Bob's *backers* taunted and teased him when he was losing, trying to rev him up more, saying, "*Dumping* me, are you, Bob? I never thought you would do this to me." This would provoke Bob to do more horrible stuff to himself. He'd reply, "I ain't tossin' you, honest. Look, look!" Then he might put the cigar out on his face, rubbing it all over.

Cigar Bob once ran his head into a paneled wall and broke through. He got stuck and couldn't pull his head out. If he tried to pull back through, Bob would have cut his throat on the sharp edges of the wall. The *sweators* had to break the wall with hammers to get his head out.

photos courtesy Bill Hermicudas

Cisero Murphy

Top *Bite-Men (smallish amounts)**

Meyer Seigel of Brooklyn, NY. In the 40s, Meyer was a top-notch middleweight prize-fighter. He moved to Chicago in the 50s and the *bite* was on. Dueces, treys and some fins were his specialties. Seigel patrolled the racetracks by day and the bars and poolrooms by night.

When he was drunk, which was often, Meyer was a lovable slob, but drunk or not Seigel had plenty of heart. I was in attendance once, when a big-time mob enforcer named **"PeePee"**, angry at Meyer, told him threateningly, "Guys like you wind up in the trunk!" Meyer instantly replied in kind, "Your fat ass ain't too big to fit in the trunk either!"

Mendy Weiss

When he was a kid in the Jewish section of Brooklyn, Seigel played the Jewish card game Klabyash with the killer, **Mendy Weiss**, who was one of the heads of the infamous Murder, Inc. Weiss was a flashy dressing, redheaded strangler who had worked his way up through the strong-arm labor rackets.

Meyer had been winning from Mendy for days. In frustration after another loss, Mendy took out his .45 pistol and pointed it at Meyer. "I oughta kill you, you son-of-a-bitch." Meyer shrugged the threat off and replied matter-of-factly, "Who are you kidding? If you kill me, who you gonna get to play with? Everybody else is too afraid of you." Mendy thought it over for a second, absorbed the logic in Meyer's statement and put the gun away. "You're right, Meyer, deal the cards."

Softest Touch For The *Bite*

Late in life, **Minnesota Fats**. Any *broke* could always get a $20 bill for eating money from him.

**bite-men*: People who borrow money for a living.

Meyer Seigel

Artie Bodendorfer. However, he turned me down once because I already owed him $3000. Out of revenge, I gave his phone number to several world-class *bitemen* I knew, along with advice as to how much to ask for.

Laziest Pool Hustler
"Canadian Pete" Tasic, a prodigy of Detroit Whitey. In gambling bars, Pete acted like he had money and wanted to play, so the *Jar* hustlers would buy him a few free beers in order to spike them with *scopalomine*. Pete didn't mind, rather enjoying the high.

One night in **Bensinger's**, Canadian Pete was awakened off the bench and was given one $20 barrel to play Nine Ball against **Jim Rempe**. With the one *barrel* Pete played Rempe to a three-hour draw.

Most Games Played *On Ass By A Bar Hustler— Career**
James "Peaches" Rochford from Chicago, IL. I saw Peaches go so far as to play a vicious mob-enforcer with only the first quarter to put in the bar table.

Top Punishment Absorbers

Bobby Strauss, champion horse-handicapper and a shortstop pool player. In Miami, FL's Congress Bowl, he went for 35 games of One-Pocket at a sawbuck a game without a raise, to top player **Harry Cohen** of NY. Strauss did try to raise the bet, but Harry wouldn't budge.

Bobby topped that masochistic effort with a 58-game One-Pocket lashing playing one of the foremost *grinders** of all-time, **Frank "Bananas" Rodriquez** from San Antonio, TX.

Strauss played Bananas for $30 a game in the 72-hour session — also without a raise. Bananas, an old school hustler, had raised pool-water-torture to a fine art. Not even 70-plus hours of pool and being a jillion games ahead could entice Bananas to loosen up and go for a marginal shot. His laborious preparation before every shot was maddening. He would take 2 to 3 minutes to drill in a *hanger* game ball. Even those *sweating* the session — of which I was one — got the shivers watching Bananas' relentless, sadistic performance.

**on ass, play on ass:* Playing for money, without any money

**grinder:* A very deliberate, workhorse type player.

James "Peaches" Rochford Playing On
Table 15 In Bensinger's

Bobby Strauss was also party to a tremendous reversal of fortune in a match with **Peter "Rabbit" Linhardt** of Philadelphia, also at the **Congress Bowl** in North Miami, FL. The game was best 2 out of 3 One-Pocket, for $200 dollars a set playing even-up. Rabbit, as usual, was getting *staked* and was *strumming** Strauss. Rabbit won the first 18 of 19 games played and was 9 sets and $1800 ahead.

It was now about 6 am and Rabbit's *backer* had to go to work, so he split up the money, giving Peter his share, $900. Rabbit wanted to quit and go home, but how could he justify quitting when he had only lost 1 game out of the last 19?

The outcome was predictable. Rabbit, now betting his own money, lost 10 games in a row and the $900. Rabbit went so far as to stiff Strauss for the last $100 of the final bet. Strauss was justifiably upset. He had *broke* the Rabbit, but was still stuck $900 and would now have to pay the time, since the Rabbit was empty.

When asked how he could have possibly *dogged it* that badly betting his own money, Peter replied candidly, "I just feel naked without a *backer*."

Greatest Pool Dogs - Literally

Jerry the Greek's wonder dog, **King**. King could spot **Rin-Tin-Tin** the six and nine when it came to smarts. King could have been a dog pimp and gotten **Lassie** to work in his stable. Jerry would be in his apartment, the phone would ring and Jerry would tell King, "I had a tough day today, King. I don't feel like getting up. Bring the phone over to me, boy." King would take the phone off the receiver, give a quick "woof" as if to say, "hold on," then put the phone in his mouth and carry it over to Jerry.

Jerry would put King on a pool table with a full set of racked balls. You could call out any number ball and King could pick it out, put it in his mouth and drop it into the pocket, honest. Jerry won some big bets with that hustle. King would "stall" on the first small bet, scattering the balls wildly and acting crazy. At this point everyone would be laughing at Jerry and deriding the dog.

Jerry would pull out a hip-flask, take a snort and blame King's performance on the noise and distractions of the sweators. Faking embarrassment and anger, Jerry would challenge the marks to a very large bet, with the proviso that they would have to keep quiet during King's performance.

**strumming*: Beating up on. Like playing a banjo.

With the big money up, Jerry would give King *the office** to come off the stall and take the money down. King would now be on the table sitting alert, with his ears sticking straight up in the air. "Get me the four ball, King." Jerry would say and King would stroll leisurely over to the rack, open the balls up with his paw and put the called ball in his mouth, bring it to the pocket and drop it in. King would then sit back on his hindquarters and await the next command.

Jerry never got turned down for the *bite* because he never asked for anything for himself, only for King. Jerry would say, "King hasn't ate today," and guys would dive into their pockets to *un-ass* eating money for King. Jerry, for himself, probably couldn't get a stick of gum.

The only known photo of King can be found in **Eddie Robin's** Winning One-Pocket book on page 247. You will find King posing with Ronnie Allen. King is the one wearing sun-glasses.

Detroit Whitey's German Shepherd, **Windy**. Windy would lay down under the pool table when Whitey was playing. When Whitey gave him *the office*, Windy would snarl, growl and sometimes fart just as Whitey's opponent was ready to shoot.

He Did A Stretch At Bensinger's

He was originally **Virginia Bob Ogburn**, then **Big Bob** and finally became **Black Bart**. He came to Chicago's **Bensinger's** from Virginia in the late 60s. He did a 6–month sentence, never missed a ball and stayed broke the whole time. Ogburn never got to play Nine Ball, a game where he could beat us; instead, he was steered into trap after trap of One-Pocket, Eight Ball and banks.

However, if you ask Bob about those days, he will tell you that that his **Bensinger's** experience was the basic training that hardened him into a top-notch road hustler. Ogburn went on to be a formidable force in the South for a long time, a high-roller and plenty tough to beat. One-Pocket was his worst game, but he still played it very solid. Bob was a diet-and-fasting freak for a long time. Unfortunately he mixed the health stuff, as we all did then, with speed pills.

**the office*: A predetermined signal to roll into action A secret tip-off.

Bob played One-Pocket a little under me, even though the last time we played he charged me $2500. I claim extenuating circumstances, because we were both being staked by killers and my killer (Sugar Shack Johnny Novak) snuck off with the stakes well before the match was over — and I knew it— and I had to try to perform under those conditions.

The Rat Story

I'm playing One-Pocket at **Bensinger's** with **Artie Bodendorfer**. The pool room was in a dismal basement that used to be an old bowling alley, with a ceiling full of old water pipes servicing the rest of the building. My opponent, Artie, was a very safe player. You might go weeks before Bodendorfer would leave you a good shot.

As usual Bodendorfer was leaving me nothing, but then, amazingly, a miracle happens and Artie sells out! He leaves me a baby layout, balls open all over the table, cue ball right in the middle, a real easy run-out. But I don't take my shot right away. I wanted Artie to suffer a little first. I wanted him to soak in it. So first I go to the bathroom to kill some time. I go in, I wash my hands, I comb my hair, I diddle around and I finally come out.

I get back to the table and I'm snookered! I haven't got a shot! The cue ball is frozen behind another ball in front of my pocket! I start hollering and screaming, saying," What the hell is this? What is going on here?" The sweators were laughing hysterically and the place was in an uproar.

You must first understand that the poolroom was infested with giant rats that ran and played all along the pipes in the ceiling. The rats ran up and down those pipes like it was The Autobahn.

Finally, a guy explains what happened. One of the rats lost its footing, slipped and fell off the pipe and onto the table. Then the rat ran off the table, scattering the balls and snookering me in the process.

I didn't know what the hell you're supposed to do in that spot. I had never heard of anything like that before. I'm still not sure what you're supposed to do. It was a weird funny kind of an incident. We wound up playing the game over, and naturally Artie never left me another good shot for the rest of the year.

This is the Stick-Up story

Years ago, back when I was seriously hustling pool, this bird-dog brought me to a bar spot to play. A bird-dog is a guy that goes around sniffing out action spots, and then he brings a player back with him to take the spot off. Sometimes they're also called steer men or backers, because they put the money up for you to play with.

So this steer man brings me to this joint and there's an old-time bar-pool champion playing. Now I knew this guy but he didn't know me, because I was just an up-and-coming player at that time. The player's name was **Sonny Garrison.** We began playing Nine Ball. He started off playing real good, but he couldn't keep that kind of pace up anymore, so I wound up breaking him. It was a real nice score back then, $800.

Garrison paid off with a lot of 5s, 10s and 20s. The steer man and I left the place feeling good. Sonny follows us outside and he pulls out a .45, cocks it in my stomach and tells me to give him the money. So I reach in my front pocket and pull out a package of money and hand it to him.

Sonny pushes the gun deeper into my stomach and says "Give me all the money!" This was not an inexperienced stick-up man. So I reach into my left front pocket and give him another package of money. With this he's satisfied and he lets us go.

We're walking down the street and the steer guy hails a passing squad car, calls them over and tells the coppers that we just got stuck up. The bird-dog told them it was Sonny Garrison. He was very excited and upset. Now I wasn't all that upset at the guy, even though he emptied out two pockets of money from me. I was a turned-out hustler in those days and I was prepared for any contingency. I had money in three pockets! And, as a matter of fact, the majority of the bankroll was in the *third* pocket. This information I did not share with the steer man. So the bottom line was, I was still ahead pretty good. I wasn't stuck at all. What the robber really stole was the steer man's money. My end and my bankroll were still safely tucked away in my back pocket.

Later the cops picked up Garrison and we were called down to the station. Garrison was in an office being interrogated by the Duty Lieutenant. When they called me into the office, the Lieutenant said he had heard a different story from Sonny. Sonny's story was that he didn't stick me up with a gun, but that he stuck me up with a pool stick. He claimed that he beat me fair and square playing pool and that I was just a sore loser.

Now I was mad. I didn't care so much that he had put a gun on me and took some money, because as I said before, I wound up ahead of the game anyway. But when Garrison started saying he could beat me playing pool, I got upset, because I had robbed him on the table. I shot his nuts off. I murdered this guy and he's saying he beat me.

Now the Lieutenant says to me, "I don't know who to believe. You guys have two different stories."

That's when I stood up and said, "Listen, we can settle this by going down to the pool room. Me and Garrison will play a Nine Ball race to eleven and the loser goes to the shit-house! Then we'll see who beat who and who robbed who."

The cops didn't take me up on the offer and I never showed up for the court date, so nothing happened to Garrison and I never saw the guy again.

Glenn "Piggy Banks" Rogers

AUTOMATIC 5/6 Full Cross Side

2 : 1 Divide The Angle Adjustment

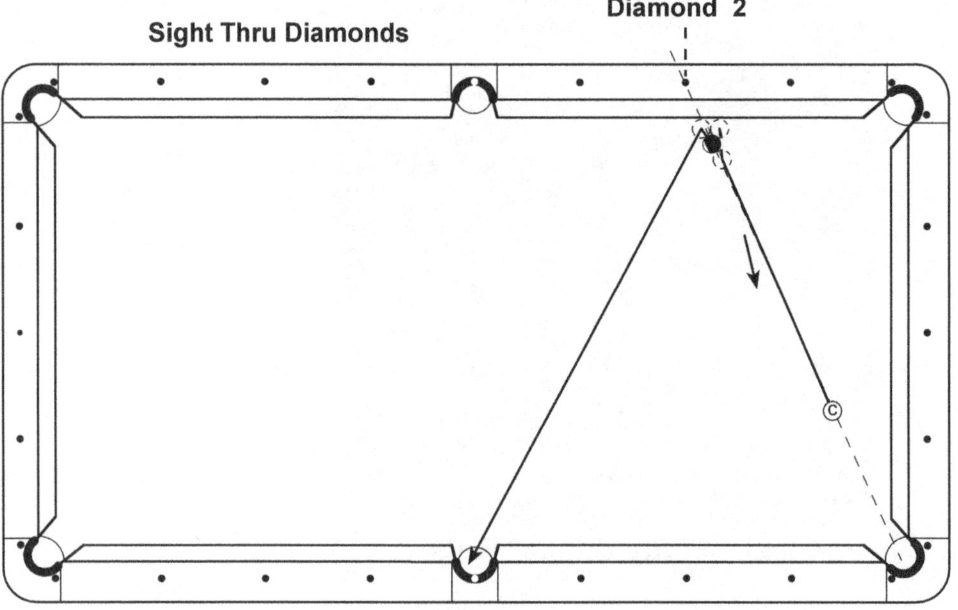

Object Ball Must Be Within 4" Of Cushion

At, or near diamond 2, we need to employ the least amount of cut to compensate for a 2 to 1 angle.

AUTOMATIC 3/4 Full Cross Side

2 : 1 Divide The Angle Adjustment

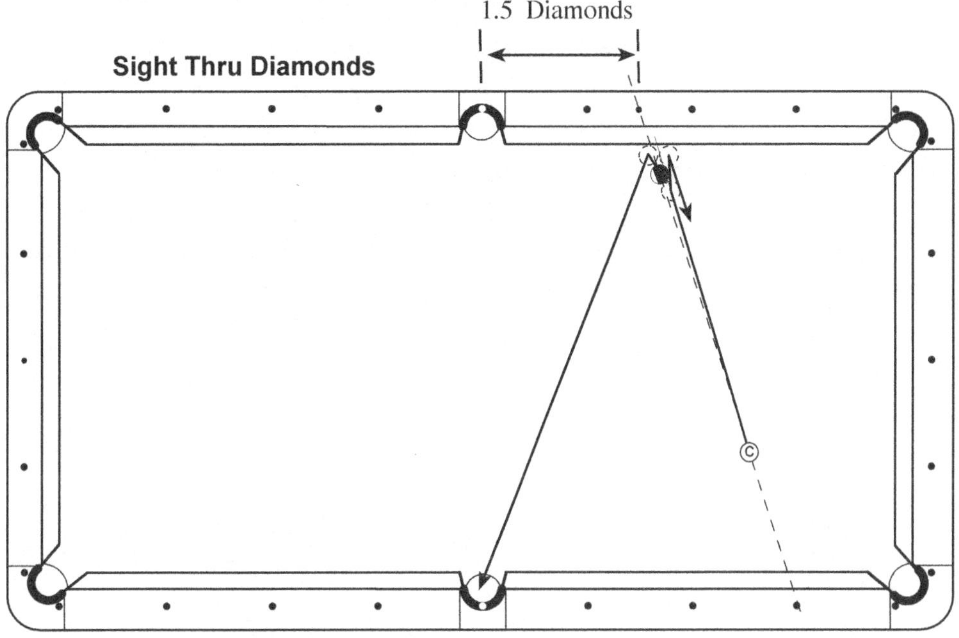

Object Ball Must Be Within 4" Of Cushion

As we move from diamond 2 toward the side pocket, we must gradually increase the amount of cut.

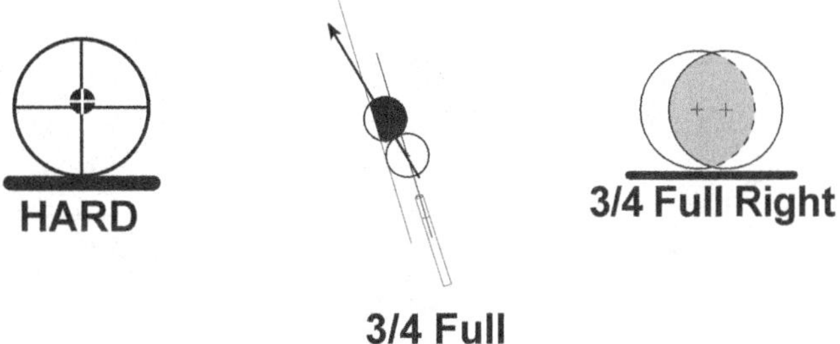

AUTOMATIC 2/3 Full Cross-Side

2 : 1 Divide The Angle Adjustment

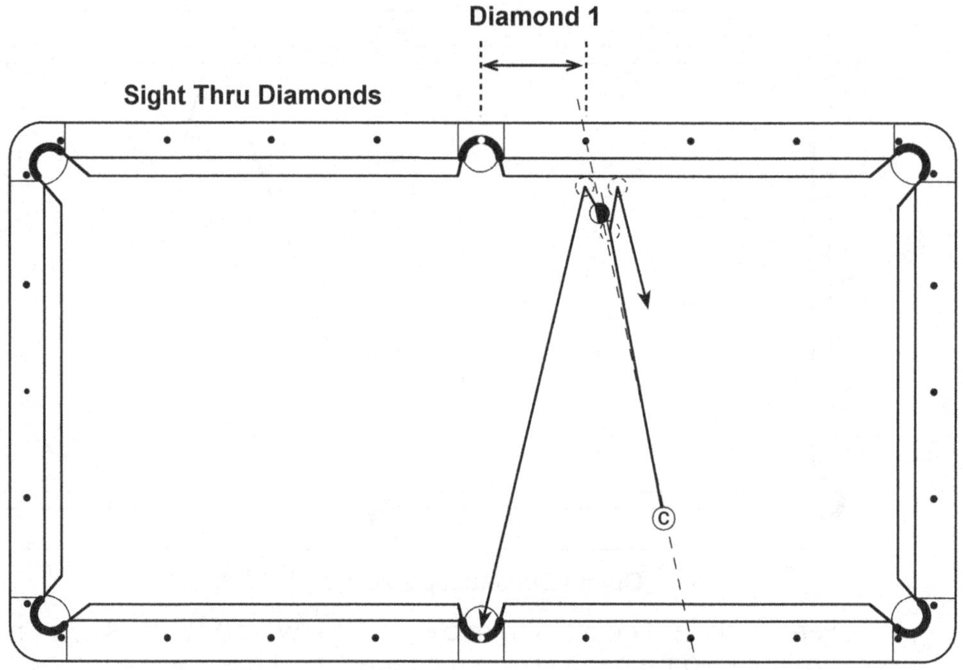

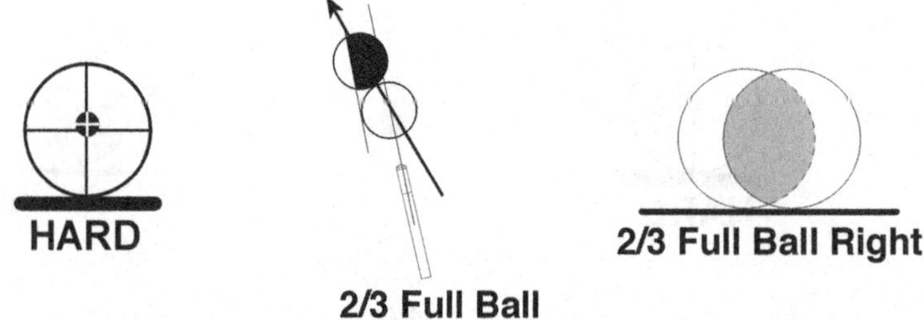

As we move from diamond 2 toward the side pocket, we must gradually increase the amount of cut.

AUTOMATIC 1/2 Full Cross-Side

2 : 1 Divide The Angle Adjustment

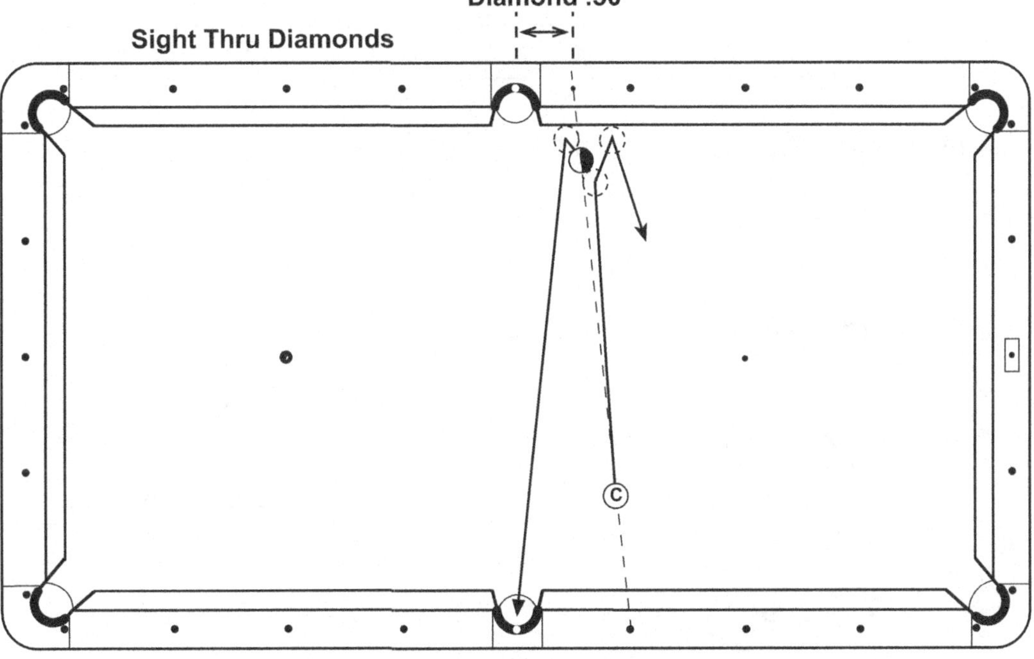

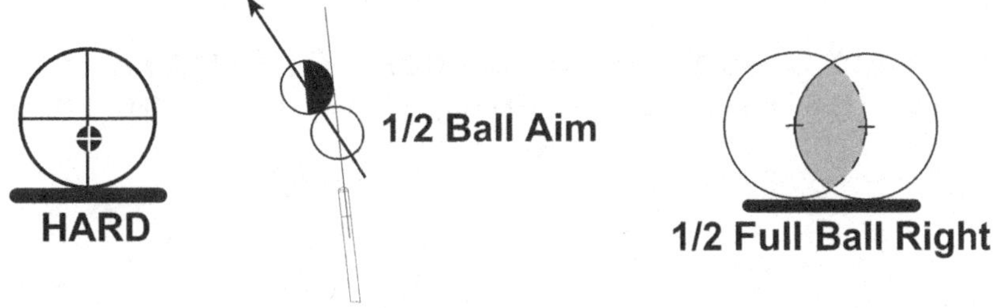

EQUAL ANGLES

Extended Rail — 2 : 1 Divide The Angle Tracks

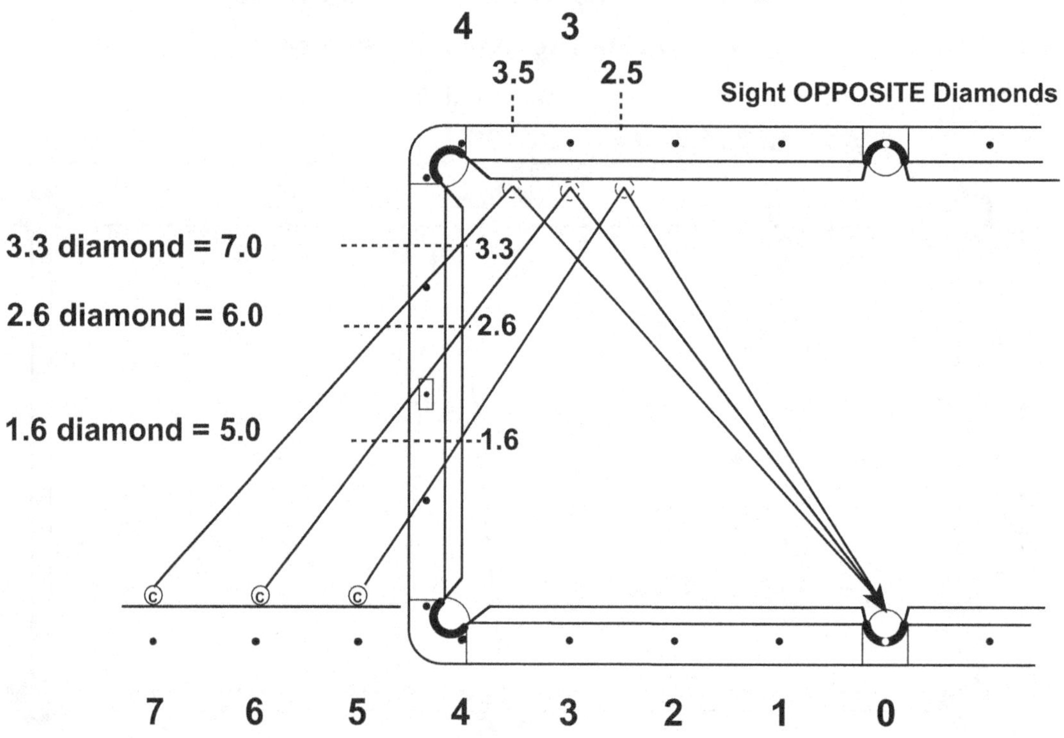

This diagram shows intersection points on the short rail for cross-side banks that start beyond the long rail.

In this system we do our calculations **OPPOSITE** the diamond positions instead of aiming through the diamonds.

AUTOMATIC 3/4 Full Cross Side

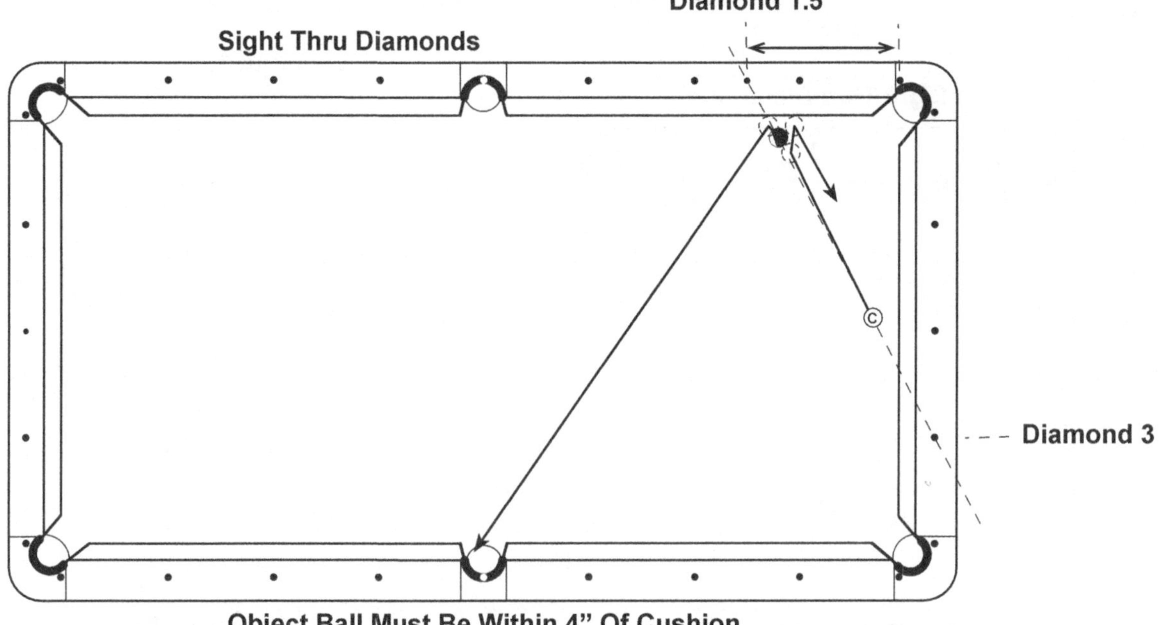

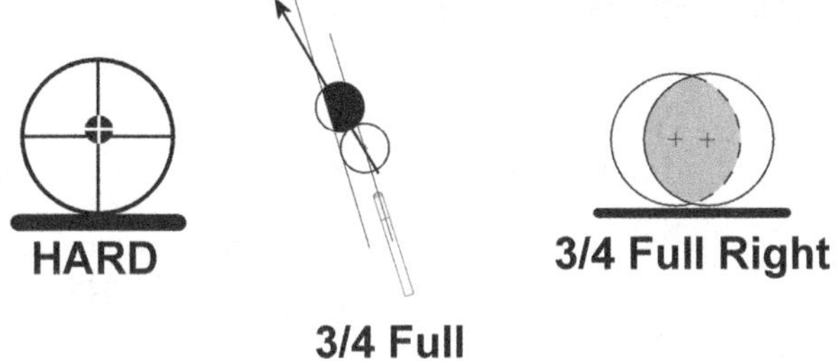

AUTOMATIC 2/3 Full Cross Side

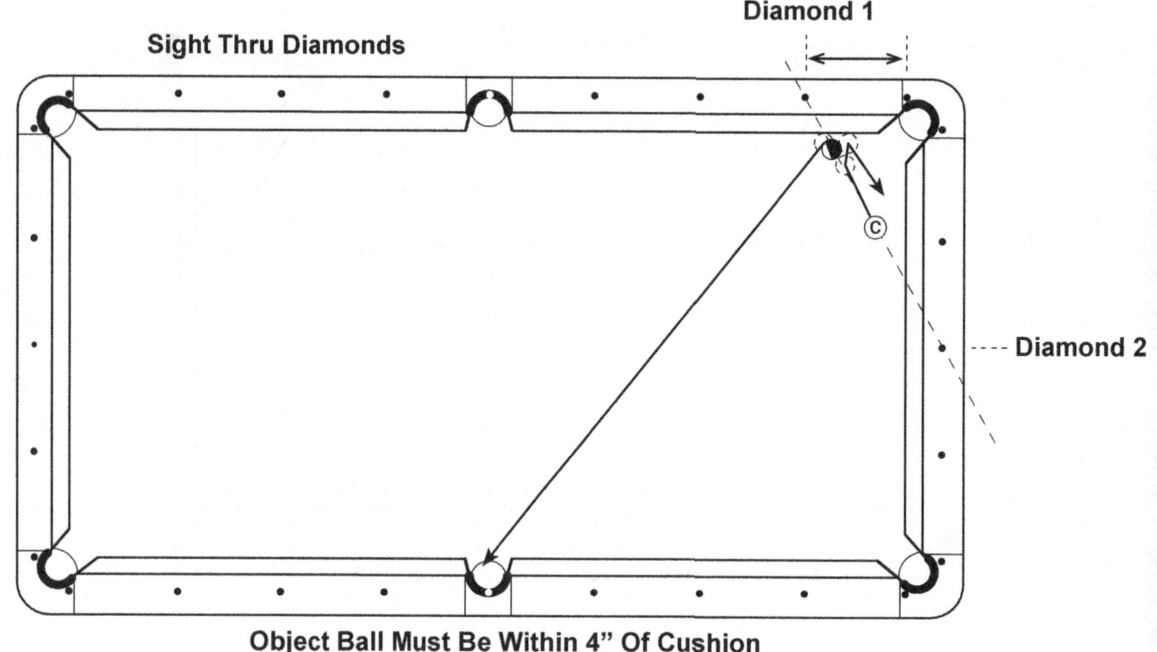

Object Ball Must Be Within 4" Of Cushion

HARD

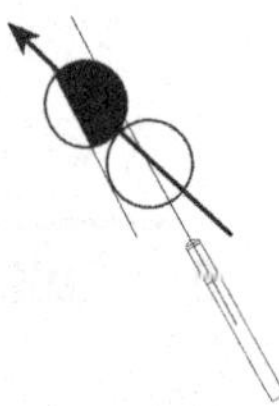

2/3 Full Aim

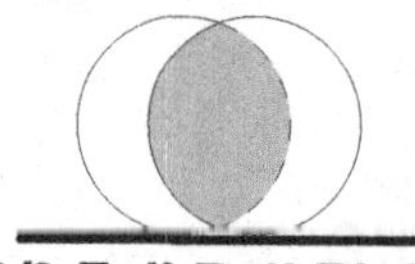

2/3 Full Ball Right

AUTOMATIC 1/2 Full Straight Back

2 : 1 Divide The Angle Adjustment

Sight Thru Diamonds

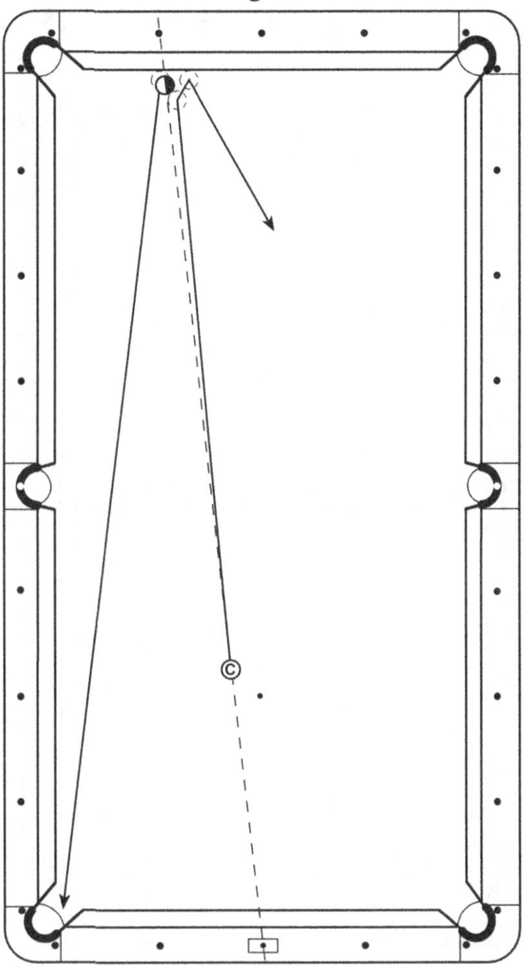

Object Ball Must Be Within 4" Of Cushion

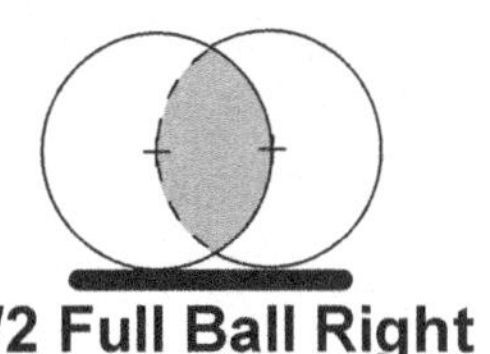

AUTOMATIC 3/5 Full Straight Back

2 : 1 Divide The Angle Adjustment

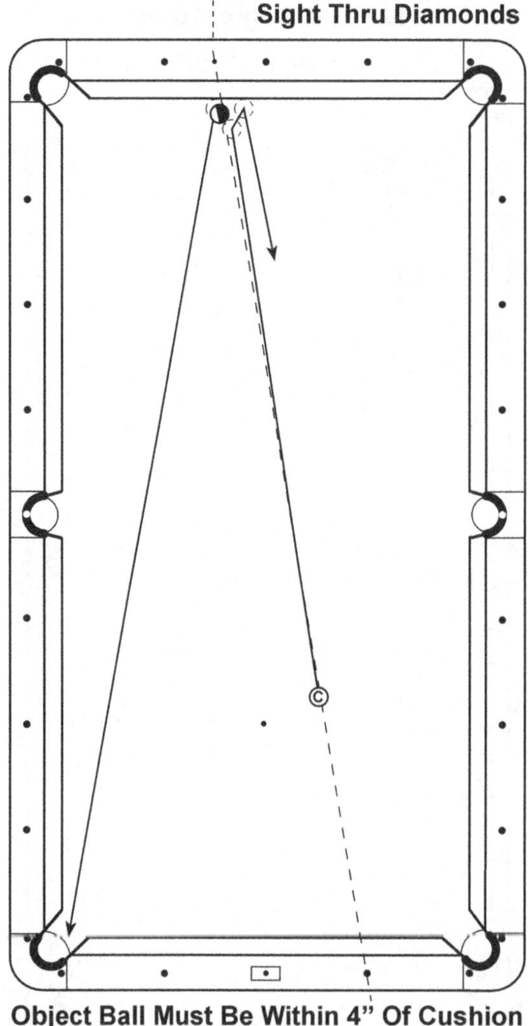

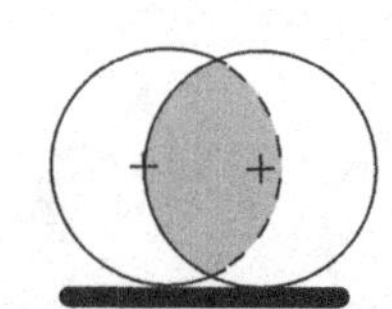

AUTOMATIC 2/3 Full Straight Back

2 : 1 Divide The Angle Adjustment

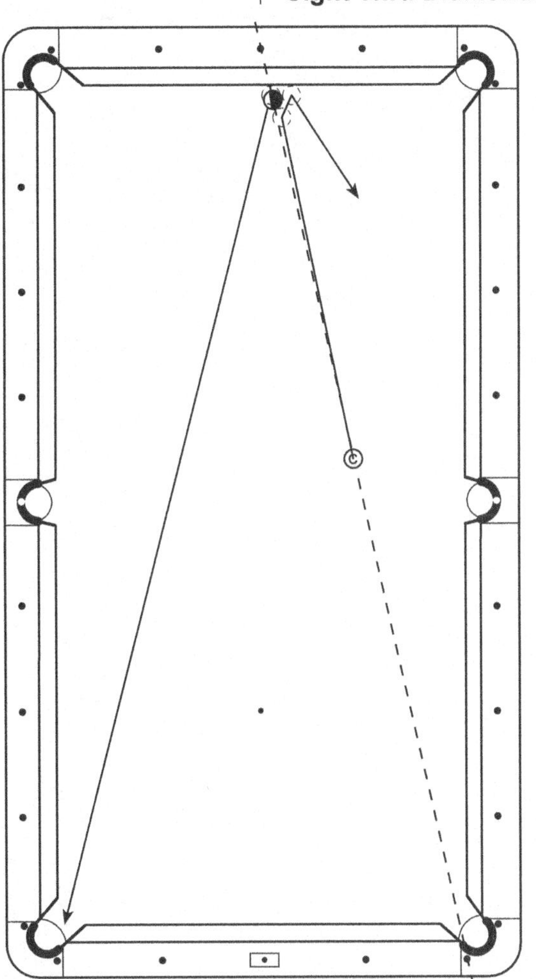

AUTOMATIC 7/10 Full STRAIGHT-BACK

2 : 1 Divide The Angle Adjustment

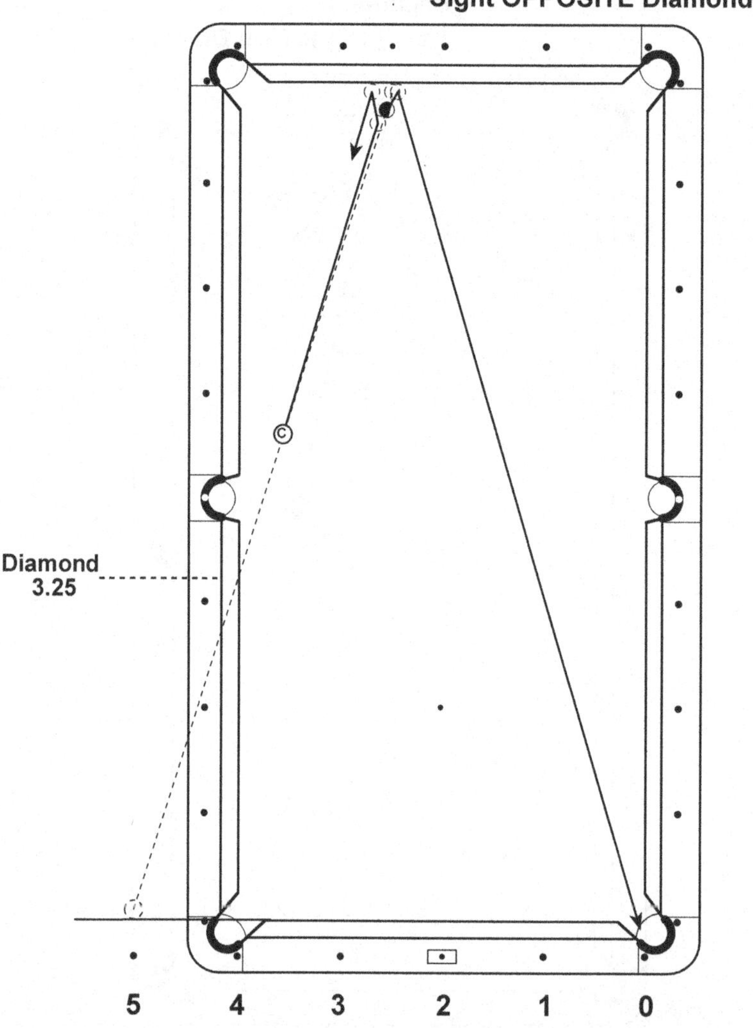

Object Ball Must Be Within 4" Of Cushion

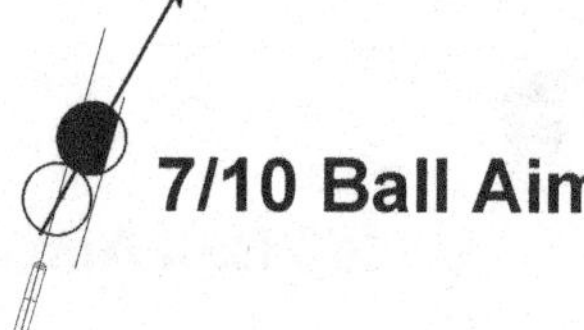

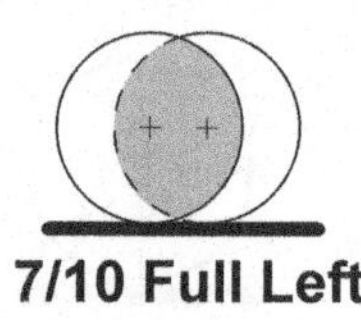

AUTOMATIC 3/4 Full STRAIGHT-BACK

2 : 1 Divide The Angle Adjustment

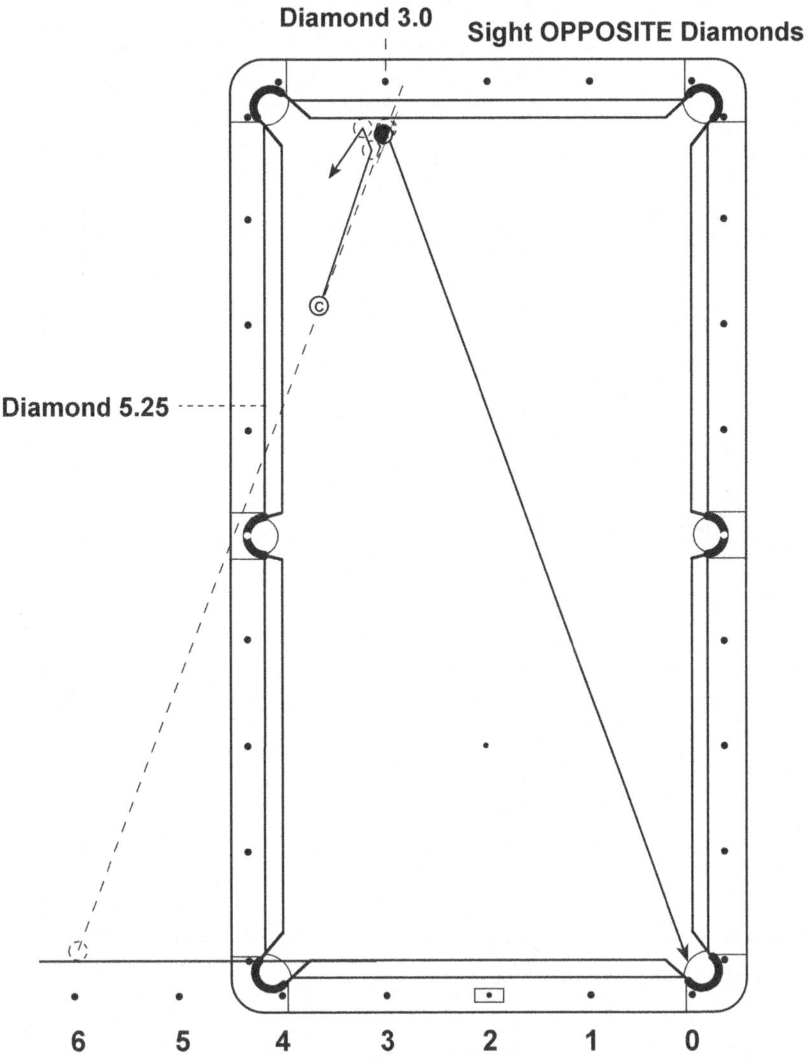

Diamond 3.0
Sight OPPOSITE Diamonds
Diamond 5.25
6
5
4
3
2
1
0

Object Ball Must Be Within 4" Of Cushion

HARD
3/4 Ball Aim
3/4 Full Left

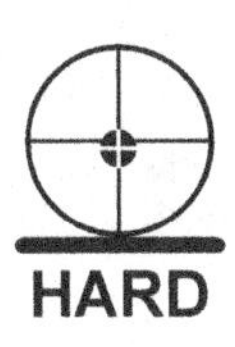

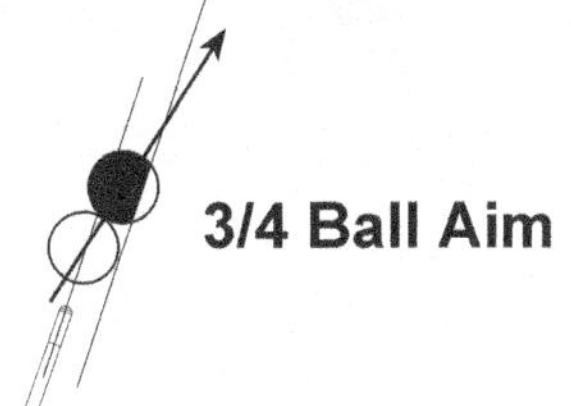

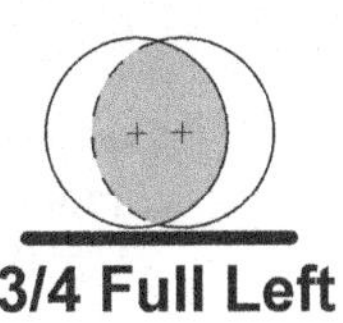

AUTOMATIC 4/5 FULL STRAIGHT-BACK

2 : 1 Divide The Angle Adjustment

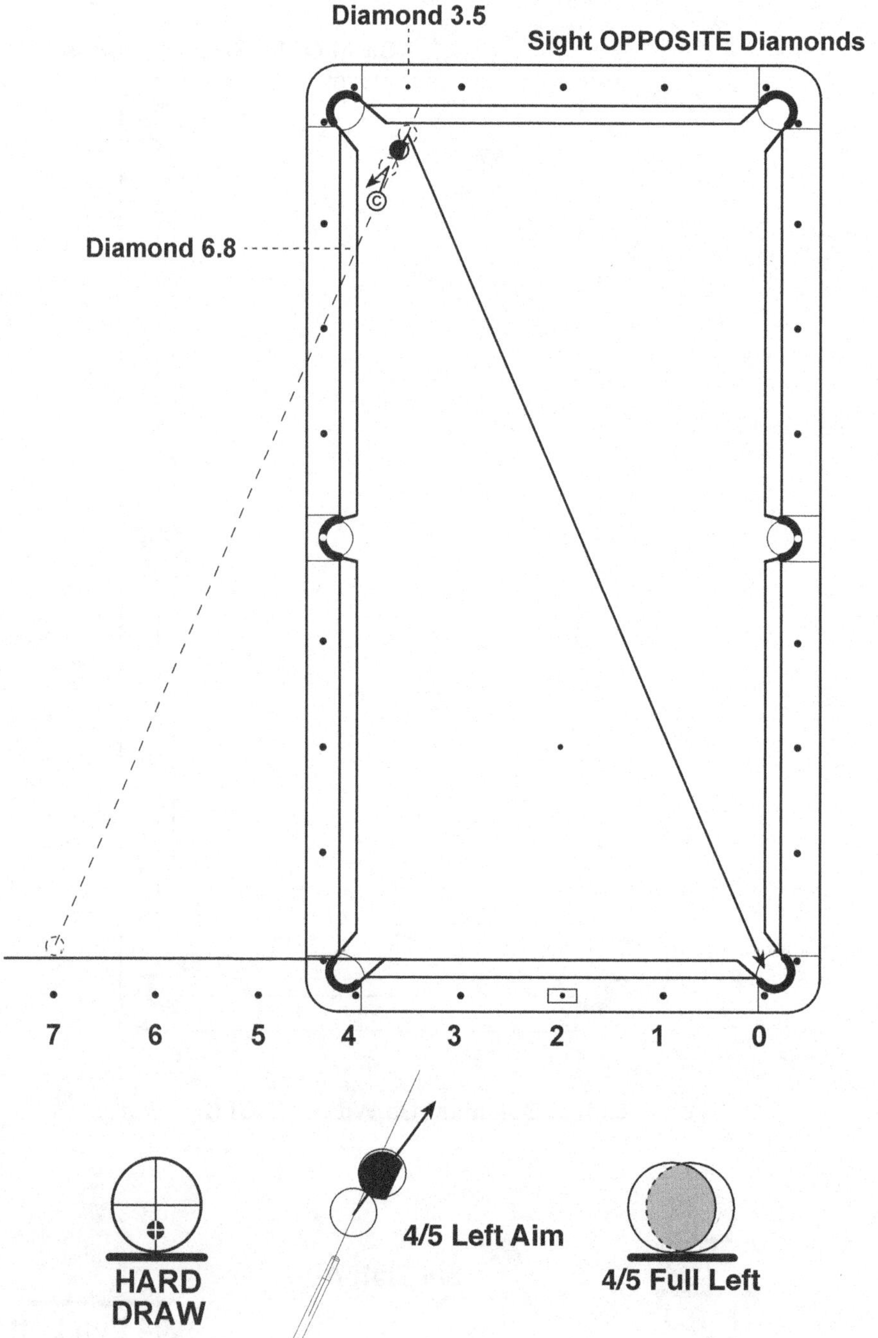

AUTOMATIC 3/4 FULL STRAIGHT-BACK

Straight-Back Parallel Angles
Adjusted Cuts

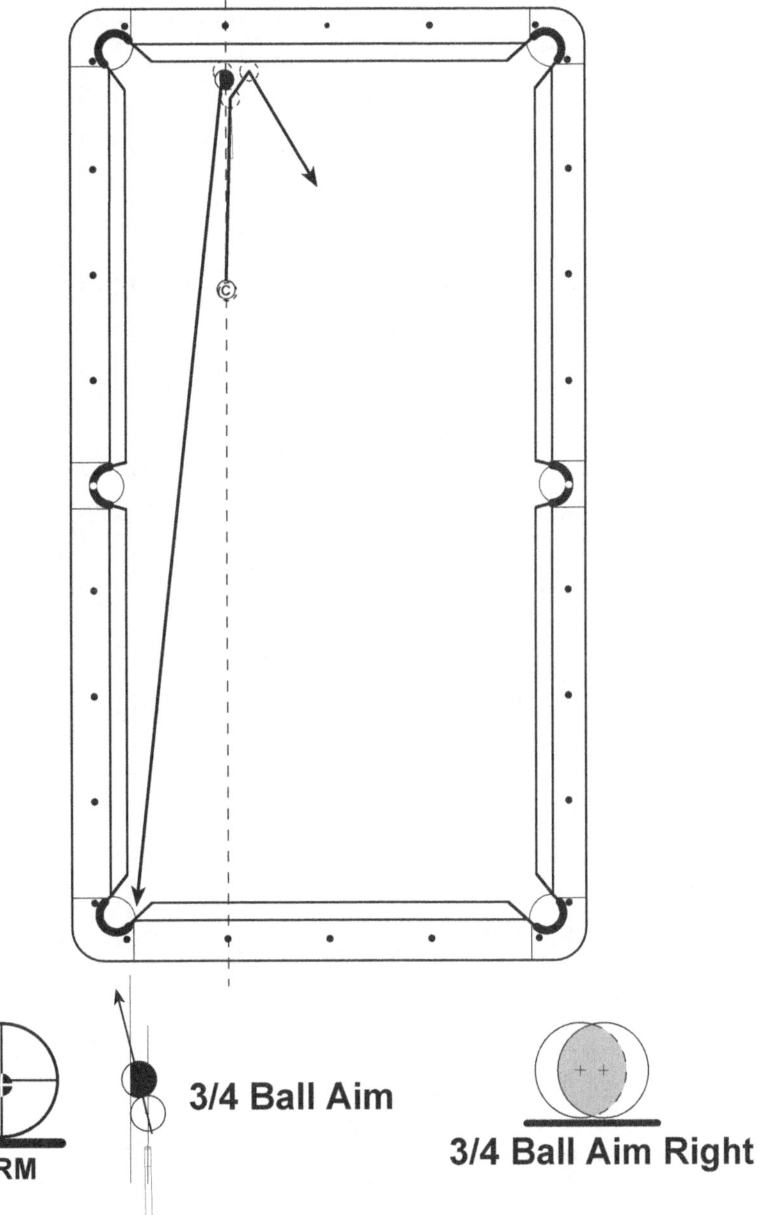

AUTOMATIC 5/6 FULL STRAIGHT-BACK

Parallel Angles Adjusted Cuts

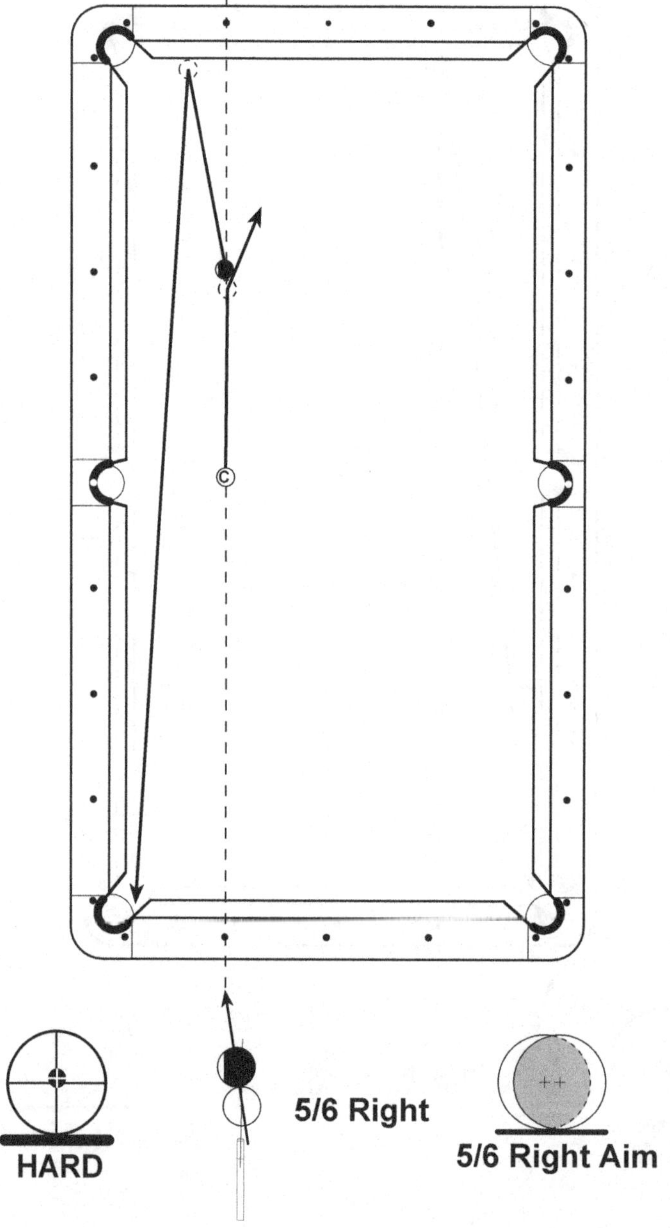

AUTOMATIC 7/8 FULL STRAIGHT-BACK

Parallel Angles Adjusted Cuts

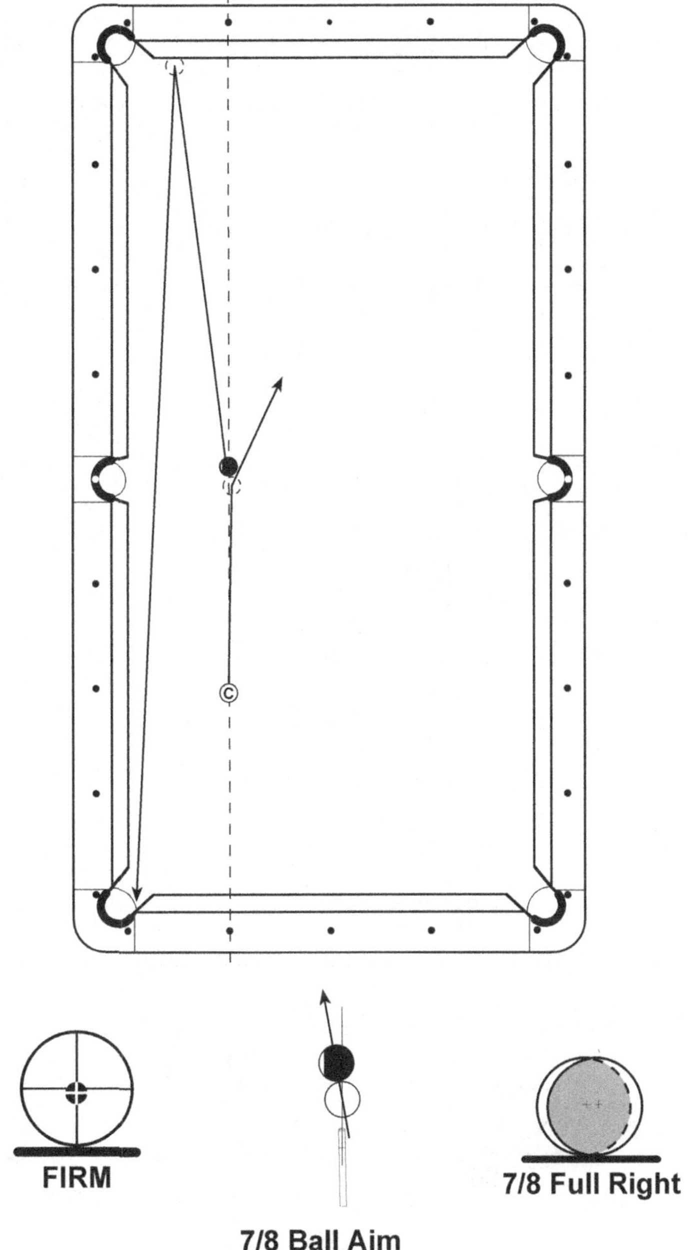

AUTOMATIC 9/10 FULL STRAIGHT-BACK

Parallel Angles Adjusted Cuts

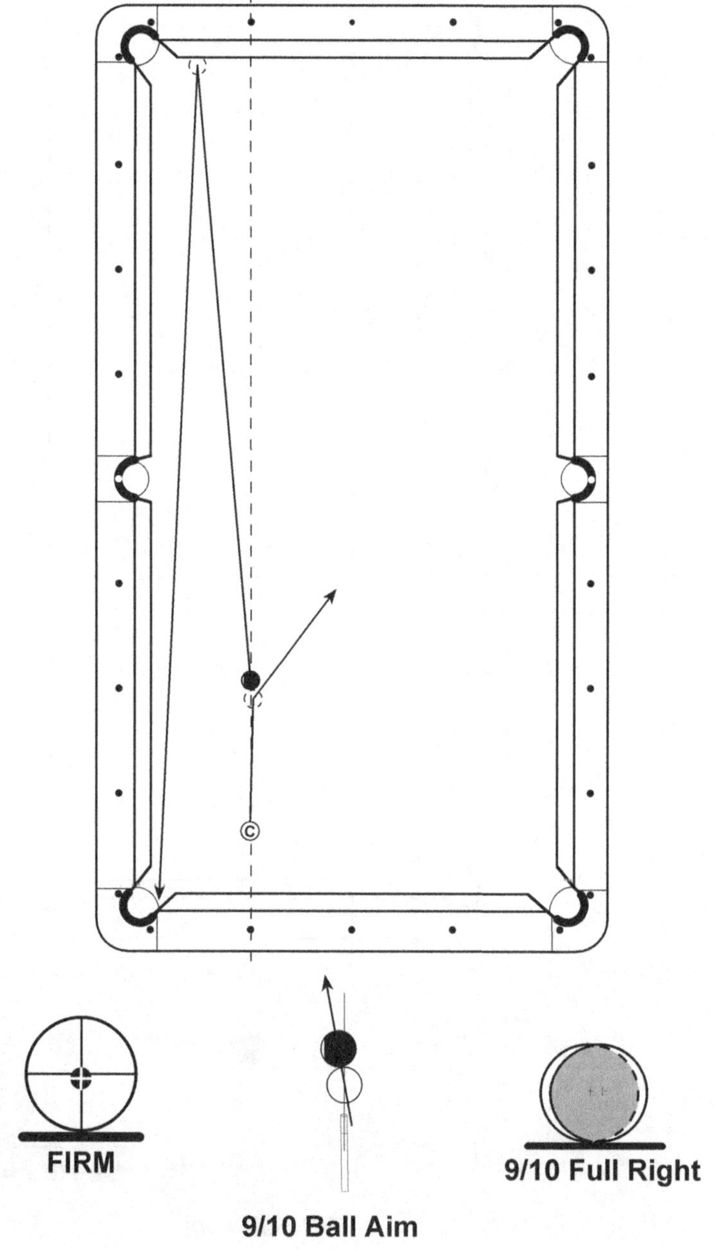

AUTOMATIC 1/2 FULL STRAIGHT-BACK

Parallel Angles Adjusted Cuts

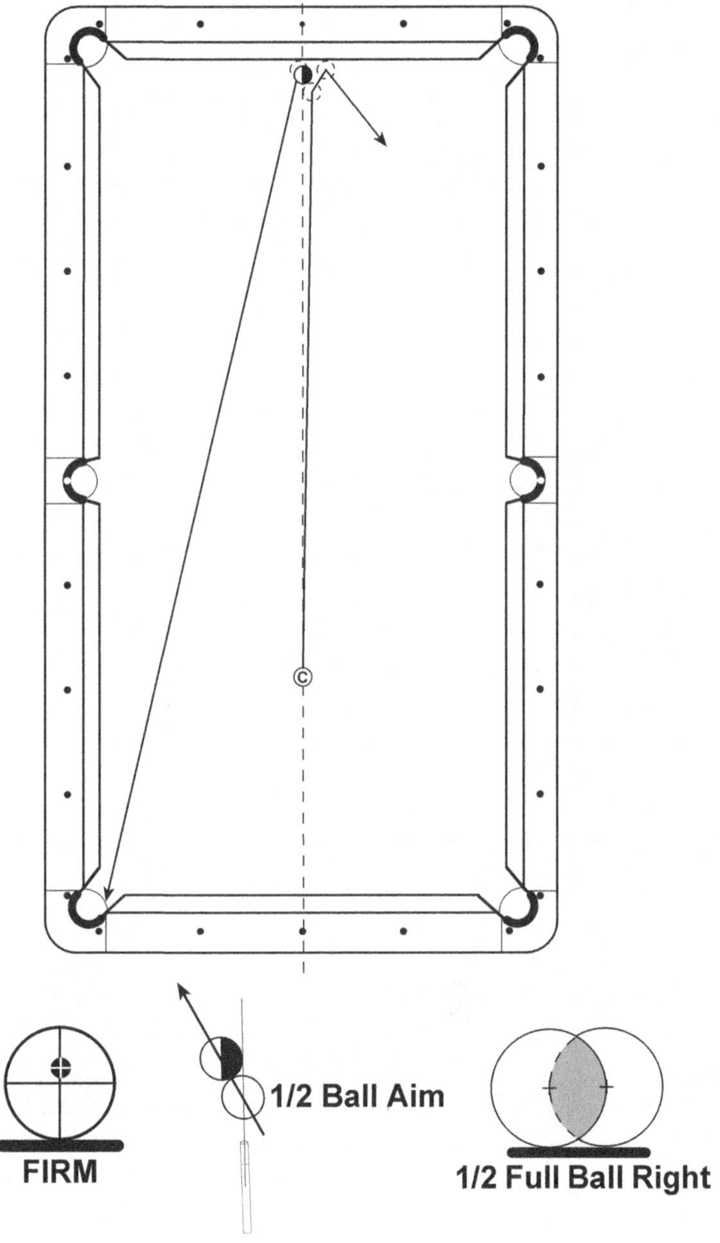

AUTOMATIC 2/3 FULL STRAIGHT-BACK

Parallel Angles Adjusted Cuts

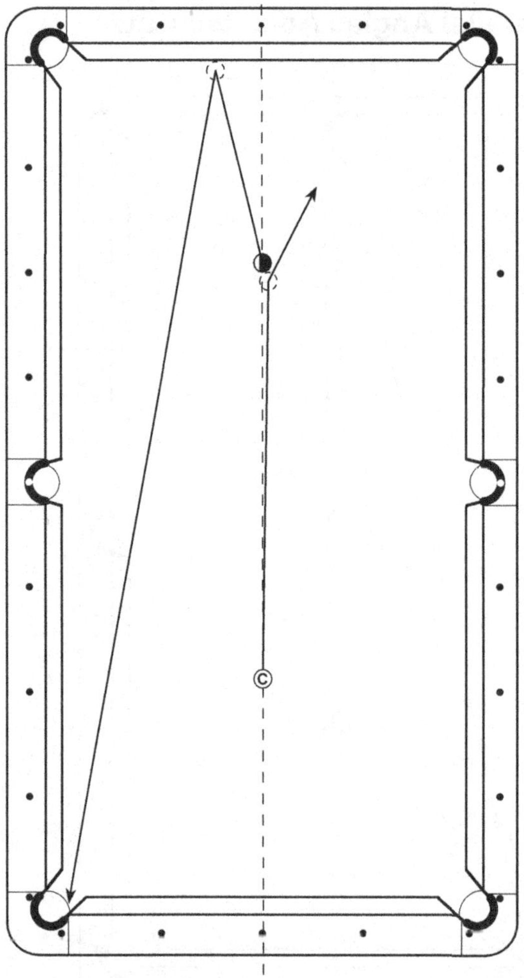

FIRM

2/3 Ball Aim

2/3 Full Ball Right

AUTOMATIC 3/4 FULL STRAIGHT-BACK

Parallel Angles Adjusted Cuts

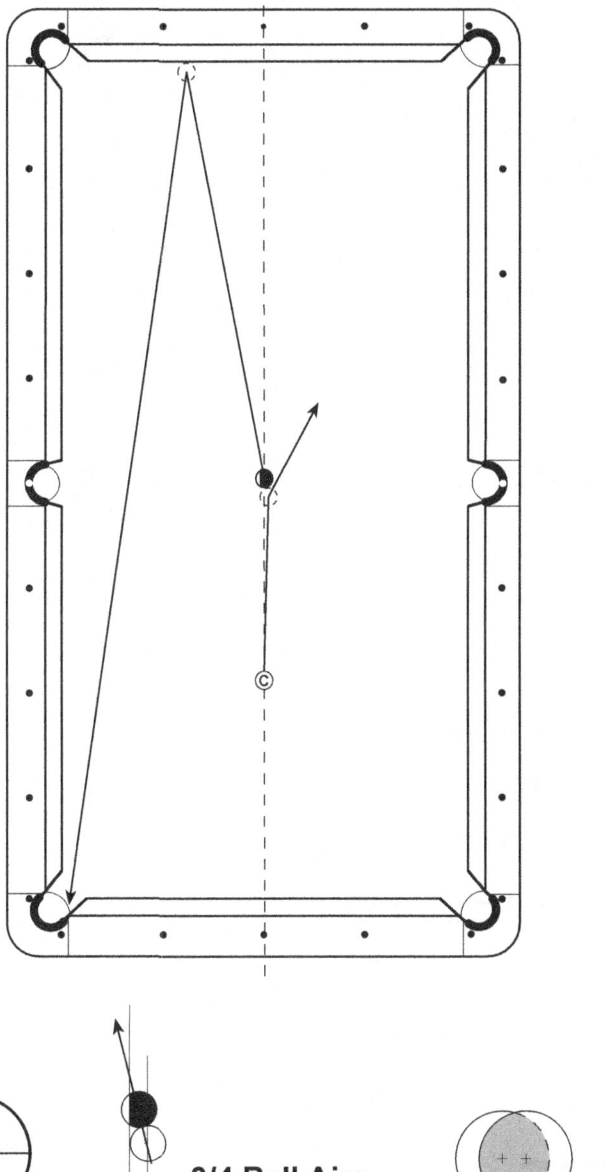

FIRM

3/4 Ball Aim

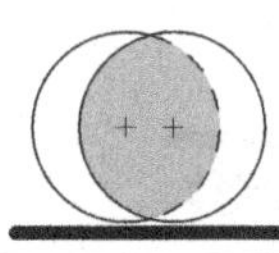
3/4 Full Ball Right

AUTOMATIC 5/6 FULL STRAIGHT-BACK

Parallel Angles Adjusted Cuts

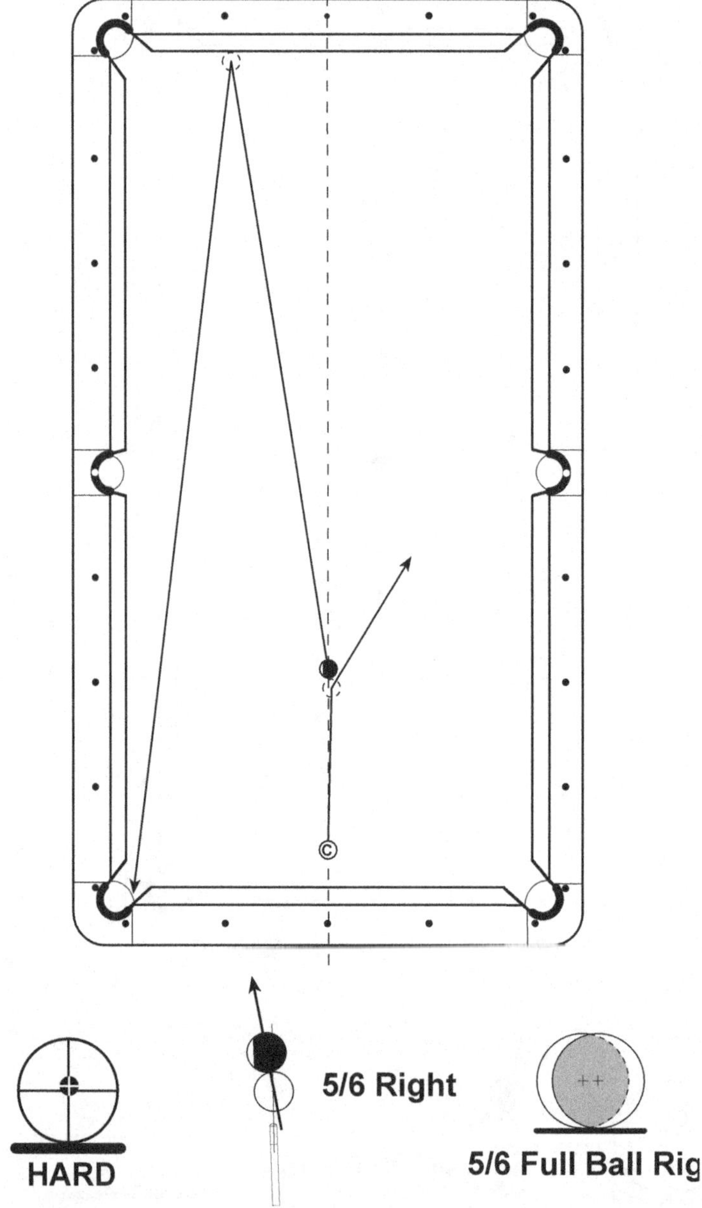

3/4 FULL LONG CROSS CORNER

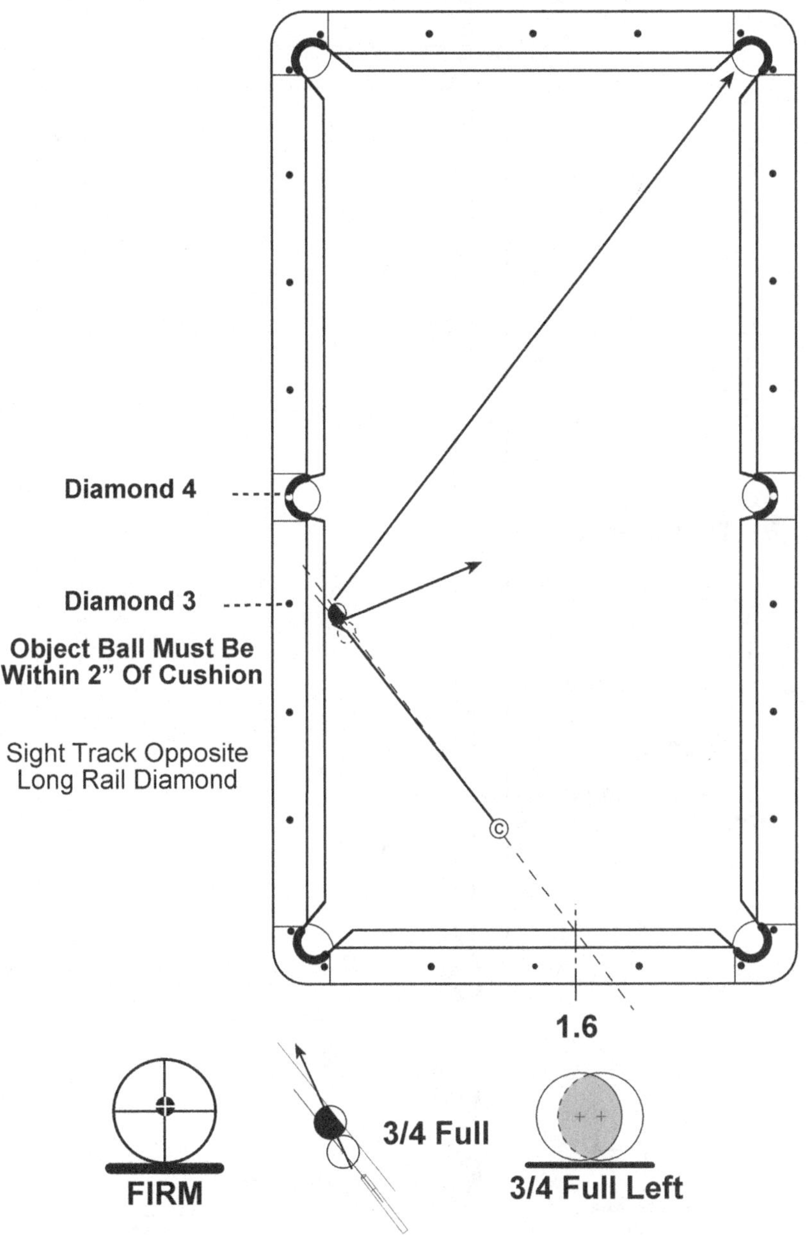

2/3 FULL LONG CROSS CORNER

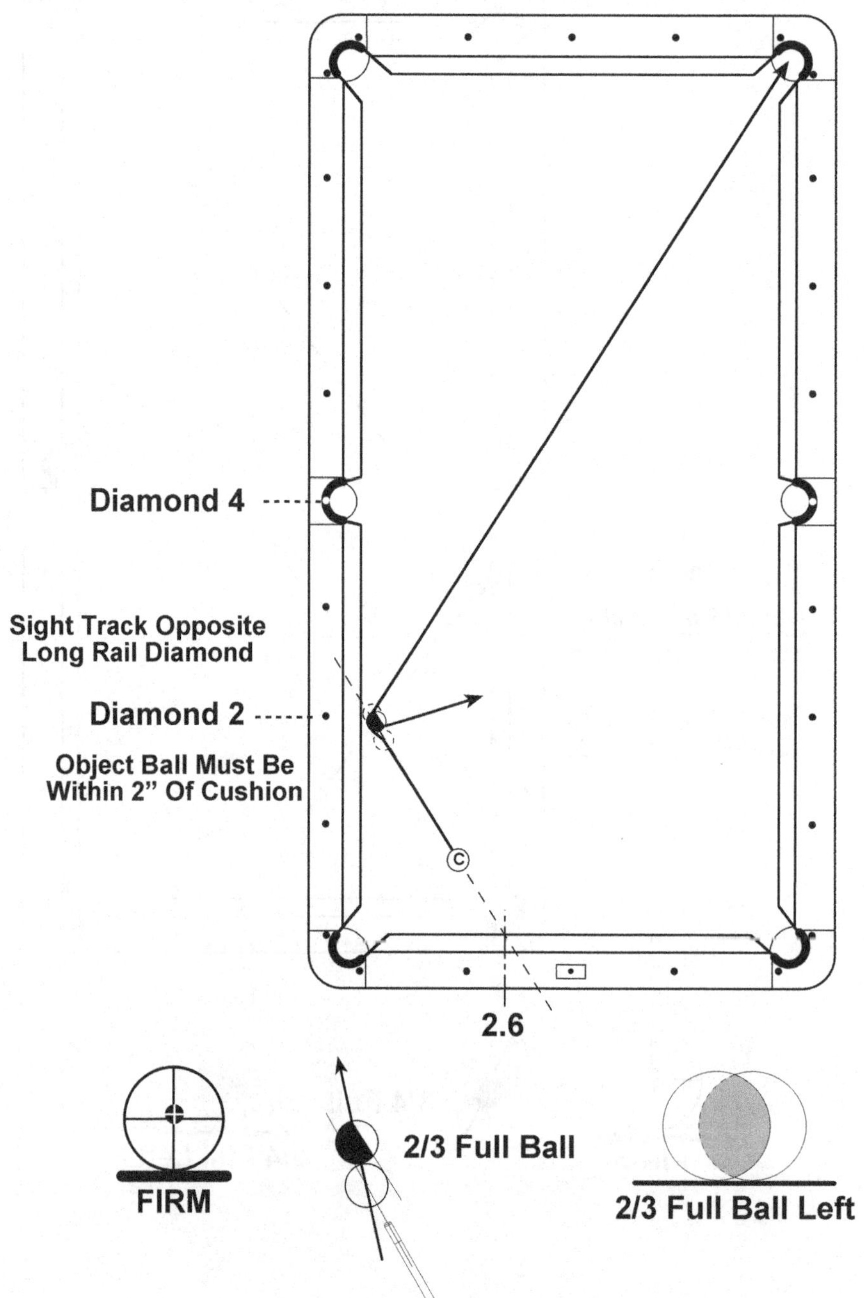

1/2 FULL LONG CROSS CORNER

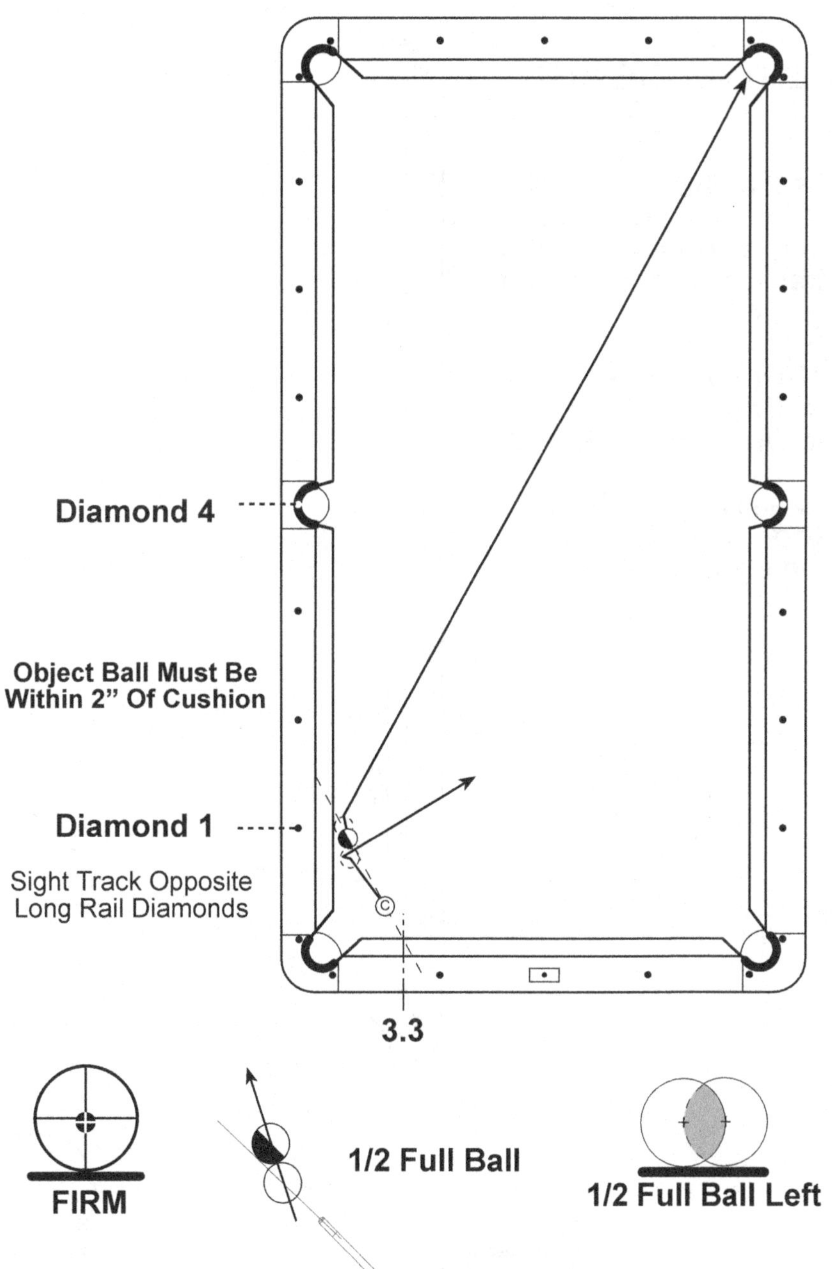

SELDOM PLAYED, BUT VERY MAKEABLE, 1 RAIL ONE POCKET BANK

EDGE TO EDGE AIM

Would I shoot this shot for the money? Yessir, and I have done so on many an occasion. With a little practice anyone can get the hang of it.

Use a **THIN** cut with extreme **Reverse English** (right) and **Extreme Draw**. **Hard Speed**.

The **Draw** and **Reverse English** keep the Cue Ball from scratching in one of the corner pockets.

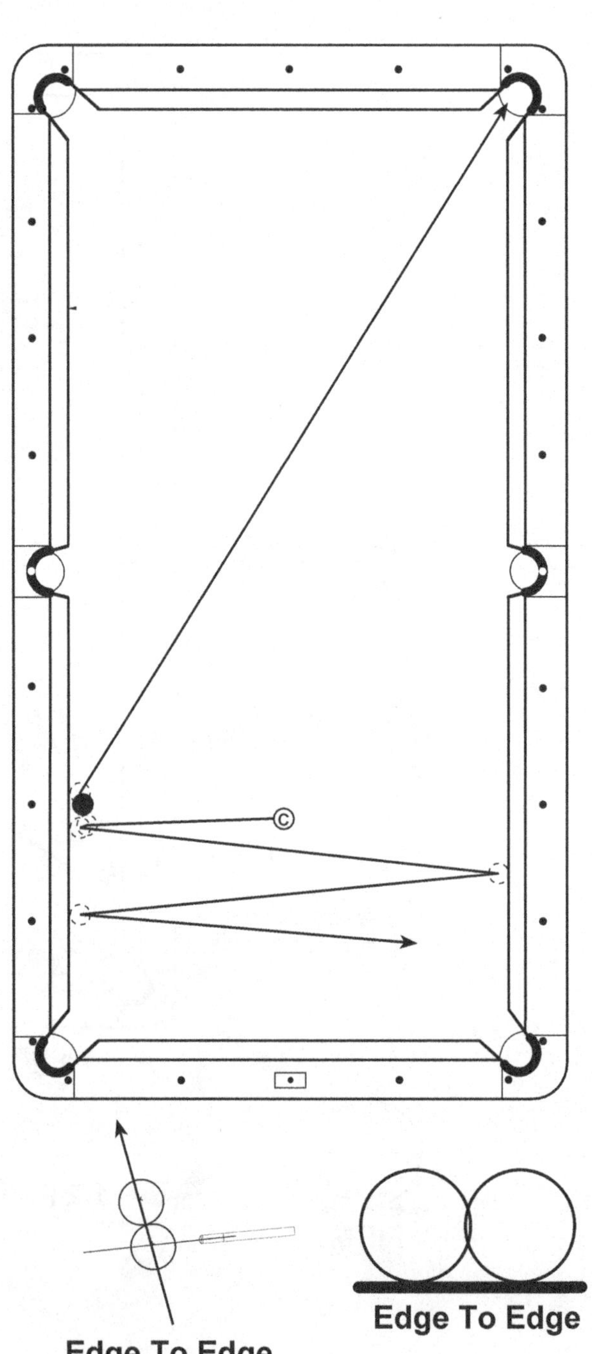

AUTOMATIC CROSS-SIDE TWICE

The next two shots are favorites of **Cross-Side Larry** of **AZ Billiard** forum (**http://www.azbilliards.com/**). Larry uses 1 Tip of Right–Hand english for this shot.

I play it a little differently than Larry.

I use center ball, **NO ENGLISH** with a 1/2 ball aim, and **HARD SPEED**.

Both the Cue ball and the Object ball are lined up dead in the middle of the side pockets.

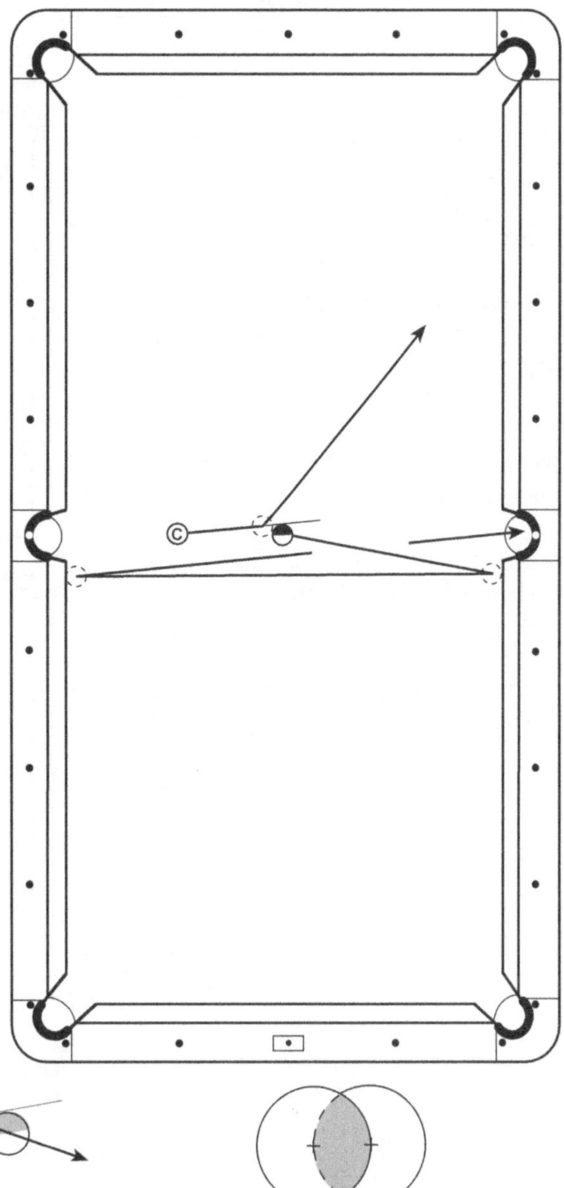

HARD

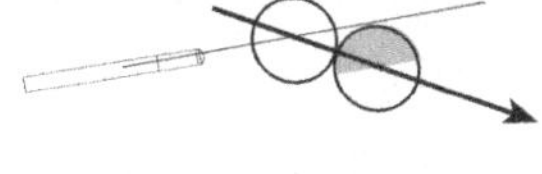

1/2 Ball Aim

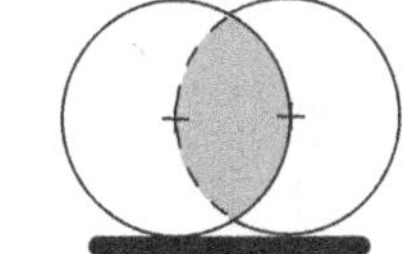

1/2 Full Ball Left

AUTOMATIC CROSS-SIDE THREE TIMES

The biggest difference between this shot and the one on the previous page is the speed used to make it.

The key is: **HARD SPEED** for twice, and **FIRM SPEED** for three times.

Cut this shot slightly more than the previous shot (1/2 ball aim on twice Across.).

Dead center ball, **NO ENGLISH**, and use **FIRM SPEED**.

Again, the Cue ball and Object ball are lined up in the middle of the side pocket.

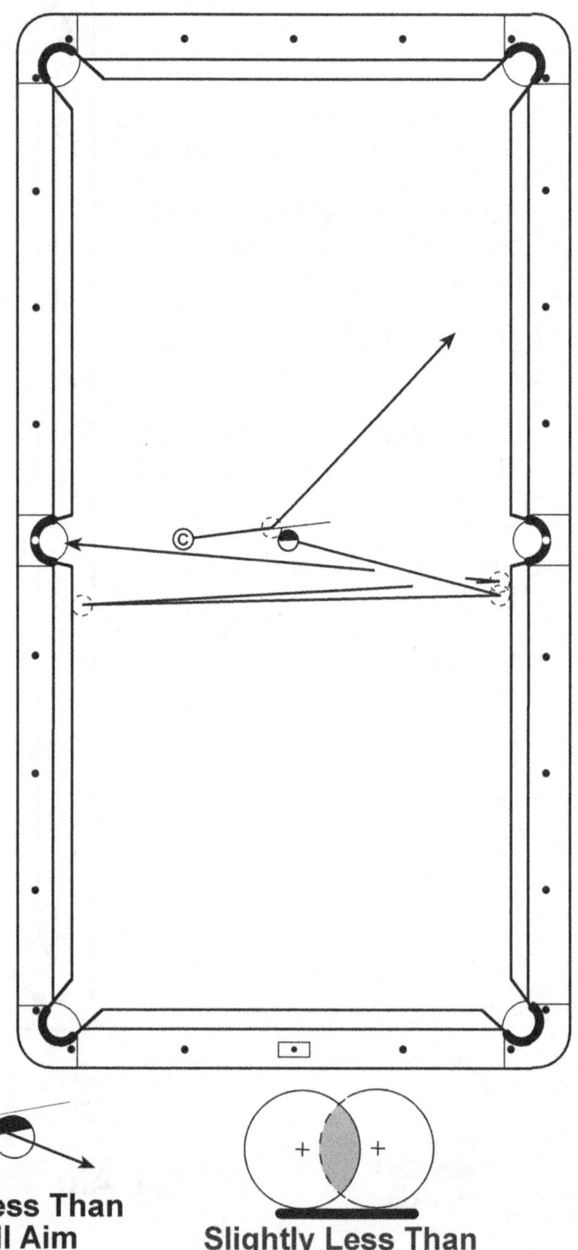

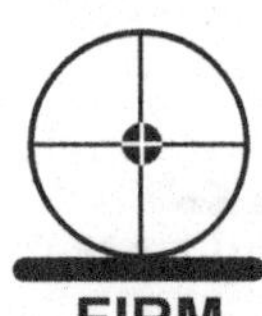

FIRM

Slightly Less Than 1/2 Ball Aim

Slightly Less Than 1/2 Ball Left

MAXIMUM CAROM ANGLE OFF A NEAR STRAIGHT–IN

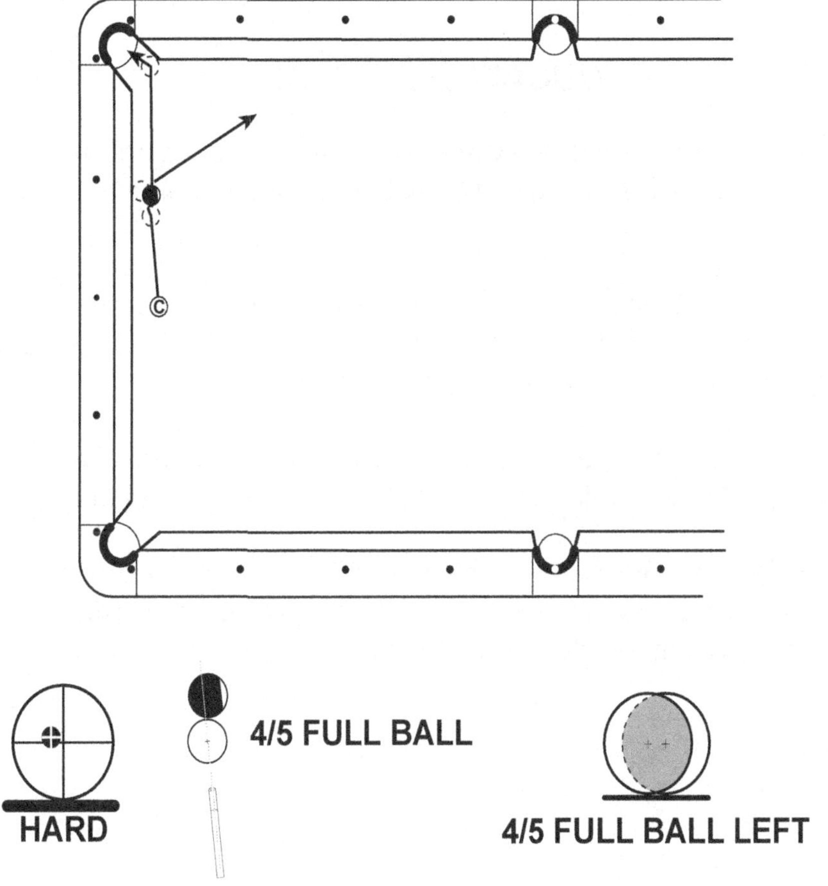

The key to this shot is using a hard 4/5 hit with left English. The usual (wrong) method is to use right English. What often happens with right English is the cue ball slides along the rail and either scratches in the corner or catches the point of the corner pocket and is stopped from getting up table.

EDUCATED BUNT SHOTS

On a rolling cue ball hit with easy speed and left or right English, the cue ball a the end of it's path will turn over slightly in the opposite direction of the applied English.

This is to say, Left English on the cue ball will make the cue ball turn over slightly and veer to the right at the end of it's roll. Conversely, right English, makes the cue ball turn over slightly to the left.

This can be easily observed if you test this principle using a striped ball instead of the cue ball. Watch which way the stripe turns at the end of its roll.

This principle does not apply if the cue ball is struck high with an elevated massé stroke or by hitting the cue ball low with an elevated stroke, as the cue ball will then curve in the direction of the applied English.

PATH DEVIATION

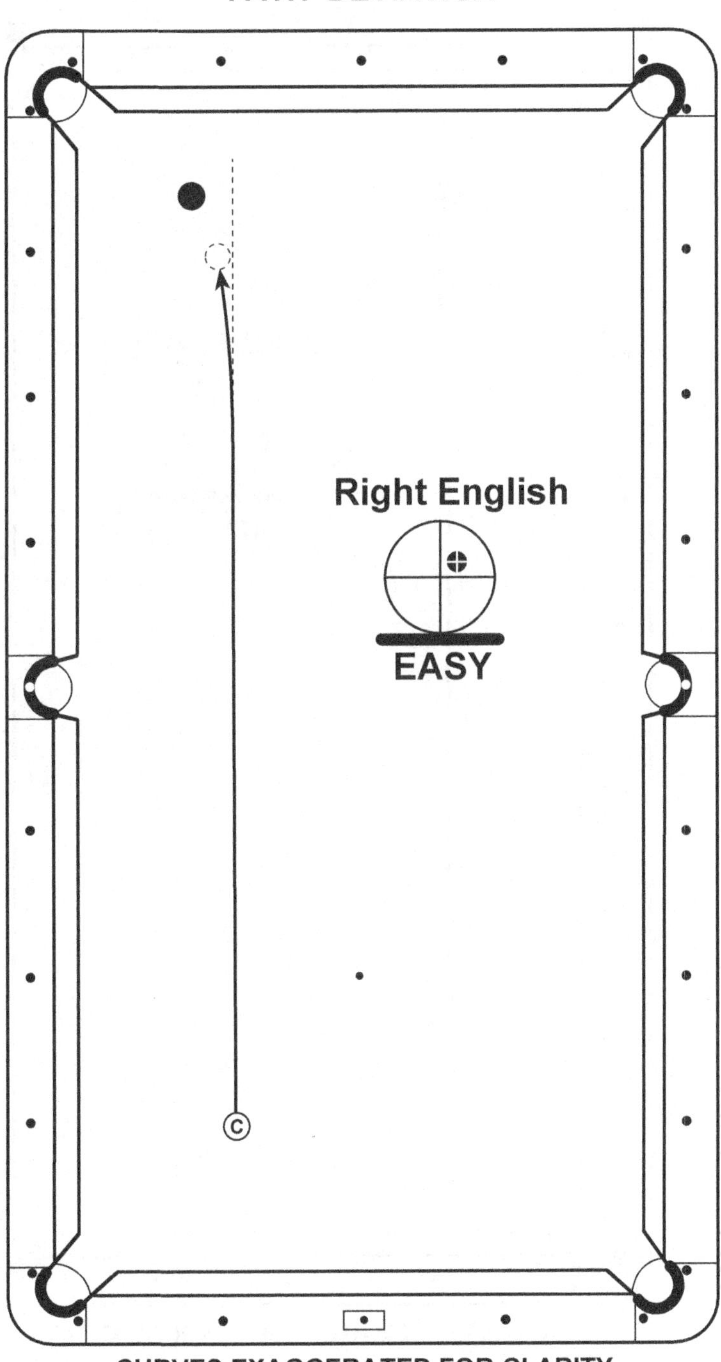

CURVES EXAGGERATED FOR CLARITY

PATH DEVIATION

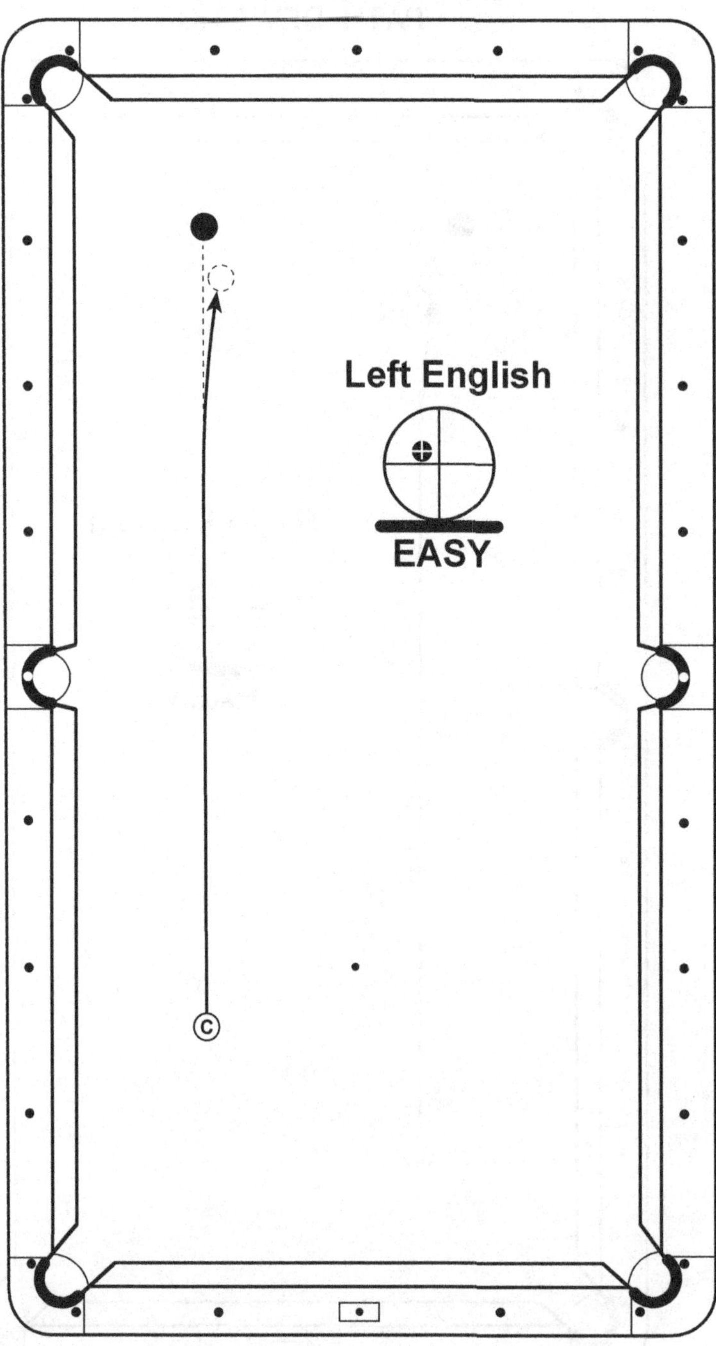

CURVES EXAGGERATED FOR CLARITY

JUST WHEN YOU THOUGHT YOU HAD HEARD EVERYTHING

This next tid-bit is for super-serious, hard-core, pool-bugs. This is a previously never reported, banking observation:

English, on a cut or pass-over bank shot will, at an easy speed on a broken-in cloth, break slightly at the end of it's roll in the same direction as the applied English. ie., Opposite or favoring English breaks short, and Reverse or holdup English breaks long.

Keep this principle in mind when playing on a table that rolls off. This is one way to get a little more "help" on your softly rolling bank shot to nullify the table roll. One Pocket and Bank Pool players who like to hit banks at "pocket speed" will find this useful.

PATH DEVIATION

Pass-over Banks
Left English, Easy Speed

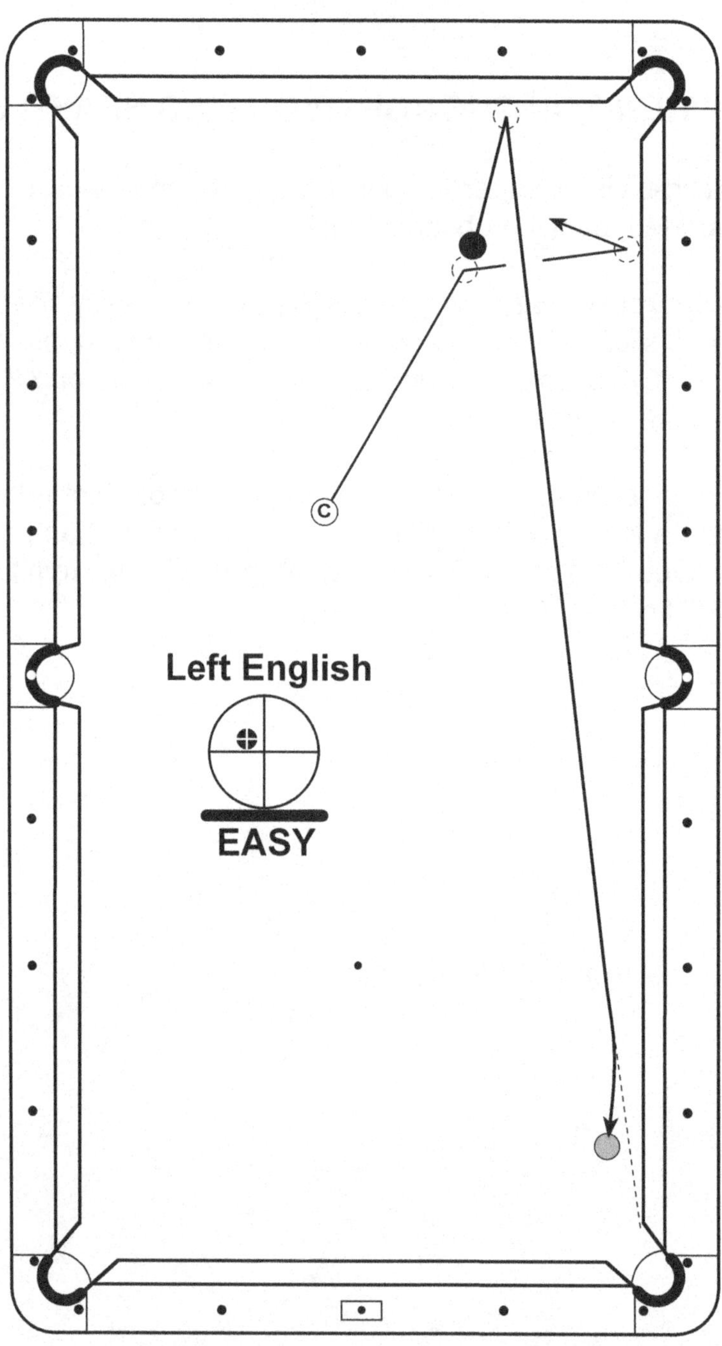

CURVES EXAGGERATED FOR CLARITY

EDUCATED BUNTS
PATH DEVIATION

Pass-over Banks
Right English Easy Speed

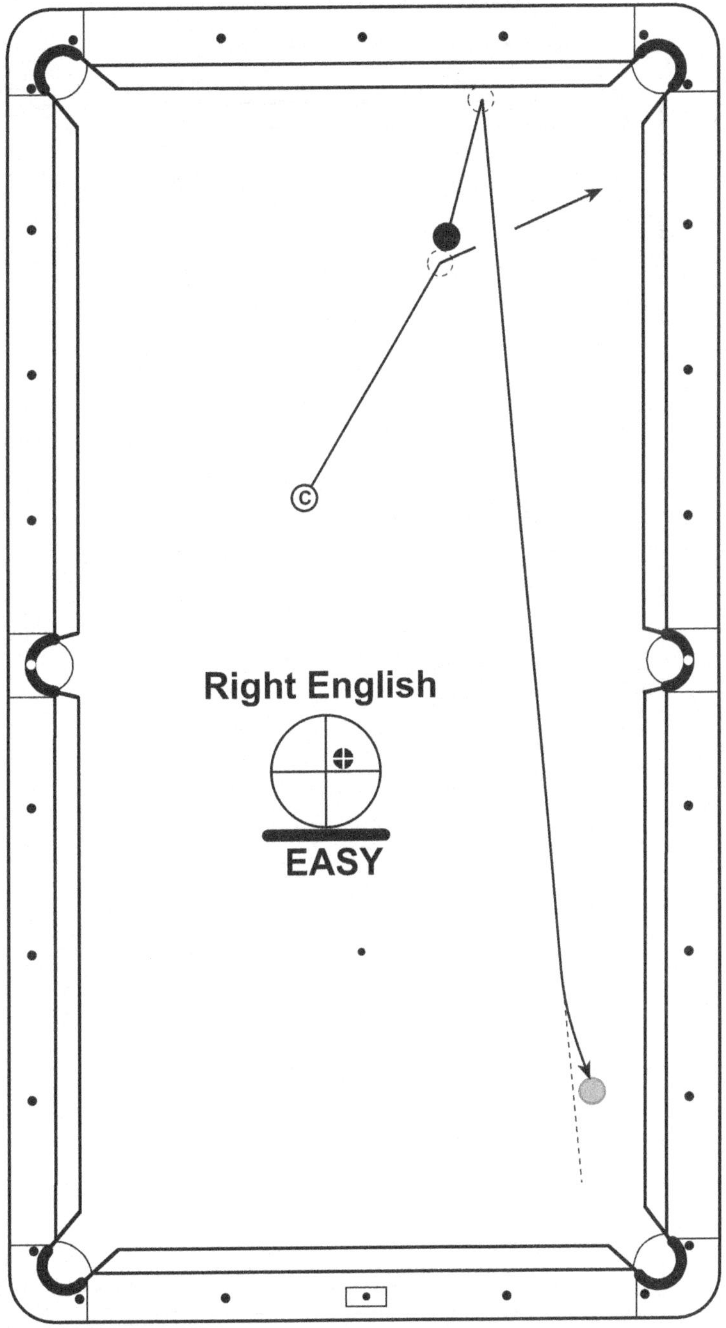

This shot breaks slightly long the last few inches.

PATH DEVIATION

Cut Banks
Left English Easy Speed

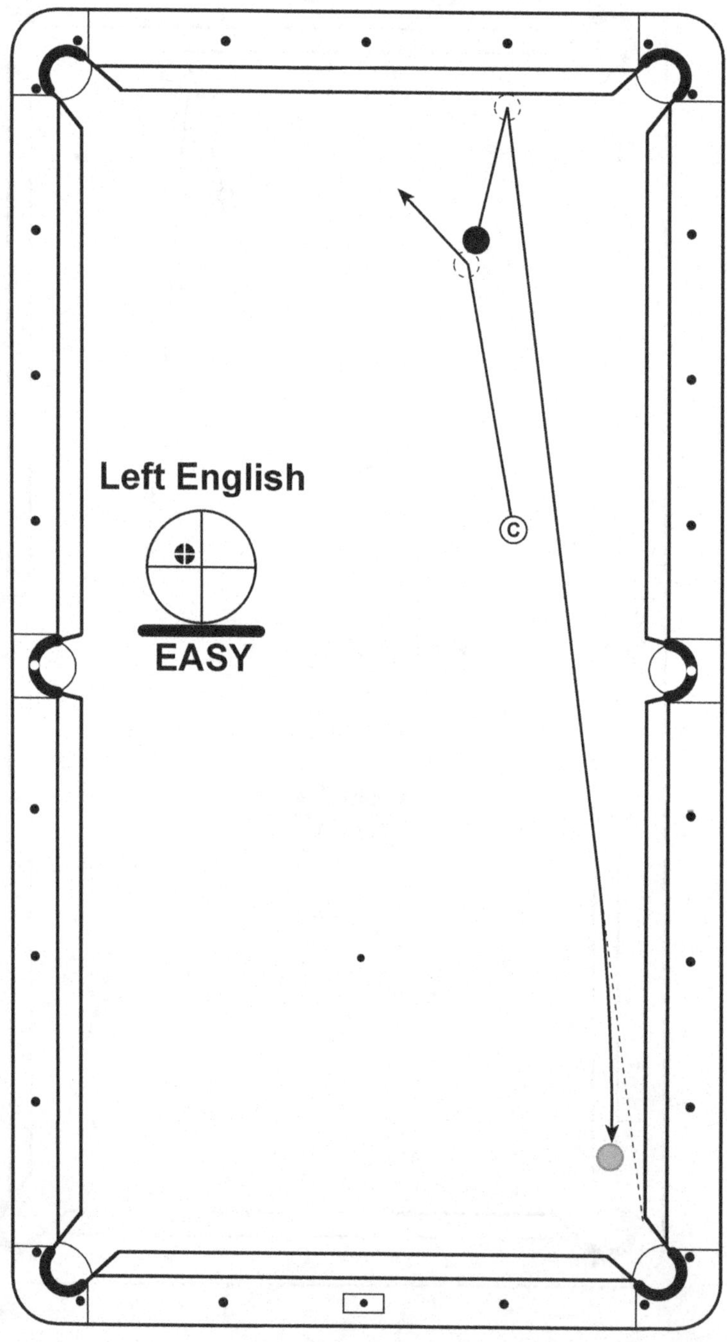

CURVES EXAGGERATED FOR CLARITY

PATH DEVIATION

Cut Banks
Right English, Easy Speed

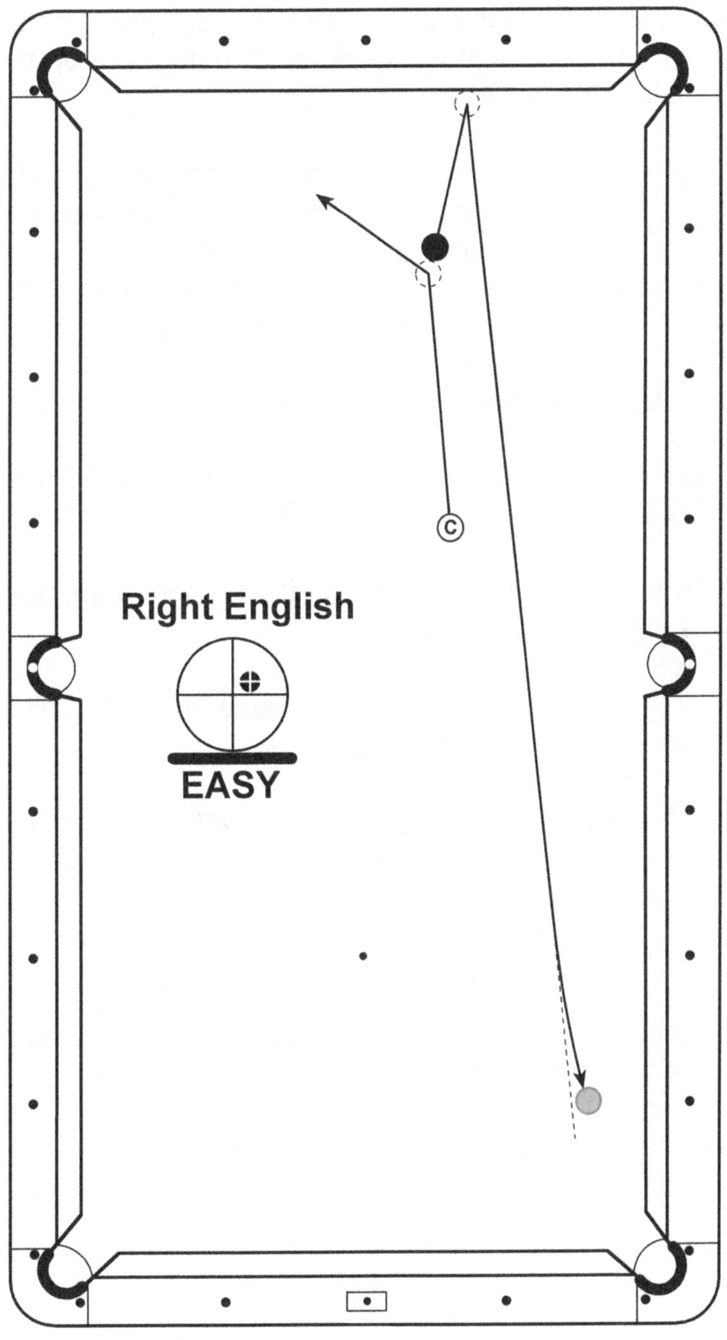

CURVES EXAGGERATED FOR CLARITY

FINAL RAMBLE

My views on pool game knockers
My fantasy is to tie a game knocker to a chair, gag him and force him to watch one player robbing another player, winning every game in a row. Seeing the knocker squirm in the bindings, desperately trying to stop the game through telepathy, would add five years to my life.

When I was a pup, if a good money game was coming up and we were worried that a certain individual would make it his business to step in and try to "queer" the action, for that evil knocker we would fix up a "shit mickey" (a concoction designed to induce diarrhea and vomiting simultaneously), put it in his drink, and then *we'd* go into the bathroom and lock the door. Those were the days.

Sage quotes from old-time road hustler, Roy "Kilroy" Kosmanski:

> Take a can opener and a spoon with you on the road— "It's easier to eat the beans if ya' got the right tools."
>
> If you see two guys shaking hands in a poolroom, one of them is a sucker.
>
> If you are in a poolroom or a card game and you can't figure out who the sucker is, it's probably you.
>
> Kilroy's advice regarding gambling with a very hard nosed player— Don't bet against him; he tries so hard he puts fingerprints in the slate.

Harold Worst
How would you like to have the money for your life saving operation on the line, and have to find somebody to beat Harold Worst playing Nine Ball? If you had Wimpy Lassiter going for you, you would have a good chance for a cure. Anybody else and you would be in bad shape. The best you could hope for would be an visitation and religious intervention from Mother Cabrini.

Youngest Hustler

Frank "Frankie Boy" Filerino of Jersey City, NJ was the youngest pool hustler at age eleven! I first met Frankie Boy in a Miami, FL poolroom. He had just came down from New York with two *backers*, one of whom was his truant officer from the Jersey school system, **Augie Catarella**.

Augie used to go into class and remove Frankie Boy on some trumped-up misdemeanor. Then Augie would take Frank hustling around the poolrooms in the northern New Jersey territory. Augie became Frankie Boy's backer after receiving a serious thrashing trying to beat the kid playing Nine Ball.

Frankie Boy was playing Nine Ball with another child-prodigy, **Mike Carella** of Hialeah, FL. It was sight to see, fifteen-year-old Carella spotting the eleven-year-old Frankie Boy the wild eight. Frankie Boy won and broke everybody (except me) in the poolroom.

Biggest Sex Degenerate

Detroit Whitey #1, no contest. He lapped up a seventy-five year old rack woman at the Rack And Cue in Detroit on a bet. He "topped" that by chewing up his female German Shepard, "**Windy**" in Sammy Blumenthal's poolroom in Jacksonville, FL for a bigger bet, remarking to his dog, "Look at this, Windy, these suckers are paying us for what we do at home for free!"

A distant second, but super-kinky in his own right, **Grady Mathews** (check out his autobiography, *Bet High And Kiss Low*). Grady may have been just as great a chewer, except that he kept his chewing to his own species.

ONCE IN A LIFETIME

I've watched and played in jillions of tournament matches, and I've only seen this once. Eddie Taylor was playing a Nine Ball match with Ronnie Allen in Johnston City. Ronnie broke and ran the first three racks. Taylor finally got a shot in the fourth game and ran to the nine. He had a super easy shot, a slight cut into the corner. Instead without hesitation, he got down and banked the ball cross-corner! It was a reminder to Ronnie about whom he was playing with. A shaken and embarrassed Ronnie never won another game in the set.

Can you imagine anybody else purposely banking the nine, in a big tournament match, down three games to none, and playing a young Ronnie Allen? That was the Knoxville Bear.

Eddie Taylor was one of the few true superstars in the game. I was familiar with most of the other top players – we all talked and interacted — but around Taylor I was in such awe that I never even attempted to talk to him, even though I was dying to.

Taylor was so good that in Johnston City, IL, a town full of the greatest players in the world, he never got asked to play! It was kind of assumed by everyone to just leave him be and go find somebody else. Taylor was even barred out of the ring Nine-Ball games. Wimpy Lassiter said the Bear was the only pool genius he had ever met, besides a trick-shot hustler named **Spin The Ball George**.

More About Danny DiLiberto

Danny had a penchant for getting into trouble in bars and then successfully defending himself.

Most people don't know that Danny won't use a curse word — ever! He would be in a tough bar and a beef would develop with the local tushhog, and they might begin wolfing at each other. While the hog was threatening Danny with every curse word he knew, Danny's mild retorts only served to encourage the quarrelsome intimidator.

Danny would bark at the tushhog and call the guy a "son of a pup" or "gall darn you!" or "What the heck do you mean by that?" Honest, that was as profane as he would get.

Overbearing thugs always thought Diliberto was some sort of sissy, and if because of a misguided ego, the bully attempted to get physical, a lightning-like right hand would beam into the ruffian's jaw and put him to sleep. This, as you can imagine, happened many times. I speak from personal experience. He felled many much-larger-than-he bruisers in this manner. I could do a book of stories about Danny, but he has already done one himself (**Road Player** *Bebob Press*).

Hayden Lingo

A great player himself, **Marshall "Squirrel" Carpenter** tells a story about the legendary **Hayden Lingo**. Squirrel went to play Lingo and was going to play him even, but before he could ask to play even, Lingo offered him 9 to 7 instead. Squirrel played with that unbelievable spot, but Lingo beat him with it!

Squirrel finished the story by saying he waited around until he caught Lingo when he was shaking like a dog shitting peach-pits off a two-day drunk. They played even this time and Squirrel broke him. Squirrel said Lingo was the best One-Pocket player in the world for years.

I just have to insert one more little tid-bit about Hayden Lingo. The first (and only) time I ever saw him was in Johnston City in the 60s. He only came there once. He looked like time was running out quickly for him. He weighed about 95 pounds and it was obvious that he was dying of cancer. However, he must have appeared differently to the older players, because when they spotted him a buzz went through the room. "It's Lingo!" "Look, it's Lingo!"

It was very perplexing, because the guy looked like death warmed over. These pool killers were reacting with what I interpreted as abject fear.

Baby-Face (Alton Whitlow) was complaining and groaning to me, "I drew Lingo for tomorrow. I gotta play Lingo!" I pondered to myself, who must this guy be to incur this kind of fear and apprehension? To me it looked like the guy wasn't gonna make it through a whole game.

But they were looking at Lingo with different eyes. He must have been some kind of sumpthin' in his day.

Brooklyn Jimmy Cassas was such a fabulous personality, most backers would rather take a chance of getting *dumped* by Jimmy, than stake a top player with a good game who was actually trying to win

More On Bodendorfer

Artie's nicknames were "Super-Punk," "Smartie-Artie," and "Soap-and-Water." The latter came from the time that he owned **Bensinger's** and ran the poolroom counter all day and then played high-stakes pool all night and never changed clothes or washed.

Cincinnati's **Joey Spaeth**, while playing in the prestigious **US Open Tournament** in Chicago, challenged a group of top players— "If you think you can play One-Pocket, there's a kid at **Bensinger's** wearing a dirty T-Shirt who will give you some action. If you beat him, then you can say you can play!"

Senior Citizen Or Not, Vernon Eliot Is No one To Make Proposition Bets With

A Vernon Elliot Warm-Up Shot

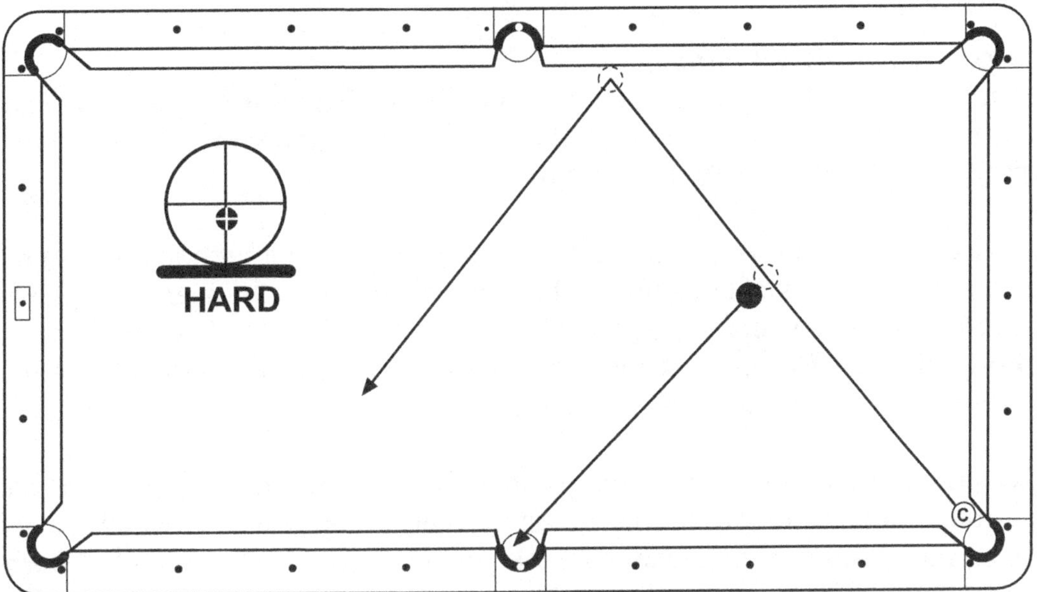

Here's a **Vernon Elliot** warm-up shot. With the cue ball hanging in the corner, cut an object ball off the spot into the side pocket on the same side of the table.

You might be tempted to bet your bankroll that Elliot can't do it, but Buddy Hall warns, "If you bet him, you'll lose."

I suspect that Elliot **BOUNCES** the Cue Ball to get the incredible hit required, but who knows for sure. Vernon Elliot is from the old school and does not reveal his secrets.

Readers can see examples of Vernon Elliot's mind bending banks on pages 166 and 167 in **BANKING WITH THE BEARD.**

The Young At Heart Award

The great player and master hustler, **Utley "U.J." Puckett** from Texas. Puck came to Hot Springs, AR in the late '80s with another Texan, **Steve "The Lizard" Smith**, for the **Oaklawn Park** racing meet.

Puck blew my mind one night when several of us were off in the corner of the poolroom doing lines of cocaine. He bullied his way through us and wanted in! Now, Puckett was a very large rangy man, known to be shoe-leather tough, a boxer in his early days, and he was not the kind of man you wanted to refuse anything, even at this late stage in his life.

I did remark, however, "Puck, you got to be kidding. You're 83 years old, and you wanna snort coke?" His reply, out of the side of his mouth, as was his style, was classic. "You punks nowadays think you're so cool sniffin' that stuff. I was snortin' that shit back in the '20s, goddamnit!" Needless to say, Puckett did his share and handled it like the champion he was.

Puckett later got mad at his road buddy, Steve "The Lizard" Smith, when Steve refused to get him down with the 19-year old girl Steve had picked up in town.

Let's Give The Final Word To Gar The Iron Man

When **Milborn "Gar" Frazier** was a young buck back home in South Carolina, he and his first wife **Diane** were in a bar and had been drinking heavily. They had become very loud and boisterous and were eventually confronted by the bouncer.

Gar's wife and the bouncer got into a heated argument when the bouncer insisted the two leave the premises. Finally, Diane asked the bouncer, "You ever been hit by a woman?" The bouncer, taken aback slightly, said, "Yeah, sure." Then Diane said, "I mean really hard!" Then she proceeded to bash him with a solid right hand that knocked him out colder than a Siberian popsicle!

Utley J Puckett

photos courtesy Bill Porter and Mike Haines

Steve "The Lizard" Smith

Five In The Side Eddie Taylor Style

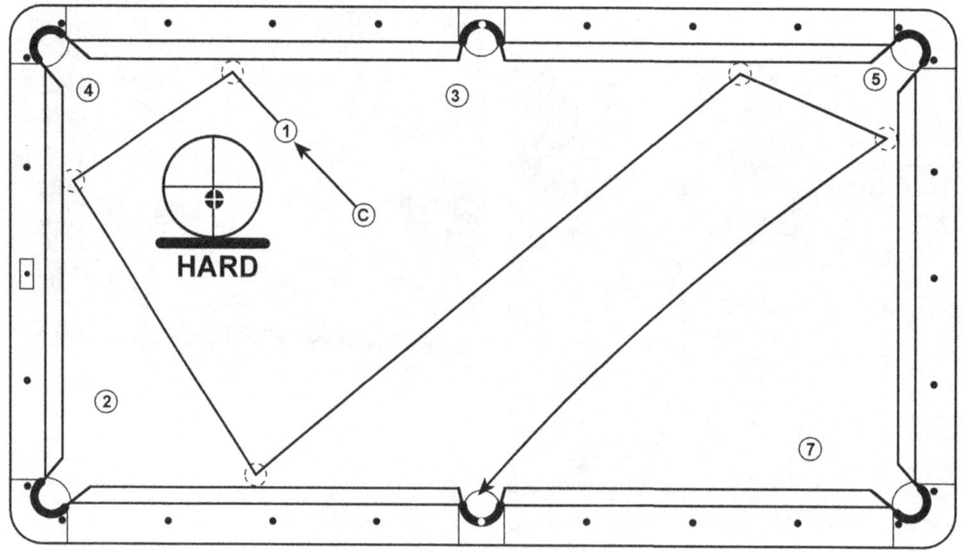

WW Woody, who hung out with Eddie Taylor for months in Louisiana, reports that Taylor made this 5–railer in the side regularly.

According to Woody, Taylor "***ARCED***" the Object Ball off the last cushion to go in the side.

Only a guy like Taylor could establish a decent percentage on the shot in game play. As a challenge shot, the odds are about 5 to 1.

The Beard's Glossary

bar spot: An action bar with money games.

barrels: Payoff units. i.e.., $30 would allow you to play 3 games for $10 each. The amount of games you can pay off measured against your bankroll.

big cue ball: An oversized cue ball, no longer in vogue, that was once used on many bar tables.

bite: A loan that is seldom paid back.

bite-men: People who borrow money for a living.

bottoms and seconds: Cards that are dealt off the bottom of the deck or to deal the second card from the top.

break someone: Win all of their money.

broke: Got broke: Lost all of his money.

business men: A business game is when a player gets staked and then loses on purpose. Times were so lean in the Old Days, that many players — myself included — occasionally fell into this despicable practice.

carry the banner: To have no place to sleep. To wind up in an all-night movie theater, a park bench, or a bus station.

cheese: Money.

cohones: Balls, testicles, courage.

cubes: Pool chalk.

dog it: To succumb to pressure and be unable to play your regular game.

dump: To lose your backer's money on purpose, as a "business man" would do and later collect 50% of his losses from your opponent who was your co-conspirator.

egg: A mark, a sucker.

eight and nine: A substantial spot in Nine Ball, whereby the spottee can win by making the eight or the nine.

8-or-no-count: A powerful handicap in One-Pocket, whereas the spotter has to run 8 balls consecutively in his One-Pocket in order to win.

fifty-or-no-count: A powerful spot playing Straight-Pool, whereby the spotter has to run at least 50 balls consecutively, or none of the balls he made previously count on his score.

5' x 10': The size of most pool tables in the 30s. Today, they are just about phased out and are a rarity. Players now play on the obviously easier, smaller sized 4 1/2' x 9' or 4' x 8' tables.

foot of the table: The table end where you rack the balls.

go off: To keep playing and lose all your money.

Great men: A *"Great"* man in hustling vernacular, is someone with unlimited bankroll who loves to play, loves to bet and has a bottomless capacity for punishment.

grinder: A very deliberate, workhorse type player.

hanger: An easy to make shot. Where the object ball is literally hanging in the pocket and a strong breeze could knock it in.

head of the table: The table end where you break the balls.

Hungarian nuts: An even greater advantage then the nuts. The term was created as a tribute to George and Paulie Jansco, the promoters of the Johnston City All-Around tournament who were of Hungarian descent.

in the one-hole: To need one more point to win the game.

Jar, Jar someone, to be Jarred: Similar to an old-fashioned "Mickey Finn." To put ***Hyacin*** or ***Scopolomine*** in someone's drink, seriously altering their vision and perceptions. Jar victims think they are playing great but can barely make a ball. It's a very dangerous drug. The KGB and the CIA used it as truth serum. Many players have died from overdoses.

Johnston City, IL. Pop.3500: Where the great hustler tournaments of the 60s were held yearly. Johnston City is located about 20 miles from Southern Illinois University (SIU) in Carbondale, IL.

kicked at a ball: Occurs when you are "snookered," and the path to the object ball you want to shoot at is blocked and you are forced to shoot the cue ball into a cushion to try and make your hit.

lemon: to lemon someone: The practice of conning a weaker player into believing that you are even weaker than they are. A pool con job.

location: The dealer unethically keeps track of several cards that he has secretly moved to the bottom of the deck.

massé: A fancy-shot, whereby the cue ball is made to curve.

Nine Ball: A type of pool game played with Nine Balls numbered 1 to 9. The object of the game is to run the balls in rotation, starting with the 1 ball going to the 9. Whoever makes the Nine Ball wins.

nuts: To have a tremendous advantage over your opponent in the game or session you are playing.

play on ass, on ass: Playing for money, without any money.

One-Hole: Another name for One-Pocket.

One-Pocket: A pool game where each player is assigned a different corner pocket. The object is to make 8 balls any way you can in your pocket before his opponent can make 8 balls in his.

Pay-Ball: The game is multi-handed Six-Ball played on a 6 x 12 snooker table. You get paid for every ball you make. The balls are to be run in rotation from one to six.

props: Slang, short for slang word "propers." That which you have coming.

pulls your coat: Alerts you to something. Knocks somebody's action to you. Think of someone tugging on your coat because he wants to tell you something.

push-out: The old rules for Nine Ball, whereby, when you were snookered on the next ball, you could push the cue ball out for a shot. Your opponent could then elect to let you shoot, or shoot the shot himself.

scooting the check: To illegally eat in a restaurant and not pay your check.

shark: Not to be confused with Pool-Shark — unethical gamesmanship. To distract your opponent while he is trying to shoot.

sharkers: Masters of gamesmanship.

shit it in: Made a lucky shot to score a ball.

short-stop: A lifetime pool player whose ability is just under the top players.

shoot his cuffs: To quickly extend the arms straight out as if preparing to start some sort of project.

shoot to hit it: Today's Nine Ball rules. You must make an attempt to hit the object ball every shot. Failure to hit the object ball gives opponent ball in hand.

slip-stroke: A fancy pool stroke, whereby your grip hand slips downward on the cue butt just before the stick is propelled forward.

spike fight: A duel where opponents wear sharpened baseball spikes and fight in a confined area like a narrow alley.

spread: Like a picnic spread. What appears to be nice things all laid out for a sucker to fall for.

stake-horse: A pool backer. He who puts up the money for you to play.

staking: Putting up the money for a pool player to play, with a deal to split the winnings 50/50.

strumming: Beating up on. Like playing a banjo.

sweator: AKA, Eye-baller, Eye-fucker, side-liner, a pool-game-watcher with no vested interest in the match, except to root for both players to somehow lose. Sweaters have zero gamble.

terps: An old brand of cough syrup that was laced with codeine

the office: A predetermined signal to roll into action. A secret tip-off.

tushhog: A strong-arm, tough-guy, bully type.

200 and out: Made 200 points consecutively, without a miss.

200-ball runner: Has run 200 balls playing straight-pool.

un-assed: Gave it up. Turned it loose. Released.

xmas trees: Barbiturates.

Index

Order The Beard's First Book   Banking With The Beard

COMPLETE YOUR BANKING EDUCATION

BANKING WITH THE BEARD

$29.95 + $4.00 S & H

180 Pages of banking goodness.

PHONE – 1—312—225—5514

ONLINE – www.BANKINGWITHTHEBEARD.COM

SEND CHECK OR MONEY ORDER TO **BANKING WITH THE BEARD**
445 West 27th Street
Chicago, IL 60616

Bentivegna has done us a great service with his new tome. **Banking With The Beard** is a masterpiece.

Mike Shamos , Billiards Digest

Banking With The Beard is written with the clarity of a natural teacher and with excellent diagrams. World-class expertise is presented brilliantly and passionately on every page. This is easily the best book on the subject ever written and will no doubt become a must-have, hands-on learning tool for both novices and "old pros." They'll upgrade their overall game many levels thanks to this veritable "banking Bible" you've given them.

Dick Sussman, Script Writer and Critic

Even pros prefer to avoid bank shots – but that may be a thing of the past. **Banking With The Beard** reveals every bit of knowledge necessary to successfully bank to the hole. The addition of great road stories, famous shots, One-Pocket info, and Bank Pool pointers make this book a treasure for serious players.

Tom Shaw, Pool & Billiard Magazine

There is simply no over-estimating the value of **Banking With The Beard** for serious players.

George Fels, Billiards Digest

Finally, a worthwhile book on Bank Pool from a Chicago banking legend. After reading this tome, you'll have no more guesswork in your Bank Pool game."

Grady "The Professor" Matthews — One Pocket Genius

Made in the USA
Middletown, DE
17 January 2024